WHEAT AND TARES

*Restoring the Moral Vision of
a Scandalized Church*

Father Mitch Pacwa, S.J.

EWTN Publishing, Inc.
Irondale, Alabama

TABLE OF CONTENTS

INTRODUCTION

Recent surveys show that the trust of church-going people in the clergy is at a very low point. A variety of reasons account for this. One reason is that many clergy have led the way in rejecting various traditional Christian doctrinal and moral teachings in favor of certain scientific claims or philosophical positions (particularly from existentialist philosophers) or changes in culture and law (particularly in the realm of sex and human reproduction). Certainly one aspect of the decline of the clergy's reputation is due to the fact that some teach and preach in a way contrary to the doctrines their churches had once held dear. The general population sees the refusal to live traditional doctrine as hypocrisy, even when they themselves do not hold to the traditional faith.

An even more serious cause for the decline in the clergy's popular loss of reputation is the wave of sexual and financial scandals found throughout the churches. Protestant ministers, Catholic priests, Orthodox rabbis, and others have been caught in patterns of sexual abuse of children and youth, in addition to affairs with consenting adults. They abused their clerical positions of trust by engaging in acts of sexual abuse of others. Most especially the victims of abuse have lost their ability to trust the clergy. Regarding victims of abuse by Catholic clergy, to whom can they go to confess their sins in private and under the seal of the confessional? Private acts that were kept secret for years are precisely the way they were victimized. How can they receive Holy Communion from the hands of a priest, when the hands of a priest touched them inappropriately? The Church itself is a sign of suffering and pain, but not because they trust that Jesus Christ took on Himself the burden of humanity's sin through His suffering and death on the Cross. Rather, it is a sign of suffering at the hands of the men who stand before the world in the Person of Christ (*in persona Christi*) and minister sacraments of forgiveness and reconciliation between God and humanity. Some of these same men have inflicted deep wounds—physical, psychological, and spiritual wounds—on the Body of Christ, whom they claimed to serve.

Compounding the tragedy has been the failure of bishops and superiors to adequately address the crisis. Too often they believed the priests rather than the victims, and in some cases they believed the accusers rather than innocent priests. This was due to a number of factors. Leaders were inexperienced in sexual abuse cases, since the number of cases increased in the mid-1970s and came to light in the mid- to late-1980s and beyond.

In effect, some Catholics, including the clergy, became ashamed of Jesus. Is it surprising then if some Catholics begin to act like the world instead of seeking to be like Christ? When the world promotes revolution against Christian moral teaching about human sexuality, is it any surprise that many Catholics take sides with the sexual revolutionaries? Some Catholic priests who taught moral theology sided with the sexual revolution after Pope St. Paul VI published his encyclical *Humanae Vitae* (July 25, 1968), even holding a press conference to dissent from an ancient Church teaching that St. Paul VI merely restated in 1968.

Catholics have always been aware that their priests are human beings with faults. Some priests are crankier than others, some are more stern, some are very funny, and some are more laid back. Some had problems with alcohol, while others seemed too focused on money. However, overall, priests were special men in the community who gave up having a family so as to commit themselves to the Church. They were involved in the depths of Catholic lives, from Baptism through the Last Rites and burial. They gave us our first Holy Communion, prepared people for marriage, and kept absolutely secret the most embarrassing sins that they heard in confession. They were held in very high respect for their hard work, their sacrifices of family and income, and their willingness to teach about God, the meaning of life, the way to heaven, and the way to avoid hell. Priests were much beloved by the people; they served them on many levels and generally did it well. All of that drew me to the priesthood, a decision I have never regretted over the past forty-three years.

Tragically, a case of a priest sexually abusing boys arose in Louisiana in the 1980s. As a relatively young priest, I was shocked and dismayed that a priest would do such a thing. Over three decades, thousands of other cases have been exposed. The majority of priest abusers did it once—which was far too many times—and stopped, realizing how wrong this was. About 15 percent lived a pattern of sexually abusing minors, most of whom were boys. Though some cases went back to the early 1950s, the patterns showed a great increase from the mid-1970s through the late 1980s and early 1990s. By that point, the bishops and superiors took more serious steps to address the problem and then began a variety of educational efforts to prevent future cases. Sadly, about 3 percent of priests engaged in the sexual abuse of minors and harmed the lives of about 13,000 young people.

The damage caused by these evils has been great. The victims have borne the brunt of the problem. Confusion, interior conflict, guilt, self-hatred, and depression have deeply harmed their lives. Many have turned to drugs and alcohol to stifle that pain; many kept it a secret for decades before finally bringing their painful memories to light; some—too many—have committed suicide. Families have been torn up, marriages split, and psyches have been destabilized. Of course, these victims have lost confidence in the Church, and a priest is the last person they would consult, especially if they had been treated badly after they reported the abuse.

The victims' families were typically committed Catholics who loved and trusted priests with their lives and with their children, only to have some priests abuse their children sexually and some engage the parents in illicit relationships. Many children became alienated from their families and from God, spouses became alienated from each other and divorced, and once-trusted priests became despised enemies. Many of the families felt betrayed by the perpetrators and by the bishops or priests to whom they reported the abuse when the latter covered up the case. They have likewise lost confidence in the Church and sometimes lost faith in God. Their lives were put into turmoil, in some cases for decades. Like the victims, the parents experienced divorce, drug and alcohol addiction, and broken hearts.

The rest of the Church has also experienced great anger, not only at the perpetrators but even more at the bishops and superiors who covered up the abuse, shuffled abusers from one parish to another for repeat performances, or used payoffs from Church funds to cope with the abuse. Too many bishops and priests approached the abuse not as pastors but as corporate officers trying to protect the institution instead of a bruised and hurting flock. Further revelations of bishops and cardinals abusing adult seminarians raised new levels of anger from the laity and the lower clergy.

Finally, priests have experienced the embarrassment and even shame of communal guilt. Many priests, myself included, have been the objects of frustration and anger at the perpetrators and the negligent hierarchy when generalized accusations of abuse were directed to us personally. Though we can theoretically know that the remarks and insults are not personal, their existence makes it painful to wear clerical garb in public. Of course, the vast majority of Catholics distinguish the guilty from the rest, but they do not know how to deal with the frustration and embarrassment they feel at being identified as Catholics whose priests have committed such grave crimes.

How Do We Deal with These Problems?

Through retirements, deaths, and removals, many of the Church leaders who failed to handle this clergy sexual abuse crisis well are gone. Over the years new leaders have tackled the situation by educating priests and seminarians about the moral and legal seriousness of the sexual abuse of minors, vulnerable adults, and anyone else. Seminaries have learned more about screening applicants for these kinds of behaviors or the signs of risk that someone might engage in them. Clear procedures for alerting law enforcement and the proper Church authorities have been set in place. As a result, the number of abuse cases has drastically fallen. Of course, the goal is total elimination of all such cases, and the Church works toward that. So successful has this been that other professions now look to the Church as having led the way in preventing child sex abuse.

Another approach is also needed, one that fits the specific mission of the Church—namely, a spiritual approach. This is particularly difficult to accept since the whole problem involved people who were seeking spiritual guidance from priests who then used the occasion to abuse them as children or as adults. How can people trust priests to guide them through a spiritual healing of problems caused by abusive and negligent priests and bishops? How can they trust the Catholic Church, the power of its sacraments, or even Jesus Christ Who gave priests their vocation?

Most Reverend Father General Arturo Sosa, S.J., has called

the Jesuits to address the present sexual abuse crisis by prayer and by leading others in prayer, and that is the purpose of this book. My method will lay out various relevant themes as they appear in Sacred Scripture so that the reader can bring these passages to personal prayer and encounter Our Lord personally. My hope is that as an individual meets the Lord and allows Him to speak in the silence of the heart, a deep spiritual healing can enter the life of the one who is hurt—the victims of sexual abuse and betrayal most especially, their families and friends who share their deep pain, the Church in general, and the bishops, priests, deacons, seminarians, and religious who suffer some of the pain because they publicly identify with the Church.

We'll begin with the many texts that recognize the sinfulness of the priests and people that God calls to follow Him. Though their sinfulness remains a scandal, we all will do well to consider that God calls sinners because they are the only kind of people who are born. Though He will treat them with justice if they refuse His mercy, the realistic expectation is that sinners will be part of the Church.

To better understand the failure of modern clergy, the second and third chapters will look at the Apostles' failures, beginning with Jesus' public ministry and then reviewing the events of Holy Thursday. Throughout their public ministry, the Apostles display self-centeredness, anger, cowardice, and other vices, which Christ corrects repeatedly. On Holy Thursday they are ordained as the first twelve bishops and receive their first Holy Communion, yet one bishop proceeds to betray Jesus with a kiss, eleven run away in abject fear, and the first pope denies even knowing Him.

Chapters 4, 5, and 6 will present Christ's arrest, trials, sufferings, and death as the experiences that best connect with the sufferings of the victims of the clerical sexual abuse crisis.

Chapter 7 will look at how the appearances of the Risen Lord to His disciples and Apostles brought about their conversions to authentic faith in Jesus. They had not expected Him to rise again, even though He had told them about it many times. Chapter 8 will look at the Ascension and the coming of the Holy Spirit at Pentecost to empower the Apostles in their mission to serve other people selflessly. Finally, the last chapter will look at the role of the Blessed Virgin Mary in the lives of the Apostles and the rest of Christ's disciples in drawing them closer together in faith and leading them to heaven.

A man, whose wife divorced him after their sons were abused by clergy, fell apart emotionally and morally. After dealing with some of the pain on a psychological and medical basis, he surprised himself by following spiritual promptings that gradually and slowly nudged him back to praying inside a church, attending Mass, confessing his sins, and seeking spiritual direction from a good, wise, and holy priest. He gently drew his son to seek this healing, and they both are discovering new and deep peace with God. This book is dedicated to them and all those like them who are finding a renewed love of God in their broken hearts and lives and are sharing it with others who suffer as they do.

CHAPTER 1

---∞∞∞---

THE CHURCH WILL
ALWAYS INCLUDE SINNERS

Jesus Christ was not at all naive; He knew that humans were fallen sinners, and he knew that His disciples were sinners. He upbraided them often enough for their pride, selfishness, and ignorance, pointing out their sin so that they might repent and enter the Kingdom of God. Furthermore, Jesus frequently taught His disciples about the coexistence of evil and good, especially in the parables in St. Matthew's Gospel: the weeds sown among the wheat (13:24–30, 36–43); the net full of good and bad fish (13:37–50); and the wedding feast where one guest failed to wear a wedding garment (22:10–14). The parables about the final judgment begin with the distinction between the good and wise steward versus the wicked one (24:44–51), followed by three parables about the foolish and wise virgins awaiting the groom (25:1–13); the industrious and lazy servants (25:14–30); and the sheep and goats who serve or fail to help the least people (25:31–46). Given the great scandal caused by bishops and priests recently, we do well to take seriously Jesus' teaching about the existence of both righteousness and evil within the Kingdom of God.

The Existence of Scandal in the Kingdom of God

Jesus taught that people who cause scandal will always be part of the Kingdom of God. When His disciples asked, "Who is the greatest in the kingdom of heaven?" (Matt. 18:1), His first response was to call a child into the middle of the disciples, saying, "Truly, I say to you, unless you turn and become like children, you will never enter the kingdom of heaven. Whoever humbles himself like this child, he is the greatest in the kingdom of heaven" (Matt. 18:3-4). Humble, innocent, childlike behavior and attitudes make it possible for someone to be great in heaven. By implication, those who are arrogant and seek prominence will be among the least.

Then Jesus warns His ambitious disciples about two antithetical choices: receive Jesus in the little ones or be severely punished for causing a little one to sin.

> "Whoever receives one such child in my name receives me;
> but whoever causes one of these little ones who believe in me
> to sin, it would be better for him to have a great millstone
> fastened round his neck and to be drowned in the depth of the
> sea." (Matt. 18:5–6)

The humble, innocent, childlike person is to be accepted with love for his or her own sake. However, causing an innocent person to sin or to be tempted to sin will lead to a punishment worse than having a millstone tied around the neck. This is not the fifty- to seventy-pound hand millstone used in homes to grind grain, but the large millstone weighing one or two tons that was pushed by draught animals in a public mill. No one can swim with such a stone attached to them, and that punishment would be better than the punishment Jesus Christ has in store for those who cause children to sin.

Jesus then proclaims a "woe," which is the opposite of a beatitude in ancient speech forms, against those who cause temptation: "Woe to the world for temptations to sin! For it is necessary that temptations come, but woe to the man by whom the temptation comes!" (Matt. 18:7).

Such tempters are inevitable because some people choose to commit sin to serve their own self-centeredness. The "woe" indicates that such tempters are already condemned for their sin, and each will be severely punished by God. This is such a serious warning that Jesus recommends drastic steps to avoid the occasions of temptations in life:

And if your hand or your foot causes you to sin, cut it off and throw it away; it is better for you to enter life maimed or lame than with two hands or two feet to be thrown into the eternal fire. And if your eye causes you to sin, pluck it out and throw it away; it is better for you to enter life with one eye than with two eyes to be thrown into the hell of fire. (Matt. 18:8–9)

These injunctions repeat Jesus' teaching in the Sermon on the Mount (see Matt. 5:29–30), but here they are directed specifically to those who tempt the innocent and bring scandal to the Church of Christ.

This is obviously applicable to the contemporary situation, and all Christians, especially the clergy, would do well to consider it.

The Good and the Wicked Live Side by Side

Two parables found only in St. Matthew address the co-existence of the good and the evil in the Kingdom of God. The first of these is the weeds among the wheat and its explanation:

Another parable he put before them, saying, "The kingdom of heaven may be compared to a man who sowed good seed in his field; but while men were sleeping, his enemy came and sowed weeds among the wheat, and went away. So when the plants came up and bore grain, then the weeds appeared also. And the servants of the householder came and said to him, 'Sir, did you not sow good seed in your field? How then has it weeds?'" (Matt. 13:24–27)

The servants are the first to observe the growth of weeds in the wheat field, so they question the landlord about the presence of weeds. The owner immediately knows that "an enemy has done this" (Matt. 13:28). When the servants suggest cutting down the weeds as a solution to the problem, the owner rejects it because uprooting the bad weeds would also harm the good wheat. Instead, the owner tells them to wait until the harvest time: "Let both grow together until the harvest; and at harvest time I will tell the reapers, Gather the weeds first and bind them in bundles to be burned, but gather the wheat into my barn" (Matt. 13:30).

This parable is so important that Jesus leaves the crowds to speak privately with His disciples in order to explain it to them.

"He who sows the good seed is the Son of man; the field is the world, and the good seed means the sons of the kingdom; the weeds are the sons of the evil one, and the enemy who sowed them is the devil; the harvest is the close of the age, and the reapers are angels. Just as the weeds are gathered and burned with fire, so will it be at the close of the age. The Son of man will send his angels, and they will gather out of his kingdom all causes of sin and all evildoers, and throw them into the furnace of fire; there men will weep and gnash their teeth." (Matt. 13:37–42)

The harvest is a metaphor of the final judgment at the end of the world, when the Son of Man and the angels will cast out and punish the wicked. Jesus frequently tells of the "wailing and gnashing of teeth" for those who are hell bent (see Matt. 8:12; 13:42, 50; 22:13; 24:51; 25:30; Luke 13:28), while "the righteous will shine like the sun in the kingdom of their Father" (Matt. 13:43), as we find in the Book of Daniel:

> And many of those who sleep in the dust of the earth shall awake, some to everlasting life, and some to shame and everlasting contempt. And those who are wise shall shine like the brightness of the firmament; and those who turn many to righteousness, like the stars for ever and ever. (Dan. 12:2–3)

Jesus concludes with "He who has ears, let him hear" (Matt. 13:43b), exhorting everyone to be among the righteous and avoid being wicked.

Another parable uses an image of a dragnet drawing in all kinds of fish:

> "Again, the kingdom of heaven is like a net which was thrown into the sea and gathered fish of every kind; when it was full, men drew it ashore and sat down and sorted the good into vessels but threw away the bad." (Matt. 13:47–48)

The term for the "bad" fish is *sapra*, the Greek word that describes bad trees and their fruit (see Matt. 7:17–18; 12:33). The Old Testament laws regarding clean and unclean animals, including aquatic animals, determined the good and bad fish by whether the fish has fins and scales (see Lev. 11:9-11; Deut. 14:9-10). The "bad" fish do not have fins and scales, but instead are bottom feeders, such as the catfish or eels found in the Sea of Galilee. Jesus uses a natural experience common to the fishermen where he preached to give an illustration of the process of God's judgment. Similarly, John the Baptist had spoken about such gathering and judgment to be accomplished by the Messiah Who comes after him:

> Even now the axe is laid to the root of the trees; every tree therefore that does not bear good fruit is cut down and thrown into the fire.... His winnowing fork is in his hand, and he will clear his threshing floor and gather his wheat into the granary, but the chaff he will burn with unquenchable fire." (Matt. 3:10, 12)

In the dragnet parable, Jesus the Messiah compares the fisherman to the angels who separate the evil from the righteous, so that the wicked can be punished in the furnace of fire, as Jesus taught elsewhere in the Gospel:

> "Whoever says, 'You fool!' shall be liable
> to the hell of fire." (Matt. 5:22)

> "It is better that you lose one of your members than that your whole body be thrown into hell." (Matt. 5:29, 30)

> "And do not fear those who kill the body but cannot kill the soul; rather fear him who can destroy both soul and body in hell." (Matt. 10:28; Luke 12:5)

> "You serpents, you brood of vipers, how are you to escape being sentenced to hell?" (Matt. 23:33)

Jesus drew upon a number of Old Testament passages for the idea of fiery punishment. For example:

> Then the Lord rained on Sodom and Gomorrah brimstone and fire from the Lord out of heaven; and he overthrew those cities, and all the valley, and all the inhabitants of the cities, and what grew on the ground. (Gen. 19:24–25)

> On the wicked he will rain coals of fire and brimstone;
> a scorching wind shall be the portion of their cup.

For the Lord is righteous, he loves righteous deeds;
the upright shall behold his face. (Ps. 11:6–7)

While such images of fiery torment in hell are unpopular in modern times, we should remember that Jesus used this common image from the Old Testament in His parables and in the Sermon on the Mount. He knew that some people do not respond to idealism very readily, and for such persons, fear of punishment is the only motive that holds them back from sin. That principle applies to clergy and laity alike. While Jesus assumes the coexistence of the good and the bad within the Church, He never condones it. Therefore, He preached these parables to remind those who are complacent about sin that they need to awaken from their delusion before the eternal punishment comes upon them.

Parables in Jerusalem Regarding the Good and Wicked Members in the Church

After His Palm Sunday triumphal procession into Jerusalem, Jesus spent three more days teaching in the Temple. A series of three parables, beginning in Matthew 21:28, address the lack of faith among the people of the holy city. The third parable fits the theme of the presence of the good and the bad existing side by side in the Church until the judgment comes.

And again Jesus spoke to them in parables, saying, "The kingdom of heaven may be compared to a king who gave a marriage feast for his son, and sent his servants to call those who were invited to the marriage feast; but they would not come. Again he sent other servants, saying, 'Tell those who are invited, Behold, I have made ready my dinner, my oxen and my fat calves are killed, and everything is ready; come to the marriage feast.' But they made light of it and went off, one to his farm, another to his business, while the rest seized his servants, treated them shamefully, and killed them. The king was angry, and he sent his troops and destroyed those murderers and burned their city. (Matt. 22:1–7)

Twice the king invited his guests to his son's wedding feast. Culturally, a wedding feast is a very important celebration with rich foods, such as meat, which was seldom eaten, sweet wines, and other delicacies. An invitation from a king was a great honor, so the rejection of that opportunity by those who were invited was shocking to Jesus' listeners, especially since the king sent the invitation twice. The concern for their personal affairs and the violence to the messengers was even more shocking. All of the ancient people would have expected the king to punish the ingrates. However, their failure to accept the invitation opened the door for other people to receive the king's summons.

"Then he said to his servants, 'The wedding is ready, but those invited were not worthy. Go therefore to the thoroughfares, and invite to the marriage feast as many as you find.' And those servants went out into the streets and gathered all whom they found, both bad and good; so the wedding hall was filled with guests. But when the king came in to look at the guests, he saw there a man who had no wedding garment; and he said to him, 'Friend, how did you get in here without a wedding garment?' And he was speechless." (Matt. 22:8–12)

Even the newly invited had to remain concerned for their righteous appearance at the wedding feast, which was symbolized by wearing proper wedding garments. The king personally addressed the problem of the one guest who failed to wear a wedding garment, leaving the man speechless. The notion that special garments were provided for the wedding reception by the host finds no parallel in literature, so the guest seems to have been required to bring a wedding garment.

The meaning of the garment may be linked to two passages in the Old Testament. The first is in Psalm 132, where priests are clothed in righteousness when they offer the liturgy: "Let your priests be clothed with righteousness, and let your saints shout for joy" (Ps. 132:9). The second is a song of praise in Isaiah 61:10, where the saved greatly rejoices and exults because the Lord effects a transformation that clothes the person in salvation and righteousness, such as one might find in a wedding feast on a groom or bride.

> I will greatly rejoice in the LORD, my soul shall exult in my God; for he has clothed me with the garments of salvation, he has covered me with the robe of righteousness, as a bridegroom decks himself with a garland, and as a bride adorns herself with her jewels.

Such imagery also appears frequently in the Book of Revelation (see Rev. 3:5, 18; 19:7; 19:14). In the context of these passages, the garment symbolizes the righteousness that each person must possess in order to remain in the wedding feast of the Lamb of God. St. Paul has a related idea of being "clothed in Christ" as a reference to Baptism: "For as many of you as were baptized into Christ have put on Christ. There is neither Jew nor Greek, there is neither slave nor free, there is neither male nor female; for you are all one in Christ Jesus" (Gal. 3:27–28).

In any case, the king therefore punishes the man, from which Jesus draws the conclusion for His disciples: "Then the king said to the attendants, 'Bind him hand and foot, and cast him into the outer darkness; there men will weep and gnash their teeth.' For many are called, but few are chosen" (Matt. 22:13–14).

The Lord Jesus is warning all of His disciples, whom He has called to the wedding feast, that if they are not properly clothed in righteousness, they too will experience "wailing and gnashing teeth" in the "outer darkness" of hell. All members of the Church must be aware that good and bad people are called to the wedding feast, and some of the people who enter fail to cover their immortal souls with the garments of righteousness and salvation. Neither ought the bishops and priests, who wear beautiful vestments to celebrate the "wedding feast of the Lamb" at Mass, forget the garment of holiness and salvation, since they can be excluded from eternal life as much as anyone.

Jesus continued teaching in Jerusalem, publicly announcing seven "woes" against the hypocrisy of the Pharisees (see Matt. 23) and privately teaching His disciples about the last judgment (see Matt. 24:1–44). He continued that private teaching with four parables about the righteous, the wise, and the industrious alongside the wicked, foolish, and lazy servants of the King, all of whom will be judged with eternal consequences for their behavior (see Matt. 24:45–25:46).

The first parable is directed to the leaders of the Church, as to whether they are faithful or wicked (see Matt. 24:45–51). Jesus posed a rhetorical question that implies its answers: "Who then is the faithful and wise servant, whom his master has set over his household, to give them their food at the proper time?" (Matt. 24:45). As a servant to his Lord, fidelity to the master who set him over the household is the most basic quality of a servant leader in charge of the "household," or church, that Christ leaves behind. Wisdom, referring to practical wisdom (*phronimos*) as distinct from a more theoretical wisdom (*sophia*), is his second qualification for leadership, so as to serve the other servants at the right time. This parable points out the servant's accountability for leading through service.

In stark contrast, Jesus describes the wicked servant in the household with a conditional statement: "But if that wicked servant says to himself, 'My master is delayed,' and begins to beat his fellow servants, and eats and drinks with the drunken ..." (Matt. 24:48–49). The "if" at the start of the sentence indicates Jesus' recognition that a servant may choose to be wicked, even if he is put in charge of the household. He describes the servant's wickedness as being motivated by a denial of the master's return. Once he thinks that he will not be punished for his wicked behavior, the servant proceeds to abuse the other servants and to gratify his self-indulgence and passions, such as the desire to get drunk. Therefore the master makes certain his threat of the inevitable punishment for the wicked servant. The arrival of the master will be on a day and an hour the wicked servant does not expect, since neither the righteous, nor the angels, nor the Son of Man know it:

> "But of that day and hour no one knows, not even the angels
> of heaven, nor the Son, but the Father only.... Watch therefore,
> for you do not know on what day your Lord is coming. But
> know this, that if the householder had known in what part of
> the night the thief was coming, he would have watched and
> would not have let his house be broken into. Therefore you also
> must be ready; for the Son of man is coming at an hour you do
> not expect." (Matt. 24:36, 42–44)

The wicked servant will be punished by being cut in two pieces (*dichotomesei*). This punishment was reserved for the person who broke a covenant, as seen in Genesis 15:9–18, when Abram splits some animals in two pieces to indicate the fate of anyone who broke the covenant. It follows logically that the wicked will experience the "wailing and gnashing of teeth" that Jesus frequently mentions. Clearly, Church leaders will receive the consequences for their behavior, whether it is faithful and wise, or self-indulgent and wicked—a point that no bishop or priest can afford to neglect.

Jesus' second parable of the judgment indicates that both wise and foolish virgins exist within the Church (see Matt. 25:1–13). He emphasizes the need for watchful preparedness for His second coming at the end of the world. Since His disciples cannot know the date of His second coming, they must all sustain constant readiness in prudent, practical wisdom until He arrives. The setting for the parable is again the image of the wedding feast, particularly favored by Jesus in Matthew's Gospel.

> "Then the kingdom of heaven shall be compared to ten maidens who took their lamps and went to meet the bridegroom. Five of them were foolish, and five were wise. For when the foolish took their lamps, they took no oil with them; but the wise took flasks of oil with their lamps." (Matt. 25:1–4)

Jesus explains that five virgins were foolish and five showed practical wisdom (*phronimoi*), indicating that He wants His disciples to be clever: "Behold, I send you out as sheep in the midst of wolves; so be wise as serpents and innocent as doves" (Matt. 10:16). The practical issue which divided the wise from the foolish was whether they brought sufficient oil for their lamps during the time of waiting for the return of the groom. The key problem of the foolish virgins is their assumption about the length of the bridegroom's delay. They expected him to arrive soon and were not prepared for a long delay. That folly turned the arrival of the bridegroom into the first crisis of the night:

> "As the bridegroom was delayed, they all slumbered and slept. But at midnight there was a cry, 'Behold, the bridegroom! Come out to meet him.' Then all those maidens rose and trimmed their lamps. And the foolish said to the wise, 'Give

us some of your oil, for our lamps are going out.' But the wise replied, 'Perhaps there will not be enough for us and for you; go rather to the dealers and buy for yourselves.'" (Matt. 25:5–9)

Such delays were common at Middle Eastern weddings because the groom and the bride's parents frequently were still negotiating the dowery or discussing other concerns. However, during the delay the foolish women ran out of oil in their lamps, so they asked the wise to solve their dilemma. Unfortunately for the foolish, taking oil from the wise would become a problem for all of them, since no one would have enough oil to keep their lamps burning. For that reason the foolish had to search for oil in the stores that had closed long before midnight, while the wise enter the wedding before the door is shut:

> "And while they went to buy, the bridegroom came, and those who were ready went in with him to the marriage feast; and the door was shut. Afterward the other maidens came also, saying, 'Lord, lord, open to us.' But he replied, 'Truly, I say to you, I do not know you.'" (Matt. 25:10–12)

Though the five foolish women eventually return to the site of the wedding feast, the door is shut to them. At this point they ask admittance to the wedding feast, but the bridegroom prohibits their entrance because he does not know them. This is the very concern with which Jesus concluded the Sermon on the Mount:

> "On that day many will say to me, 'Lord, Lord, did we not prophesy in your name, and cast out demons in your name, and do many mighty works in your name?' And then will I declare to them, 'I never knew you; depart from me, you evildoers.'" (Matt. 7:22–23)

The connection of the parable about the five foolish, unprepared virgins with the conclusion of the Sermon indicates that foolishness characterizes the people Jesus does not know. In conclusion He says, "Watch therefore, for you know neither the day nor the hour" (Matt. 25:13). Disciples may not use the delay of His second coming as an excuse for their lack of preparation. Rather, He will hold each of them responsible for their foolish lack of expectant preparedness.

The third parable about the last judgment presents a mixture of industrious and lazy servants whose Master gives them responsibility for a number of talents (Matt. 25:14-30). The focus is on the faithful disciples' activity during the master's absence, or the lack thereof. The master prepares for a journey, during which he entrusts his property to his servants. As in the preceding parables, his absence is the occasion for a testing process, here to determine whether the servants are industrious or lazy. The Lord's absence actually demonstrates each servant's capacity for the responsibility entrusted to each: "For it will be as when a man going on a journey called his servants and entrusted to them his property; to one he gave five talents, to another two, to another one, to each according to his ability. Then he went away" (Matt. 25:14–15).

The master is well familiar with each servant's abilities and limitations, but the differences of capacity do not diminish the opportunities possible for each servant. They will not be judged by the standard of the other servants' abilities but by the ways they seize the opportunities available to each of them: nothing more, and nothing less. This, too, is a component of the Lord's judgment of each person.

A talent was a denomination of money composed of 6,000 denarii, while a denarius was the minimum day's wage. Another measurement of a talent was 60 pounds of gold or silver. In either measure, this was an enormous amount of money. The modern American equivalent for one talent would be about three hundred thousand dollars. No matter how one figures the precise value today, the amounts were quite large.

Each servant responded differently with his talents: The first two servants traded with the money and doubled it, while the third servant hid his talent, though no motive is given for his action quite yet.

> "He who had received the five talents went at once and traded with them; and he made five talents more. So also, he who had the two talents made two talents more. But he who had received the one talent went and dug in the ground and hid his master's money." (Matt. 25:16–18)

As in the preceding parables, the crisis occurs when the master returns to settle the accounts.

> "Now after a long time the master of those servants came and settled accounts with them. And he who had received the five talents came forward, bringing five talents more, saying, 'Master, you delivered to me five talents; here I have made five talents more.' His master said to him, 'Well done, good and faithful servant; you have been faithful over a little, I will set you over much; enter into the joy of your master.' And he also who had the two talents came forward, saying, 'Master, you delivered to me two talents; here I have made two talents more.' His master said to him, 'Well done, good and faithful servant; you have been faithful over a little, I will set you over much; enter into the joy of your master.'" (Matt. 25:19–23)

The master's return after a long delay is a symbol of Christ at the last judgment. Both of the first two servants are good and faithful because of their industrious effort to increase the master's money. Their reward is twofold: First, they receive an increase in responsibility because they demonstrated their capabilities; second, they enter into their master's joy, which derives from their increased responsibility. Their joy is also a new level of fellowship with the master.

Finally, the master settles accounts with the third servant, who approaches his master with the original talent and an excuse for not prospering.

> "He also who had received the one talent came forward, saying, 'Master, I knew you to be a hard man, reaping where you did not sow, and gathering where you did not winnow; so I was afraid, and I went and hid your talent in the ground. Here you have what is yours.'" (Matt. 25:24–25)

Instead of mentioning the amount he had received, as the other servants had done, this servant immediately excuses himself by describing the hardness of his master. He judges the master and out of fear fails to take proper action with the talent. The master responds by rebuking the servant:

> "'You wicked and slothful servant! You knew that I reap where I have not sowed, and gather where I have not winnowed? Then you ought to have invested my money with the bankers, and at my coming I should have received what was my own with interest.'" (Matt. 25:26–27)

His fear has made him lazy and wicked, and thereby the epitome of the servant who is neither awake nor watchful, as Jesus had commanded: "Watch therefore, for you do not know on what day your Lord is coming. Therefore you also must be ready; for the Son of man is coming at an hour you do not expect" (Matt. 24:42, 44). The servant's moral fault lies in sloth, his lack of industrious activity, and initiative rather than in the lack of increase for its own sake. He is therefore punished in two stages. First, his talent is removed (see Matt. 24:28–29) and second, he is sent outside to weep and gnash his teeth (see Matt. 24:30).

The fourth parable concerns the judgment of the sheep and the goats (see Matt. 25:31-46) as a separation of the good and the wicked at the end of time:

> "When the Son of man comes in his glory, and all the angels with him, then he will sit on his glorious throne. Before him will be gathered all the nations, and he will separate them one from another as a shepherd separates the sheep from the goats, and he will place the sheep at his right hand, but the goats at the left." (Matt. 25:31–33)

Two images of Jesus Christ are joined here. First, He is the Son of Man who comes with His own angels and with the authority to judge humans, as in the prophecy in Daniel 7:

> I saw in the night visions, and behold, with the clouds of heaven there came one like a son of man, and he came to the Ancient of Days and was presented before him. 14 And to him was given dominion and glory and kingdom, that all peoples, nations, and languages should serve him; his dominion is an everlasting dominion, which shall not pass away, and his kingdom one that shall not be destroyed. (Dan. 7:13–14; see also Matt. 16:27; 19:28; 26:64)

Second, Jesus is a shepherd, with the authority to separate the good from the evil among the "nations," or Gentile peoples. The King begins with His judgment of the righteous sheep, whom He invites to enter the kingdom that had been prepared from the foundation of the world (see Matt. 25:34). Jesus identifies

Himself as "the King," which is not used very often in Matthew, except for His birth: "Where is he who has been born king of the Jews?" (Matt. 2:2); and Palm Sunday, which fulfills Zechariah 9:10: "Tell the daughter of Zion, Behold, your king is coming to you, humble, and mounted on an ass, and on a colt, the foal of an ass." (Matt 21:5). Otherwise, Jesus proclaims the "Kingdom of God" and the Kingdom of Heaven," without identifying Himself as the king (see Matt. 4:17; Mark 1:15).

The righteous are quite surprised at the criteria they had fulfilled to enter the kingdom prepared for them, since they ask: "Lord, when did we see you hungry and feed you, or thirsty and give you drink? And when did we see you a stranger and welcome you, or naked and clothe you? And when did we see you sick or in prison and visit you?" (Matt. 25:37–39). Jesus responds that their good deeds to others were done to Him: "Truly, I say to you, as you did it to one of the least of these my brethren, you did it to me" (Matt. 25:40).

Then the King judges the goats on His left, with His reasons for their condemnation to hell:

> "Depart from me, you cursed, into the eternal fire prepared
> for the devil and his angels; for I was hungry and you gave
> me no food, I was thirsty and you gave me no drink, I was
> a stranger and you did not welcome me, naked and you did
> not clothe me, sick and in prison and you did not visit me."
> (Matt. 25:41–43)

Despite the excuses offered by the accursed, they remain condemned:

> "Then they also will answer, 'Lord, when did we see you hungry
> or thirsty or a stranger or naked or sick or in prison, and did
> not minister to you?' Then he will answer them, 'Truly, I say to

you, as you did it not to one of the least of these, you did it not to me.'" (Matt. 25:44–45)

The righteous sheep and the wicked goats live side by side, unwittingly doing or neglecting good deeds. As in the rest of the parables about the final judgment, Jesus Christ will judge each person according to His standards, not theirs, either for good or ill. The wicked "will go away into eternal punishment, but the righteous into eternal life" (Matt. 25:46). Until then, neither society nor the Church are exempt from this mixture of good and bad people.

Conclusion

As scandalous as the sex abuse and financial scandals might be, no one ought to be so surprised that they lose faith in Christ or His Church. Jesus was well aware of the varying qualities of human beings, so He knew that the Kingdom of God and His Church would have saints and sinners alike. He will be the final arbiter who judges the distinctions between good and evil, wisdom and folly in each and every human heart. Likewise, He promises eternal reward to the just and condemnation to the wicked.

People throughout the centuries have been scandalized by wickedness among Church members, including clergy and hierarchy, as well they ought to be. However, wisdom equally should induce us to expect that some members of the Church and its leadership are going to be wicked. In the face of that inevitability, each of us must choose to do the righteous and good that God desires for us. Failure due to weakness can be corrected; the choice to be self-centered and seek one's own gratification, pride, ambition, and advancement at the expense of obeying God's commandments and laws and of respecting the inherent dignity of every other person will lead to condemnation in hell.

Tensions rooted in sin existed among the Apostles that

Jesus called as His closest associates, and these appear throughout the public ministry. We turn to the Gospel episodes about those failures and tensions in the next chapter.

CHAPTER 2

—⚬⚬⚬—

PRELUDE TO THE FAILURES
OF THE APOSTLES

Amazingly, all four Gospels portray the Twelve Apostles as men who were willing to leave their former ways of life and follow Jesus, and at the same time as men filled with envy, ambition, anger, and greed. Jesus had to correct their vices many times throughout His public ministry, both in private and in front of the large crowds. These honest portrayals distinguish themselves from other ancient (and modern) histories that criticize opponents and enemies but overlook the faults of rulers and heroes. The Gospels lay out the sins and failings of their own authors and heroes, except for Jesus and His mother, Mary, who are presented without sin or fault.

The honest presentation of the flaws in New Testament heroes is particularly seen in St. Peter, who is the second most frequently mentioned person in the New Testament; only Jesus Christ is mentioned more often. Mark's Gospel portrays Peter in a worse light than any New Testament book, which is particularly interesting in light of the Fathers of the Church consistently teaching that St. Mark was St. Peter's secretary who recorded Peter's memoirs. In other words, Peter himself was the primary source for the Gospel account that is most critical of him. This indicates that the Apostles themselves were the sources of the stories about their personal flaws and moral failures. Such honesty places them into the general line of Israelite literature, which recognizes the sinfulness of all of its heroes; the Old Testament narratives include the sins and faults of Abraham, Isaac, Jacob, David, Solomon, and the prophets. Humble honesty about human sin is one of the most endearing qualities of biblical literature, in both the Old and New Testaments.

The Gospel accounts of the types of men called by Christ are worthy of meditation by bishops and priests as an honest examination of their own lives. Of course, the lay faithful can find fruitful reflection on their own flaws and failures within their vocations and personal lives, as well as reflecting upon the situation of the clergy. This does not give anyone permission to justify existing bad behavior, but rather leads us to consider how Jesus Christ dealt with the faults and sins of the men He called to lead His new Church. The goal here is to let Christ correct each of us in the present as we examine the weak Apostles of the past. The Gospels can open our imaginations to see our life stories in their truest, deepest light—which is the light provided by Jesus Christ on our lives.

Jesus Selects The Twelve

The three Synoptic Gospels (Matthew, Mark, and Luke) relate that Jesus chose twelve men to formHis inner circle of disciples. Clearly, the selection of twelve men parallels the twelve tribes of Israel, to indicate that Jesus was founding a new Israel. However, they would not become the physical progenitors of twelve new tribes named after each of them. Instead, they were to sow an "imperishable seed," which is "the living and abiding word of God," the "word [that] is the good news" they preached. Through preaching the "imperishable seed of God's word," they brought people of faith to be "born anew" through that word (see 1 Pet. 1:23, 25). They became the spiritual fathers of the Church through their preaching, as St. Paul wrote: "For I became your father in Christ Jesus through the gospel" (1 Cor. 4:15), and people were "born anew" of "water and the Spirit" (John 3:3, 5) as the Apostles and their disciples baptized people throughout the world. Yet the Christians who followed the Twelve were not separated into twelve groups named after the Twelve Apostles, but became "one body and one Spirit ... called to the one hope ... one Lord, one faith, one baptism, one God and Father all, who is above all and through all and in all" (Eph. 4:4–6). They were called to preach the Kingdom of God just as Jesus had done, even though each Apostle was a very limited person and a sinner.

Significance of the Lists of the Apostles

There are four lists of the names of the Twelve Apostles (see Matt. 10:2-4; Mark 3:16-19; Luke 6:12-16; Acts 1:13), each of which organizes the names into three groups of four names. All four lists begin their three groups with the names Peter, Philip, and James the son of Alphaeus, and the names within each group are the same, though appearing in different order. Some names fluctuate: Thaddaeus is called Judas the son of James in the Gospels of Matthew and Mark; Simon the Kananaios is parallel to Simon the Zealot. However, the names of the twelve tribes of Israel in the various lists also fluctuate (see Gen. 49; Deut. 33; Judg. 5; Rev. 7:5–8), so there is no need to exaggerate the importance of these variations.

In this first section we will examine the lists of the Twelve in the Gospels to learn more about Jesus' purposes in calling them. We will also pay attention to various clues about the personalities of each Apostle, noting the first hints of their faults and sins.

Matthew 10:1–4

After Jesus noticed how the crowds were "harassed and helpless, like sheep without a shepherd" (Matt. 9:36), He instructed His disciples to "pray therefore the Lord of the harvest to send out laborers into his harvest" (Matt. 9:38). He then chose twelve men as the inner core within His larger group of disciples so as to commission them with His own authority.

> And he called to him his twelve disciples and gave them authority over unclean spirits, to cast them out, and to heal every disease and every infirmity. The names of the twelve apostles are these: first, Simon, who is called Peter, and Andrew his brother; James the son of Zebedee, and John his brother; Philip and Bartholomew; Thomas and Matthew the tax collector; James the son of Alphaeus, and Thaddaeus; Simon the Cananaean, and Judas Iscariot, who betrayed him. (Matt. 10:1–4)

First, Jesus gave the Twelve the very power over unclean spirits, disease, and infirmity that He possessed. A few verses later He commanded them to preach, cast out demons, and heal sicknesses: "And preach as you go, saying, 'The kingdom of heaven is at hand.' Heal the sick, raise the dead, cleanse lepers, cast out demons" (Matt. 10:7–8). Clearly, He intended the Twelve to share in His authority and power, and their message is to be the same as His (see Matt. 4:17). These disciples were in some ways to embody Christ (see Matt. 10:24–25, 40; see also Luke 6:40; Luke 10:16; John 13:16, 20; John 15:20).

Christ wanted to make the disciples like Himself in both power and in holiness, but He started with very flawed men who very much needed His correction and guidance.

Mark 3:13-19

Jesus climbed a mountain to make His choice of the Twelve in parallel with Moses, who climbed Mount Sinai to mediate the covenant with the twelve tribes of Israel (see Ex. 19:4–6). He had two reasons to "call to himself" the men He desired. First, He appointed twelve "to be with him" as companions who would form the nucleus of the Church. Second, He wanted to send them out to preach His Gospel and cast out demons, enabling them to minister just as He does.

> And he went up on the mountain, and called to him those whom he desired; and they came to him. And he appointed twelve, to be with him, and to be sent out to preach and have authority to cast out demons. (Mark 3:13–15)

St. Mark arranges the names of the twelve in three groups of four Apostles each, with the first name in each subgroup indicating a certain preeminence, or leadership, within it. The evangelist's notes about the individuals indicate both the diversity among them and the tensions that later erupt into disputes.

The first group included four fishing partners: Simon whom He surnamed Peter; James the son of Zebedee and John his brother, whom He surnamed Boanerges, that is, sons of thunder; and Peter's brother Andrew (see Mark 3:16–18a). *Simon* was the most commonly used name among Jews during the period of Roman occupation, according to contemporary inscriptions. The Aramaic name *Kepha* (rock, crag) appears only once before Peter, in a fifth-century marriage contract on Elephantine Island in Egypt. The Greek form *Petros* is never used as a name until the Christian era, when Christian parents started to give this name to their sons.

Peter's fishing partners include James and John, the sons of

Zebedee, whose nickname is Boanerges, or "sons of thunder." They are never addressed by this name anywhere else, so it is not a name change, as in the case of Simon being called Peter. That title is less a reflection on their father Zebedee than it is on their own temper and aggressive self-promotion. A testimony to the just application of this epithet to the brothers is found in a different Gospel:

> And he sent messengers ahead of him, who went and entered a village of the Samaritans, to make ready for him; but the people would not receive him, because his face was set toward Jerusalem. And when his disciples James and John saw it, they said, "Lord, do you want us to bid fire come down from heaven and consume them?" But he turned and rebuked them. (Luke 9:52–55)

Note that Jesus rebuked their thunderous attitude and their later attempt to put them in prominent seats at His right and His left (see Mark 10:35-52). Most of us with brothers have little doubt that had Christ acceded to their request, they would have fought over taking the position on Christ's right side.

Peter, James, and John will be the three intimates of Jesus who are admitted to events from which the others were excluded — the raising of Jairus's daughter (see Mark 5:37), the Transfiguration of Jesus (see Mark 9:2), and Jesus' prayer in Gethsemane (see Mark 14:33).

Peter's brother and partner, Andrew, however, is the fourth in this list, apparently as the one who was still outside that intimate group of three disciples. Other than his call from Jesus, and his inclusion in all the lists of the apostles, he is only mentioned twice more in the Synoptic Gospels. He was co-owner of the house in Capernaum with Peter, to which this very group of four fishing partners enter after the synagogue service (see Mark

1:29). Andrew was with the other three partners again when they marvel at the Temple and Jesus gives them His discourse on the end of Jerusalem and the end of the world (see Mark 13:3). Only in John's Gospel does Andrew have much prominence: he is one of the two disciples of John the Baptist who are the first to follow Jesus, he points out the lad with five barley loaves and two fish, and Philip brings some Greeks to Andrew (whose name is Greek, like Philip's) to introduce them to Jesus, perhaps as a translator (see Mark 12:22).

The second subgroup includes Philip, and Bartholomew, and Matthew, and Thomas (see Mark 3:18b). The call of Matthew the tax collector is an important episode in Mark 2:14–17, where he is known as Levi (see also Luke 5:27–31; Matt. 9:9–13 is the only Gospel that mentions him as Matthew). The dislike of tax collectors led to a Jewish prohibition against anyone marrying a tax collector or the relative of a tax collector. Matthew's presence among the Twelve was certainly a cause of tension, especially for Simon the Cananaean, who was a member of the super patriotic Zealot faction.

The other three disciples—Philip, Bartholomew, and Thomas—do not have any prominence in Mark, Matthew, or Luke, but they each play significant roles in episodes of John's Gospel. Jesus calls Philip (see John 1:43-48), and subsequently Philip calls Bartholomew/Nathaniel in John 1:45. In fact, the reason to identify Bartholomew with Nathaniel is that his name is immediately after Philip's, perhaps an indication of their relationship to each other; *Bartholomew* means "Son of Tolmai," while Nathaniel would be his first name.

Philip is the one whom Jesus asks about feeding the crowd, and he points out the boy with five loaves and two fish (see John 6:5–7); some Greeks approach Philip, whose name is Greek, in order to go meet Jesus (see John 12:21–22); Jesus corrects Philip's lack of comprehension that seeing Jesus means seeing the Father also (see John 14:8–9); Thomas is famous for doubting the claims of the ten disciples that Jesus had truly risen from the dead (John 20:24-29); and both Thomas and Bartholomew/Nathaniel were in the fishing boat with Peter and his partners when Jesus appeared to them at the Sea of Galilee (see John 21:2).

The third apostolic subgroup is "James the son of Alphaeus, and Thaddaeus, and Simon the Cananaean, and Judas Iscariot, who betrayed him" (Mark 3:18c–19). Levi/Matthew is also called a son of Alphaeus, indicating that this "James the Less" may be his natural brother. Simon the Cananaean is a name derived from Aramaic *qan`ana`* (in Hebrew, *qan`a*), which means "zealous." That is why St. Luke simply translates the title into the Greek "Zealot," indicating his radical nationalistic politics.

Thaddaeus is the Latin form of the Aramaic word *Taddai*, meaning "courageous." He is also known as Judas or Jude (see Luke 6:16, where he is "Judas of James," which the Aramaic Peshitto translation and many modern translations interpret as "Judas son of James," which is a very solid interpretation.

Finally, Judas Iscariot is mentioned, with the editorial note by St. Mark that he was the disciple who betrayed Jesus (see Mark 14:10–11, 18–21, 41–44). The meaning of *Iscariot* is not clear. One interpretation bases Iscariot in two Hebrew words, *ish Qerioth*, meaning "a man of Qerioth," which was a Judaean town mentioned in Joshua 15:25. Judas's father is identified as "Simon Iscariot" (John 6:71), which could be interpreted the same way. One difficulty is that this interpretation depends on using Hebrew rather than Aramaic, which was more commonly spoken at the time of Christ. Yet, since Hebrew was still in use, as evidenced in the Dead Sea Scrolls, it remains the easiest interpretation of the name. Another possibility is to derive Iscariot from the Aramaic root *scr*, meaning "liar, fraud, false one." That causes problems of interpreting John 6:71 and 13:36, where the word refers to the name of a place, thereby indicating that John forgot the meaning of the nickname given after the betrayal. A third possibility is to derive the word from the Latin *sicarius*, which means "assassin," which was then given a Semitic form "Iscariot."

Luke 6:12-16

More than the other Gospel writers, St. Luke highlights how frequently Jesus prayed, so before choosing the Twelve, Jesus "went out to the mountain to pray; and all night he continued in prayer to God" (Luke 6:12). Only after that night vigil did He call His disciples together and "chose from them twelve, whom he named apostles" (Luke 6:13). His list of the Twelve has but a few notes on certain individuals, similar to the information given by St. Mark:

> … Simon, whom he named Peter, and Andrew his brother, and James and John, and Philip, and Bartholomew, and Matthew, and Thomas, and James the son of Alphaeus, and Simon who was called the Zealot, and Judas the son of James, and Judas Iscariot, who became a traitor. (Luke 6:14–16)

St. Luke also wrote Acts of the Apostles, where he lists the eleven apostles remaining after Judas's betrayal of Jesus: "Peter and John and James and Andrew, Philip and Thomas, Bartholomew and Matthew, James the son of Alphaeus and Simon the Zealot and Judas the son of James" (Acts 1:13). Jesus had ascended into heaven and was not present with them in the Upper Room as they devoted themselves to prayer, just as He had done on the night He chose them. Luke gives no additional notes about any of the individuals.

The Apostles' Blind Inability to Understand Jesus

As the Twelve follow Jesus during the public ministry, they show a spiritual blindness to Jesus' message, despite His preaching, miracles, and exorcisms. We will look at them as a way to examine the consciences of all Christians, but particularly the clergy—bishops, priests, deacons, and seminarians—who succeed the Apostles. Spiritual blindness regarding Jesus Christ and His teachings affects the moral life of the clergy and lay faithful, so every modern disciple needs to examine himself or herself for the logs of sin that block Christ's light from their own eyes (see Matt. 7:1–5) and prevents understanding the Gospel. Failure to admit our spiritual blindness keeps even the well-intentioned away from the healing that brings Christ's light to our souls. Therefore, it is essential to prayerfully examine our consciences and humbly pursue Christ's truth before our sins overwhelm us. Authentic insight and faith in Jesus' teaching opens our way to holiness and virtue instead of blind pursuit of self-centered vice.

Failing to Focus on the Bread of Life

Following the second time Jesus multiplied loaves and fish (see Mark 8:1–9), He and the disciples sailed from the eastern shore of the Sea of Galilee to the western shore. Mark says that they brought only one loaf of bread with them (8:14), which forms the background for misunderstanding Jesus' warning against the leaven of the Pharisees. The disciples focused on their lack of bread, which they needed to give them energy to row across the lake. They may even have thought about breaking the bread into thirteen little pieces that would leave each of them hungry. They may have blamed themselves, but more likely they blamed each other for failing to bring bread from the seven baskets of leftovers after the preceding miracle.

However, their focus on the lack of loaves and the presence of only one loaf was a failure to pay attention to Jesus, the Bread of Life present with them. How different is this from modern people who concern themselves with the lack of things in their lives, or who focus on the things they actually do have while missing the presence of Jesus Christ in their midst? People so focus on material things that they neglect to center themselves on Jesus' presence in the tabernacles of our churches. On Sundays, some people are so attentive to the need to get out of the church parking lot ahead of everyone else for brunch at the local restaurant that they fail listen to Jesus, the Bread of life, Whom they just received in Holy Communion. Even some of the clergy, whose proximity to the church would make prayer and meditation before the Bread of Life easy, ignore him.

Jesus responds to the Apostles' worries about bread by warning them to "beware of the leaven of the Pharisees and the leaven of Herod" (Mark 8:15). The admonition immediately follows Jesus' encounter with the Pharisees (see Mark 8:11–13) in which they demand a sign from Him, but He refuses to give one. It was part of a history of tension with the Pharisees that began with Jesus forgiving the paralytic (Mark 2:1–12), eating with the tax collectors (Mark 2:13–17), claiming lordship over the Sabbath (Mark 2:23–27), healing a man on the Sabbath (Mark 3:1–6), and casting out demons (Mark 3:22–29). He condemned both their hypocrisy about small issues over larger moral issues (Mark 7:1–23) and their demand for a sign to prove Jesus' claims (Mark 8:11–12). This tension increased as Jesus taught and acted beyond their tradition, while they refused to believe in Him, despite witnessing exorcisms and miracles. For these reasons Jesus warns the disciples against the leaven—i.e., the influence of the Pharisees that rejects faith in Him.

The Herodians, in league with the Pharisees, plotted to kill Jesus after He healed a man in a synagogue on a Sabbath (see Mark 3:6) and they would later try to entrap Him by asking about paying taxes to Caesar (see Mark 12:13–17; Matt. 22:16–21). Most importantly, Herod had heard of Jesus but interpreted Him through the prism of his own deeds—specifically the killing of John the Baptist to please his stepdaughter Salome after a sensuous dance (see Mark 6:14–29). Apparently Herod accepted that the miracles had happened, but he misinterpreted them as the deeds of a resurrected John the Baptist instead of Jesus. Herod's leaven, or influence, refers to misdirected faith in Jesus' miracles.

Of course, the disciples misinterpret Jesus' saying in terms of their failure to bring bread with them, announcing, "We have no bread" (Mark 8:16). They reduce Christ's warning from one of concern over the bad influences of the Pharisees and the Herodians. They miss the Pharisees' and Herodians' hardness of heart because both their stomachs and their heads were empty.

Jesus rebuked them, "Why do you discuss the fact that you have no bread? Do you not yet perceive or understand? Are your hearts hardened? Having eyes do you not see, and having ears do you not hear? And do you not remember?" (Mark 8:17–18). Through these rhetorical questions, Jesus directs their attention to their lack of comprehension of His Gospel and the possibility that their hearts are hardened. St. Mark had noted this same issue after Jesus walked on the water: "They were utterly astounded, for they did not understand about the loaves, but their hearts were hardened" (Mark 6:51–52). Despite having been given the "secret" (*mysterion*) of the kingdom of God, they were unable to see or hear what Jesus was doing.

In order to evoke greater comprehension, Jesus questioned them about the two multiplications of loaves and fish.

"When I broke the five loaves for the five thousand, how many baskets full of broken pieces did you take up?" They said to him, "Twelve." "And the seven for the four thousand, how many baskets full of broken pieces did you take up?" And they said to him, "Seven." (Mark 8:19–20)

Jesus makes them repeat symbolic numbers — twelve (for the number of tribes of Israel) and seven (a sign of perfection) — but they still do not understand. Though Jesus had instructed them privately as privileged insiders, they fail to understand Him, just like the Pharisee and Herodian outsiders.

Jesus' final question is also the final rebuke of the first half of the Gospel: "Do you not yet understand?" (Mark 8:21). Jesus' question is clearly rhetorical, with the aim of rebuking them for not understanding the meaning of the miracles and signs He does, or the "mystery" of the kingdom of God. Yet they continue to follow Him, and they continue to accept His rebukes — except for Judas Iscariot, who never seems to understand. The disciples remained with Jesus and sought to understand Him, while the Pharisees and Herodians refused to accept His rebukes and became ever more hostile toward Jesus as the Gospel progresses.

As was true during Jesus' public ministry, modern disciples must examine their consciences to see whether they fail to understand Him and His Gospel mysteries. Outside the Church are the Pharisees and Herodians, those various forces of society that reject faith in Christ or want to see it work for their own self-centered and egotistical purposes. These can be contemporary atheists who hate God and religion, or cynical politicians and businesspeople who want to manipulate religion and the Church in order to gain power or money.

The question for disciples continues to be whether they will accept God's rebukes, with the knowledge that God is correct and humans are wrong, or whether they will join the modern Pharisees and Herodians. Judas Iscariot ultimately did the latter. Many other bishops and priests through history and in the modern times have chosen self-centered power, money, sex, and possessions as their own version of the thirty pieces of silver. When the Catholic faith seems unclear or incomprehensible, each of us must respond to Christ's question: "Do you not understand?" Will we follow Him despite His rebuke, or will we look for silver pieces?

The Apostles Reject the Suffering and Death of Jesus and Want Their Own Desires

After they debark from the boat, Jesus and the disciples go to Bethsaida, where Jesus heals a blind man. Jesus spat on his eyes and then laid hands on him twice, and the man gained his sight in two stages (see Mark 8:22–26). This opens the way to a large section of Jesus' teaching along the route to Jerusalem that concludes with the healing of blind Bartimaeus in Jericho (see Mark 8:27—10:52). Between these two healings of the blind, Jesus will heal the spiritual blindness of His disciples step-by-step, not unlike the blind man of Bethsaida.

The most important theme of Jesus' teaching will be His repeated predictions of His coming suffering, death, and resurrection in Jerusalem. Each time He makes these predictions, the disciples reject it or change the subject to their own desires—not unlike their change of subject from the leaven of the Pharisees and Herodians to their own desire for more bread. Peter rebukes Jesus for speaking about His coming suffering and crucifixion. All of them want to know which of them is the greatest; who will have the first places in the kingdom of God; and what benefit will they get from following Jesus.

Modern disciples can examine their own consciences in light of these passages, to see how they resemble the self-centeredness of the Apostles. Keeping an open mind and conscience in regard to personal similarities with the ancient Apostles will help us repent of the egoism that they and we so readily demonstrate in our fallen state.

Peter's Confession of Christ, Rebuke of Christ, and Rebuke from Christ

In a well-known episode near Caesarea Philippi, the Lord Jesus asked His disciples, "Who do men say that I am?" They knew the popular opinions about Jesus, so they told Him, "John the Baptist; and others say, Elijah; and others one of the prophets." When Jesus asked, "But who do you say that I am?" it was Peter who answered, "You are the Christ."

Matthew's Gospel presents a fuller dialogue, but Mark's brevity highlights the next step in the conversation, when Jesus "began to teach them that the Son of man must suffer many things, and be rejected by the elders and the chief priests and the scribes, and be killed, and after three days rise again" (Mark 8:31). This is the first announcement of His coming suffering and death, and it was met with rejection from Simon, who had just been renamed Peter, the rock: "Peter took him, and began to rebuke him" (Mark 8:32). Peter accepted that Jesus is the Christ—that is, the long-awaited Messiah—but he could not accept a suffering Messiah. Suffering and crucifixion spoke of failure and criminal punishment, and therefore Peter rebuked Jesus, using a Greek term commonly used to rebuke demons (see Matt. 17:18; Mark 1:25; 9:25; Luke 4:35; 4:41; 9:42), sinners (see Luke 17:3), and the Apostles. In response, Jesus "rebuked Peter, and said, 'Get behind me, Satan! For you are not on the side of God, but of men'" (Mark 8:33).

At this point Jesus teaches both His disciples and the whole crowd about the necessity for every one of His followers to suffer like Him:

> "If any man would come after me, let him deny himself and take up his cross and follow me. For whoever would save his life will lose it; and whoever loses his life for my sake and the gospel's will save it" (Mark 8:34–35).

Jesus teaches His disciples the absolute necessity of suffering to the point of taking up of the cross. This is particularly telling in the contemporary Church, when a fad for removing crosses from churches gained a foothold for a while. A desire to focus on the Resurrection was behind the exclusion of crucifixes, even from within churches and from altars. Often enough, this was followed by the removal of the tabernacles because the presence of Jesus Christ in the Blessed Sacrament was perceived as a distraction at Mass. If His Eucharistic presence was a distraction, then who exactly was to become the main attraction? Sometimes the priests were tempted to see themselves the center of attention at Mass as well as outside of Mass.

Using two rhetorical questions about the profit and value of gaining great possessions, even to acquiring the whole world, Jesus presented the true values of life in the context of His Second Coming, when He will judge everyone's deeds.

> "For what does it profit a man, to gain the whole world and
> forfeit his life? For what can a man give in return for his
> life? For whoever is ashamed of me and of my words in this
> adulterous and sinful generation, of him will the Son of man
> also be ashamed, when he comes in the glory of his Father
> with the holy angels." (Mark 8:36–38)

The obvious answer to the questions about gaining the whole world but losing eternal life is that such success would profit a person nothing. Anyone with good sense knows that even the wealthiest and most powerful people end up being buried in the earth. No possession or position of power can help anyone after death.

What *does* matter is losing one's life in this world for the sake of Jesus Christ and His Gospel; that is the ultimate and eternal gain for every person. Jesus Christ is the final Judge at the end of the world, and the angels are His servants who execute divine justice, as was stated in the parables of the weeds and wheat, good and bad fish, the wise and foolish virgins, and the servants with the talents. Christ's judgment determines the eternal fate of each person: either decide for Jesus Christ and acknowledge Him before all people throughout one's life both in word and deed or deny Him. Does this entail picking up the Cross and dying with Christ? Yes, indeed. Does shame for knowing Jesus mean the loss of eternal life? Yes, indeed. Therefore, each person in the world must decide must choose Christ's way to eternal life or suffer eternal loss.

Jesus' Second Prediction of His Death and the Need for Humility

After the Transfiguration, Jesus continued His journey south through Galilee toward Jerusalem, the location of His coming execution. He kept secret His destination (see Mark 9:30-31) and His teachings about His upcoming suffering, just as He had kept secret His identity as the Messiah throughout Mark. On that journey He told the disciples a second time, "The Son of man will be delivered into the hands of men, and they will kill him; and when he is killed, after three days he will rise" (Mark 9:31). This prediction has three points: 1) He will be handed over to men; 2) they will kill Him; and 3) He will rise after three days. However, the disciples "did not understand the saying, and they were afraid to ask him" (9:32). Just as they had difficulty understanding His parables, the leaven of the Pharisees and Herodians, and the Transfiguration, now they do not understand the importance of the suffering, death, and Resurrection in Jesus' ministry.

Their misunderstanding leads them to change the subject to themselves. Though Mark skillfully omits the disciples' actual discussion about their own greatness, it comes out when Jesus asks, "What were you discussing on the way?" (Mark 9:33). They had no answer, probably due to embarrassment over the topic, but Jesus clearly knew the answer anyway since He always knows what is in human hearts. The Apostles chose pride and self-exaltation over Jesus' message of emptying himself and dying on a cross like a slave.

Unlike his other rebukes, Jesus does not correct them directly, but instead gathers the Twelve to teach two points. First He lays down the principle, "If any one would be first, he must be last of all and servant of all" (Mark 9:35). Having prominence and importance does not come from self-assertion in Jesus' mind. Rather, humble service in the last place is Jesus' norm for greatness. Second, He proposes a child's humility as the model for His disciples: "Whoever receives one such child in my name receives me; and whoever receives me, receives not me but him who sent me" (Mark 9:37). He warmly embraces the child in His arms and declares that the loving reception of a child is the basis for the reception of Jesus and His Father. There is no room for seeking higher positions of authority and prestige out of personal pride, which is a stance of looking down on other people. Humility does not entail putting oneself down nor speaking badly of oneself, since that still makes one the center of attention, albeit a negative attention. Humility looks up to God's infinite goodness, majesty, and beauty, a perspective that offers a vivid sense of personal smallness. Yet when we look up to God in wonder and love, we become better persons for it, just as beautiful art, great music, or nature's magnificence make us better in their own ways.

This is a tremendous lesson for contemporary clergy. Popes Benedict XVI and Francis have frequently criticized bishops and priests who seek prominent assignments, larger sees, episcopal honors—the "scarlet fever" identified by the scarlet on bishops' robes. Such ambition is a serious temptation that contradicts the goodness of Jesus Christ, and the clergy need to repent of it if they are to be authentic disciples of Christ.

The other obvious point is that the reception and embrace of a child is the equivalent of receiving Jesus Christ and God the

Father. Any priest who embraces a child for self-serving desire is doing the same to Jesus and His Father. Any form of abuse of children, including sexual abuse, is an abuse of God as well. Jesus Himself establishes that norm for judgment, not only here but in Matthew 25:40, 45: "Whatever you do to the least one, you do to me." Who would want to stand before God's judgment seat and face the fire in Jesus' eyes as He accuses someone of sexual abuse of Himself through the person of a child, an adolescent, a handicapped or otherwise vulnerable person? Instead, Jesus calls everyone, clergy and lay faithful alike, to humbly serve Christ's smallest brethren and consider it as having been done to the Lord Himself.

The Rich Young Man

Later on the journey, a wealthy man asked Jesus, "Good Teacher, what must I do to inherit eternal life?" (Mark 10:17). Jesus answered on two levels. First, He told him to keep all the commandments, which the man says he has done since his youth (see Mark 10:19–20). The second level was to tell him to "go, sell what you have, and give to the poor, and you will have treasure in heaven; and come, follow me." Due to his great wealth, the young man was unwilling to do that, and he went away sad (see Mark 10:21–22).

At that point, Jesus addressed His disciples about the uselessness of riches in the kingdom of God: "How hard it will be for those who have riches to enter the kingdom of God!" And when the disciples find it difficult to accept this teaching, He again said:

> "Children, how hard it is to enter the kingdom of God! It is easier for a camel to go through the eye of a needle than for a rich man to enter the kingdom of God." They were so astonished that they asked, "Then who can be saved?" (Mark 10:23–26).

Jesus assured them that "with men it is impossible, but not with God; for all things are possible with God" (Mark 10:27). Therefore they would have to become even more dependent on God than on themselves. Yet Peter reminded Him that they had already given up a lot in order to become disciples: "We have left everything and followed you" (Mark 10: 28). Peter's statement implied that he and the others had expected to acquire significant material gains from being disciples. This is understandable in light of Deuteronomy 26—27, where curses are proclaimed for those who failed to obey God's commandments but prosperity and comfort were the blessings due to those who faithfully kept the commandments.

Many Christians, Catholic and non-Catholic alike, hold a Deuteronomistic theology that links obedience to God with the blessings of prosperity. Throughout Catholic history there have been clergy who use the Church as a way to become wealthy, and some have lived luxurious lifestyles. This continues among some of the clergy today, despite the call of the Vatican Council and the popes to live a simpler life. Over the centuries, the heroes of the faith—that is, the saints—lived greater poverty and simplicity, whether as religious, as diocesan priests, or lay faithful. Those who attained great wealth and lived luxurious lives are not among the rolls of the saints. Therefore, in the face of self-indulgence in a very wealthy, modern society, Our Lord clearly teaches us that material success in this world must be measured in the light of the shortness of life, the inevitability of death, and God's true judgment:

> Jesus said, "Truly, I say to you, there is no one who has left
> house or brothers or sisters or mother or father or children or
> lands, for my sake and for the gospel, who will not receive a
> hundredfold now in this time, houses and brothers and sisters
> and mothers and children and lands, with persecutions, and in

the age to come eternal life. But many that are first will be last, and the last first." (Mark 10:29–31)

Third Prediction of the Crucifixion

As Jesus and His disciples continued walking toward Jerusalem, He makes a third prediction of His suffering and death and Resurrection:

"Behold, we are going up to Jerusalem; and the Son of man will be delivered to the chief priests and the scribes, and they will condemn him to death, and deliver him to the Gentiles; and they will mock him, and spit upon him, and scourge him, and kill him; and after three days he will rise" (Mark 10:33–34).

He gives them more details of His suffering and death than in the previous predictions, but that does not prevent the disciples from changing the subject to themselves and their status. James and John, two of the first four disciples, approached Jesus about their status among the rest of the disciples. "Grant us to sit, one at your right hand and one at your left, in your glory" (Mark 10:37). Rather than argue amongst themselves, "the sons of thunder" avoid a discussion with the other ten disciples and ask Jesus directly to grant them higher status in the group. Jesus recognized their failure to understand the meaning of higher status in Christianity:

"You do not know what you are asking. Are you able to drink the cup that I drink, or to be baptized with the baptism with which I am baptized?" And they said to him, "We are able." And Jesus said to them, "The cup that I drink you will drink; and with the baptism with which I am baptized, you will be baptized; but to sit at my right hand or at my left is not mine to grant, but it is for those for whom it has been prepared." (Mark 10:38–40)

Jesus emphasizes that being at His right and left does not entail honors as much as it means a baptism into suffering and a drink from the bitter cup of pain (see "the cup of wrath" in Jer. 25:15; Is. 51:17,22; Ps. 11:6; 60:3; 75:8; Job 21:20). Jesus here builds on His teaching that His disciples must pick up their crosses and follow Him (Mark 8:34–35). The "sons of thunder" were looking for glory, but Jesus promised them suffering like His own. Though they claimed they accepted the suffering, he could not grant their request to sit on His right and left because it had been prepared those whom the Father had chosen for such a position.

The other ten react indignantly, so Jesus continues teaching them further:

> "You know that those who are supposed to rule over the
> Gentiles lord it over them, and their great men exercise
> authority over them. But it shall not be so among you; but
> whoever would be great among you must be your servant, and
> whoever would be first among you must be slave of all. For the
> Son of man also came not to be served but to serve, and to give
> his life as a ransom for many." (Mark 10:42–45)

Jesus pointed out that self-seeking use of power belongs to the Gentiles, not His disciples. The people did not like Roman oppression, their high taxes, and the politicians' use of oppressed provinces as stepping-stones to more important government positions. If they did not like the Gentiles climbing to power, then His disciples had to avoid such behavior within the Church. They must learn from their experience and avoid doing what they dislike. The disciples must look to His life as their model: Jesus came to serve them and give up His life as a ransom for the many; all those who exercise leadership in the Church must do the same.

The Failure of Faith Among Jesus' Disciples

After teaching the crowds and His disciples inside the synagogue at Capernaum about the necessity of faith in Him and of receiving His flesh and blood in order to gain eternal life, many disciples rejected Jesus' teaching and left Him (see John 6:59–64). Those disciples "murmured" against Him, as had the ancient Israelites in the Sinai desert when they had run out of bread, saying, "This is a hard saying; who can listen to it?" (John 6:60). Jesus knew their inner thoughts, which is yet again another indication of His divinity, since only God knows the mind and the heart. He then asked them, "Do you take offense at this? (John 6:61). He offers them the ultimate proof: they will witness Jesus' Ascension into heaven, and they need to decide how they will react to that. He asks them, "Then what if you were to see the Son of man ascending where he was before?" (John 6:62). Next He sets down a principle by which they ought to judge His teaching on the Eucharist: "It is the spirit that gives life, the flesh is of no avail; the words that I have spoken to you are spirit and life" (John 6:63).

Still, Jesus knows their hearts, so He can tell them that some do not have faith in Him and one of them would betray Him: "'But there are some of you that do not believe. For Jesus knew from the first who those were that did not believe, and who it was that would betray him. 'This is why I told you that no one can come to me unless it is granted him by the Father'" (John 6:64-65). This first reference to the betrayer in John's Gospel is important because it occurs during Jesus' teaching on the Eucharist, and Judas's betrayal would take place during the Last Supper, when Judas goes out into the night, a symbol of the darkness that is within him.

The turning point of this section occurs when "many of his disciples drew back and no longer went about with him" (John 6:66). His teaching about the Eucharist became decisive for those who left Jesus' company because they could not accept that eating his Body and Blood was a necessary precondition for eternal life. Then Jesus challenged the Twelve Apostles with an option to leave him: "Do you also wish to go away?" Simon Peter answered him, "Lord, to whom shall we go? You have the words of eternal life; and we have believed, and have come to know, that you are the Holy One of God" (John 6:67–69).

Simon Peter spoke up for the group, again exercising his leadership among them, and professed faith that Jesus had the words of life and is the Holy One of God, the Messiah. In response, Jesus again exercises His divine prerogative by which He knows that one of the twelve will betray Him (see John 6:70–71). Judas was one of His chosen twelve disciples, and yet Jesus is fully aware that Judas "is a devil" who will betray Him later.

John 6 contains important parallels to Holy Thursday: the mention of Passover (John 6:4; 11:55), the multiplication of bread and the Eucharistic meal (which is not described in John), Jesus' walking on water (John 6:19–21), and His washing of the disciples' feet at the Last Supper (John 13:3–12). The long discourse on faith and the meaning of the Eucharist (John 6:25–58) parallels the long discourse at the Last Supper (John 13—17), and the disciples' who rejected Jesus and His teaching (John 6:66) parallels the disciples' abandonment of Jesus in Gethsemane. Finally, Judas's betrayal is mentioned here twice (John 6:64, 70), and it was accomplished in Gethsemane (John 18:2–5).

In regard to the present crisis among the clergy, it is worth noting that Jesus spoke about Judas Iscariot's betrayal in the context of addressing the loss of faith among His disciples, specifically regarding the Eucharist. Judas, however, remained within the inner circle of the Twelve, even though he did not believe. He eventually compensated for his hypocrisy by taking monetary compensation—Judas became a thief from the common purse (see John 12:6) and betrayed Jesus for thirty pieces of silver.

In some cases, priests and bishops over the centuries whose faith was weakened or who lost their faith sought to compensate by trying to make money for themselves. This is not a problem limited to the Medieval or Renaissance times; modern people still steal money from their churches and other institutions in order to feather their own beds with comforts and luxuries. Reflection on the person of Judas may spur such men to ask God for the gift of faith by which they can restore the salvation that may be slipping through their fingers. They can turn away from theft, sins of lust, and other evil deeds and return to Jesus Christ. Otherwise, their fate is utter doom in the next life, not to mention problems they may encounter in this one from the loss of integrity and pursuit by law enforcement.

Christians of every age would do well to consider themselves in light of these first disciples. Jesus Christ is the one who calls us to follow Him while we are still sinners, still self-oriented, and still ignorant of His wisdom. He even sends us out to the world before we have overcome all of our moral and personal limitations. Why does He do this? In part because, as we confront our personal limitations and sinful desires, we can learn about our need for His divine power, wisdom, truth, and goodness. Precisely as we engage in the mission and are confronted with our own limitations, we realize how weak we are and how we need to depend on Our Lord rather than ourselves. Like the Twelve, we will need Jesus Christ to forgive our sins, correct our mistakes, and strengthen our weaknesses. We need time for prayer and reflection to learn Christ's deeper wisdom and to receive His gracious help. As was true of the Apostles, we may change gradually, but humble acceptance of correction enables disciples to grow in holiness. Refusing Christ's correction puts us with Judas, the "devil" who rejected Jesus' teaching about faith and the Eucharist, sought money even through theft, and then betrayed Jesus. His end was a despair that drove him to suicide. Which approach will we choose, whether we are clergy or lay faithful? The failure to choose the good will end in eternal damnation; the choice to humbly stay with Jesus Christ leads to eternal life.

CHAPTER 3

———— ∞∞∞ ————

THE LAST SUPPER: SOURCE AND FOUNT, BETRAYAL AND FAILURE

One reason for the shock and tremendous scandal associated with the clergy sexual abuse scandal is that people have high regard for the Eucharist, which the Catholic Church believes is the Body and Blood, Soul and Divinity of Jesus Christ.[1] Because Christ Himself is truly present, the Blessed Sacrament is food for eternal life, and Jesus promises to dwell with those who receive His Body and Blood (see John 6:51–56). Jesus taught about the Eucharist during Passover, one year before He was crucified, and then instituted the Eucharist on the night before His saving death.

He personally celebrated that first Eucharist, but He empowered and commanded the Twelve Apostles attending the Last Supper to do the same. They and their successors, the bishops and priests, have continued to speak Jesus' words, "This is my Body, this is the cup of my Blood," for two thousand years. They say these words as if Jesus were speaking them because they act in the Person of Christ (*in Persona Christi*), and only the validly ordained priests may celebrate a valid sacrament. The

---

[1] Council of Trent, Session XIII, Chapter III.

years of training for the priesthood are meant to prepare them for the tremendous responsibilities their role entails. The candidates think and pray diligently to determine whether they are called to this ministry and are capable of living out the holiness and celibacy that Jesus Himself lived and which are attached to this office. The shock of the people of God is all the greater when priests fail to live in a holy manner and respect the dignity of the priesthood of Jesus Christ and of His Eucharist. The shock only increases the anger when the innocence of children and other vulnerable people is a further indication of the sin.

As another way to pray through the sexual abuse crisis, we turn now to consider the Apostles' behavior at the Last Supper when Jesus ordained them to His priesthood and gave them His Eucharistic Body and Blood. He taught the Twelve about service to all (see Luke 22:25–30) and demonstrated it by washing their feet (see John 13:1–32). He gave them His most intimate teaching about the Father, Son, and Holy Spirit (John 14—17), but the Apostles continued to show their typical pattern of misunderstanding Jesus, His teachings, and themselves, as well as Judas's well-established pattern of betrayal.

These reflections will especially draw from the Last Supper passages in Luke and John, who offer more detail in actions and teaching than the other two Gospel writers. Our purpose is to see the present crisis of faith and moral breakdown among some priests reflected in the description of the ordination of the first twelve bishops, though every Christian can likewise examine his or her conscience through the same texts. The goal is to deepen repentance for present or past sins and to discover Christ's healing, forgiveness of sins, and strengthening of the will to serve Him better in the future.

The First Steps in Betraying Jesus

After Jesus' triumphal entry into Jerusalem on Palm Sunday, after which He cleansed the Temple of money-changers, sellers, and buyers (see Matt. 21:12–13; Mark 11:15–17; Luke 19:45–46), He spent a few days teaching people in the Temple. By these actions, Jesus stirred up the fear and anger of the Sadducee and Pharisee leaders, so they engaged Him in a number of disputes in order "to entangle him in his talk" (Matt. 22:15). His parables and questions bested them every time, so when "the feast of Unleavened Bread drew near, which is called the Passover ... the chief priests and the scribes were seeking how to put him to death; for they feared the people" (Luke 22:1–2).

Throughout those days of controversy, the fear of the people was a larger concern for the leadership than was a desire for the truth about Jesus. On four different occasions, the priests and Pharisees chose not to apprehend Jesus. First, they did nothing after He overturned the money-changers' tables in the Temple, since the people knew that the Sadducees were corrupt in selling the animals and Jesus' teaching pleased them (see Luke 19:47–48). Second, they questioned His authority but then refused to explain the source of John the Baptist's authority (see Luke 20:1–8). Third, they were outraged at His parable about the vineyard and their moral failures, but they were afraid to arrest Him (see Luke 20:10–19). Fourth, they tried to trick Him into speaking against paying taxes to Caesar, but He was wiser than they were (see Luke 20:20–26). Therefore, they decided to arrest Jesus in secret. But how?

After these days of dispute, a spiritual battle between the Kingdom of God and the kingdom of darkness occurs in the Upper Room as intently as it had in the desert of temptation. The Apostles were weak men prone to pride and self-promotion, but Judas was engaged in more serious sin, so he is the initial focus of the temptations: "The devil had already put it into the heart of Judas Iscariot, Simon's son, to betray him" (John 13:2), so "Satan entered into Judas called Iscariot." He "conferred with the chief priests and officers how he might betray him to them" and "agreed" to accept money for this deed. After Satan had turned Judas to his side, he "sought an opportunity to betray him to them in the absence of the multitude" (Luke 22:3–5). St. Paul's words on spiritual warfare are appropriate to understand this scene:

> For we are not contending against flesh and blood, but against the principalities, against the powers, against the world rulers of this present darkness, against the spiritual hosts of wickedness in the heavenly places. (Eph. 6:12)

Judas would find his opportunity when Jesus celebrated the First Eucharist and ordained His first bishops during the Last Supper.

Preparation for the Last Supper

The Last Supper occurred "before the feast of the Passover, when Jesus knew that his hour had come to depart out of this world to the Father, having loved his own who were in the world, he loved them to the end" (John 13:1). The explanation for the Apostles finding a room prepared for the Passover before the Passover began is that the Essene sect followed a solar calendar by which they always started their Passover on a Wednesday, while the Pharisees and Sadducees followed a lunar calendar and began their Passover on Good Friday evening that year.

St. Luke gives a number of interesting details that confirm this idea. When the time came close, Jesus sent Peter and John to the city saying, "Go and prepare the Passover for us, that we may eat it" (Luke 22:8). When they asked for a location, He told them to find "a man carrying a jar of water" and "follow him into the house which he enters" (Luke 22:10). Carrying water was typically done by women, so a man with a water jar would have stood out in the crowd at the Pool of Siloam, the water source on the southeast side of the city. This indicates that the man was not married, and since the Upper Room was located in the Essene quarter of Jerusalem, he may well have been a member of that sect, which had already begun their Passover celebrations. For that reason the two Apostles were to tell the owner of the house, "The Teacher says to you, Where is the guest room, where I am to eat the Passover with my disciples?" (Luke 22:11). Jesus told them they would be shown a large, furnished upper room.

Very importantly, Jesus did not reveal the name of the place or its owner, so that the location of the Upper Room would be unknown to Judas, who was looking for the opportunity to betray Him. Judas could not tip off the Sanhedrin as to Jesus' whereabouts and interrupt the Last Supper with His arrest. Only when Jesus went to Gethsemane, as was His custom, could Judas know where to lead the soldiers to arrest Jesus.

Jesus' Hour

At the beginning of the Last Supper, Jesus announced that "the hour" had arrived (John 13:1; Luke 22:14). What does this mean? At first glance, it refers to the proper time after sunset to begin the meal in the Jewish context of Passover, but Jesus gives "the hour" a much deeper importance.

After the "Book of Signs" (see John 1—12), which covered Jesus' public ministry, John 13:1 opens a new section, sometimes called the "Book of Glory" (John 13—21), which includes the Last Supper, Christ's suffering, death, Resurrection, and His return to glory. While the signs and their discourses were meant for the general public, the Book of Glory is directed to the smaller group of faithful disciples who remain with Jesus from His suffering to His glory.

Earlier in the Gospel John gives two other notifications of the approach of this particular Passover. The first comes after the raising of Lazarus: "Now the Passover of the Jews was at hand, and many went up from the country to Jerusalem before the Passover, to purify themselves" (John 11:55). The second comes just before the meal in Bethany celebrating Lazarus's resuscitation, Mary's anointing of Jesus' feet, and mention of Judas's thievery (see John 12:1). Finally, the all-important Passover arrives as Jesus' "hour" to depart from the world to His Father.

Likewise, St. Luke acknowledges the hour: "And when the hour came, he sat at table, and the apostles with him" (Luke 22:14). Jesus emphasized this hour as a turning point in His redemptive mission:

> "I have earnestly desired to eat this Passover with you before
> I suffer; for I tell you I shall not eat it until it is fulfilled in the
> kingdom of God." And he took a cup, and when he had given
> thanks he said, "Take this, and divide it among yourselves; for
> I tell you that from now on I shall not drink of the fruit of the
> vine until the kingdom of God comes." (Luke 22:15–18)

First, Jesus' great desire to eat this Passover with His Apostles before His Passion explains the great care He took to keep the location of the Last Supper secret from Judas, whose betrayal would initiate Jesus' suffering. The suffering is itself an essential element of Jesus' mission, since the kingdom of God would come as the result of Jesus' death and Resurrection (see Luke 22:18). Until that was accomplished, He proclaimed that He would not drink "of the fruit of the vine" (a rare expression that may be related to the Jewish blessing over wine; see Mishna, Berakoth 6:1). While Jesus commands the Apostles to drink the wine, He refrains Himself in expectation of drinking it later in the kingdom of God.

The Last Supper and Institution of the Eucharist

The next event in the Last Supper is the institution of the Eucharist and the ordination of the Twelve Apostles as priests of Jesus' new covenant. This is Christ's primary attack against the evil forces of darkness, so a close examination of his institution of these two sacraments is a very important aspect of counteracting the present crisis in the Church. Some members of the Church, including some clergy, have diminished both sacraments. For some, their faith in the reality of Christ's unbloody sacrifice and Real Presence has been diminished, while others focus on their own versions of thirty pieces of silver instead of Christ.

In the Eucharist, Jesus gives human beings Himself, His very Body and Blood, Soul and Divinity, as the summit of all God's gifts from which all other gifts come. Some theologians emphasize that the Eucharist is a communal meal that builds up fellowship among believers, an idea that has even affected architecture and liturgical practices, both licit and illicit. The sacrificial nature of the Mass, the teaching that the Mass is the re-presentation of Christ's death on Calvary in an unbloody way, and the Real Presence of Jesus in the Blessed Sacrament are the specific ideas that have been diminished, so that in the minds of many, including some priests and bishops, the Mass is not the self-gift of Jesus Christ, God made man. Instead, it is reduced to a celebration of the presence of the congregation, or even to a politicized event meant to promote or detract from an issue, such as contraception, women's ordination, or political and economic partisan concerns.

In the priesthood, Jesus Christ unites His Apostles to Himself in a particular way, by which He gives them a share in His priestly action. However, for some Catholics, His command to "do this in remembrance of me" becomes a mere act of recollecting. This attitude appears when some priests even change Jesus' words of institution to "When you do this, remember me." This mistranslation of Christ's words becomes a false understanding of the priests' role at Mass. The result of these teachings about the Eucharist and the priesthood is a diminishment of the dignity of both sacraments, their ministers, and their effects. Ironically, it encourages forgetfulness of the great dignity to which Jesus calls His Church and ministers.

The central action of the Last Supper is the institution of the two sacraments, whose celebration is here intertwined: "And he took bread, and when he had given thanks he broke it and gave it to them, saying, 'This is my body which is given for you. Do this in remembrance of me.' And likewise the cup after supper, saying, 'This cup which is poured out for you is the new covenant in my blood'" (Luke 22:19–20).

As is true of every sacrament, both the "form," the words spoken, and the "matter," or physical things used as the outward sign of Christ's grace, are essential. The "form," i.e., Jesus' words, are effective because He is the Word of God made flesh. Just as God spoke eight times in Genesis 1:3–26 in order to bring about the whole of creation, so also does Jesus speak His word over bread and wine so as to re-create them as His Body and Blood. The power of God's word undergirds the truth of each sacrament.

The redemptive quality of the Eucharist is further emphasized by stating that Christ's Blood is directed toward the forgiveness of sins. St. Matthew includes with the words that this is for the forgiveness of sins (see Matt. 26:28—"This is my blood of the covenant, which is poured out for many for the forgiveness of sins."). Those words help us understand Jesus' teaching about the necessity of receiving His Body and Blood.

In John 6 Jesus teaches that receiving His Body and Blood is necessary for eternal life:

> So Jesus said to them, "Truly, truly, I say to you, unless you
> eat the flesh of the Son of man and drink his blood, you have
> no life in you; he who eats my flesh and drinks my blood has
> eternal life, and I will raise him up at the last day. For my flesh

is food indeed, and my blood is drink indeed. He who eats my flesh and drinks my blood abides in me, and I in him. As the living Father sent me, and I live because of the Father, so he who eats me will live because of me." (John 6:53–57)

Secondly, when He identifies the cup of wine as "the new covenant in my blood," Jesus indicates that the Eucharist is the new beginning that had been prophesied in the Old Testament. He uses terms from Moses' liturgy for establishing the covenant at Mount Sinai:

Moses took the blood and threw it upon the people, and said, "Behold the blood of the covenant which the LORD has made with you in accordance with all these words." (Exod. 24:8).

The Greek word for "poured out" (the passive participle of *egcheo*) is the same word used in Exodus 24:6 for "pouring" the blood into basins. Both at Mount Sinai and in the Upper Room the pouring out of blood is essential to making the covenant. Furthermore, by decreeing that the cup was "the new covenant in my Blood," Jesus also calls to mind prophecies of a new covenant by Jeremiah and Ezekiel:

"Behold, the days are coming, says the LORD,
when I will make a new covenant with the house
of Israel and the house of Judah." (Jer. 31:31)

"I will make a covenant of peace with them; it shall be
an everlasting covenant with them." (Ezek. 37:26)

Both Jeremiah and Ezekiel had declared that the Sinai covenant had been broken. Now, at the Last Supper, Jesus announced the New Covenant in His Blood. No passage in the Old Testament ever spoke of the renewal of the covenant; no passage in the rabbinic texts, such as the Mishna or Talmud, or any other Jewish literature ever spoke of the restoration of the "New Covenant" that had been prophesied by Jeremiah and Ezekiel. Jesus opens this new beginning very quietly in the presence of His Twelve Apostles as He institutes His Eucharist.

Thirdly, the words of institution include the phrase "Do this in remembrance of me" (Luke 22:19; see also 1 Cor. 11:25). The verb *do* is a plural imperative, meaning that Jesus is commanding everyone present at the Last Supper to "do this in remembrance of me." The Church rightly considers this command to be the form of the Apostles' ordination to the priesthood. In most languages, the word *do* has a wide range of meanings, and Hebrew is no exception. Among its meanings is the idea "to offer sacrifice," as in Exodus 10:25, when Moses said, "You must also let us have sacrifices and burnt offerings, that we may sacrifice to the Lord our God." The word translated as "sacrifice" is *asinu*, "we may do," and the Greek translation of the Old Testament uses the word meaning "we may do" (*poiesomen*). Yet it clearly means "sacrifice," as the Latin Vulgate translates it (*offeramus*) and in the *Revised Standard* and *King James Versions*, it is "sacrifice." This is a common expression in the Old Testament, and the Apostles would have easily understood this as command to offer a sacrifice. This would be all the more clear from the words "in remembrance of me."

The term *memorial* occurs several times in the Old Testament in connection with the sweet-smelling smoke of incense offered with a sacrifice of meal and oil (see Lev. 2:1, 16; 5:12, 26; 24:7). It is associated with a term for other sacrifices:

> "The cereal offering of remembrance..." (Num. 5:18)

> "You shall blow the trumpets over your burnt offerings and over the sacrifices of your peace offerings; they shall serve you for remembrance before your God." (Num 10:10)

> "Moreover he appointed certain of the Levites as ministers

before the ark of the Lord, to invoke, to thank, and to praise the Lord, the God of Israel." (1 Chron. 16:14)

The word *memorial* also appears in the titles of Psalm 38:1, "A Psalm of David, for the memorial offering," and Psalm 70:1, "A Psalm of David, for the memorial offering," probably to indicate that they were to be sung at memorial sacrifices in the Temple. (See my book *Eucharist: A Bible Study for Catholics*, for a fuller study of these topics.)

The combination of the plural command "do this," plus the identification of "in memory of me," would lead these twelve Jewish Apostles to recognize the priestly and sacrificial nature of what Jesus was commanding them to do. None of the Apostles had been identified as Levitical priests of the old covenant, and neither was Jesus, Who belonged to the tribe of Judah and the family of David (see genealogies in Matt. 1:1–18 and Luke 3:23–38). If Jesus is claiming a priestly authority in instituting the Eucharist, as well as the authority to command the Twelve Apostles to continue to do this sacrifice, it can only mean that Jesus was the source of a priesthood different from the Levitical priesthood, and that this new priesthood was a component of the "New Covenant" He had established in His blood.

By giving the Apostles a share in His priestly authority, Jesus provided for the continuation of the celebration of the Eucharist so that all generations would be able to "eat his flesh and drink his blood" in order to have eternal life. They have passed this gift on to the following generations, through which men have received this great dignity of Christ's eternal priesthood. Some of our later reflections will show that the Apostles did not appreciate the dignity Jesus had given them at that moment, and they would continue their old pattern of seeking a dignity of their own making instead — tragically, a mistake made by some bishops and priests throughout the centuries and even into the present time.

Jesus then distributed His Body and Blood to the Apostles, and they each receive their first Holy Communion. These actions within the traditional Passover prayers marked out a radically new beginning. How deeply the Apostles understood it at the time is a useless speculation. However, the fact that the Eucharist had such an important place in the Gospels and in the writings of St. Paul and in the subsequent history of the Church indicates that they reflected on it deeply at some point. This holds true for the role of the priesthood as well.

Jesus Announces His Betrayal and Identifies the Traitor

With the institution of the Eucharist, the New Covenant, and the new priesthood, Jesus' next announcement is all the more astounding: His betrayer is present at the Eucharistic table, among those who were just ordained:

> "But behold the hand of him who betrays me is with me on the table. For the Son of man goes as it has been determined; but woe to that man by whom he is betrayed!' And they began to question one another, which of them it was that would do this." (Luke 22:21–23)

The three Synoptic Gospels mention that the Apostles questioned themselves, asking, "Is it I, Lord?" (Matt. 26:22; Mark 14:19; see also Luke 22:23). In John, "The disciples looked at one another, uncertain of whom he spoke" (John 13:22). Such questions and "uncertain" glances at one another are themselves a recognition that any one of them had the capacity to betray Jesus, yet they did not examine the evidence carefully enough to find out who it might be. They seemed afraid to find out the actual identity of the traitorous culprit. After their earlier arguments about who was the greatest, they may have all feared the discovery of their own sins, mendacity, greed, and the pride that lies at the root of most other sins.

The Apostles' shock and nervous uncertainty corresponds to reactions among some modern clergy in regard to the sexual abuse and financial crises. The actions of the first twelve bishops may help present-day reflection on the betrayals of young people's trust through sexual abuse or the sexual predation of adults. Such sins flow from lust and betray the legitimate expectation that celibate priests will be faithful to their promises and vows.

More important than looking at the sins committed by others, a personal examination of conscience serves us better. *How have I turned other people into objects of my desires? Is pornography a factor in my life? Have I entered illicit relationships to gratify my lust? Have I used Church money for my own self-indulgence?* Self-examination, acceptance of responsibility for sins, sacramental confession, restitution, and amendment form the personal foundation for helping other clergy and laity to do the same. If they do not repent, or if they are guilty of a crime, this can help guilty clergy depart responsibly from the clerical state and deal with the consequences of their criminality.

Jesus did not name Judas, but He identified the traitor as "he who has dipped his hand in the dish with me" (Matt. 26:23; Mark 14:20). Dipping bread into a sauce was, and still is, a Middle Eastern sign of friendship. In effect, as Jesus predicted the betrayal and identified the traitor, He extended His hand to restore their relationship at this last moment. Also, by mentioning the dipping of the morsel of bread, Jesus allowed Judas to act with complete freedom of will; had He mentioned his name, the other eleven would have harmed and restrained Judas. The clergy today also have free will to commit sin or to be celibate and holy. They can choose to gratify their sensual desires, or they can return to the dignity of the priesthood and conformity to the holiness and virtue of Jesus Christ. Each time they celebrate Mass, Jesus offers Himself in Holy Communion. The issue is whether they sacrilegiously accept Jesus' self-offering with an intention to continue sinning or accept His offer to cleanse their souls and enter into a saving personal union with Christ.

After sharing of the morsel of bread in the dish, Jesus speaks a severe warning to Judas: "The Son of man goes as it is written of him, but woe to that man by whom the Son of man is betrayed! It would have been better for that man if he had not been born" (Matt. 26:24; see Mark 14:21).

Even though Judas's betrayal fulfills Old Testament prophecies and his deeds set in motion the actions that lead to the saving death of Jesus, he is still fully responsible for his evil deed. He will suffer the consequences of his decision to betray Jesus because the end does not justify the means. The way a person accomplishes a good end matters greatly in the moral judgment of his or her actions. In Judas's case, the evil is so great that Jesus decreed that it would be better not to have been born than to perpetrate this betrayal.

This reminds us of one of Jesus' warnings against causing scandal to children (see Matt. 18:5–7). No matter what thoughts, intentions, or personal difficulties may go into the decision by any adult to abuse or harm a child, the punishment due to such sin is as sure and certain as the threat Jesus issued to Judas Iscariot. This lends weight in the minds of many who compare priests who abuse children and adolescents as being akin to Judas. Jesus instructs His disciples to see Him in other persons, particularly in the weak and vulnerable. Therefore whatever anyone does to the least of His brothers and sisters, they do to Him. He will judge every person according to their actions regarding the least little ones, either for eternal reward or eternal condemnation, as in His judgment of the sheep and the goats (see Matt. 25:31–46). Bishops and priests who betray Jesus by harming the young should consider the reality of being condemned in hell and then refrain from the sin. Perhaps the fear of punishment will help them recognize the goodness of the virtue they are missing.

Despite both Jesus' last-ditch offer of friendship and His final warning and threat, Judas did not change his mind. Knowing his own treason and possessing the thirty pieces of silver, he cynically asks Jesus, "Is it I, Master?" Jesus responds, "You have said so" (Matt. 26:25). In saying this, Jesus places full responsibility for the betrayal back on Judas. Judas then exits the place of his ordination as a bishop and the reception of his first Holy Communion in order to betray Jesus in the darkness of that night.

The Disciples Again Dispute Their Own Greatness

After Judas's departure, St. Luke describes how, after Judas's departure, the Apostles change the subject from something as uncomfortable as the presence of the traitor among their number to issues of their own importance and greatness: "A dispute also arose among them, which of them was to be regarded as the greatest" (Luke 22:24). St. Luke does not lay out their precise arguments, since they amounted to nothing important; the only worthwhile response came from Jesus:

> "The kings of the Gentiles exercise lordship over them; and those in authority over them are called benefactors. But not so with you; rather let the greatest among you become as the youngest, and the leader as one who serves. For which is the greater, one who sits at table, or one who serves? Is it not the one who sits at table? But I am among you as one who serves. You are those who have continued with me in my trials; and I assign to you, as my Father assigned to me, a kingdom, that you may eat and drink at my table in my kingdom, and sit on thrones judging the twelve tribes of Israel." (Luke 22:25–30)

Jesus repeats the same message He gave to the Apostles when

they were upset over James and John in regard to leadership; in order to lead, they must serve others, particularly serving at table. Only at the end of a long life of service will they inherit a kingdom from God the Father, and then they will exercise an eternal leadership by judging Israel; then they will feast at the Lord's table.

Jesus Predicts Peter's Denials

Then Jesus turned His attention to Peter, the Apostle who had shown leadership among the Twelve, even if it was frequently very impetuous.

> "Simon, Simon, behold, Satan demanded to have you, that he might sift you like wheat, but I have prayed for you that your faith may not fail; and when you have turned again, strengthen your brethren." (Luke 22:31–32)

Jesus confirmed Peter's leadership, but He strongly warned him about Satan's demands to gain enough control over the Apostles. (The Greek word here is the plural form of "you.") The devil's plan to "sift you like wheat" refers to removing the chaff from the wheat—that is, the useless from the seed that can bear fruit. His judgment inevitably separates the good from the bad, and Jesus warns that Satan wants to be in charge of the process, even though ultimately Jesus will be the judge. Satan, which in Hebrew means "adversary" (especially in a judicial or courtroom sense) is elsewhere identified as "the accuser of our brethren" (Rev. 12:10; see also Ps. 109:6). This highlights the fact that Satan wants to sift and judge the Apostles, and their successors, the bishops, in order to destroy the Church. Jesus will separate the wheat from the chaff in order to purify the Church and pay each member the rewards or punishments due each one.

St. John Paul II placed much of his attention on Luke 22:32, because he depended on the intercession of Jesus Christ so that his own faith would not fail during the trials he faced; his hope was that his strengthened faith could support the other bishops.

However, the words directed to Peter, "when you have turned again," implied that Peter would fail to maintain his faith. In response to that implication, Peter responded, "Lord, I am ready to go with you to prison and to death" (Luke 22:33). Jesus does not accept mere good intentions, however, and soberly predicted, "I tell you, Peter, the cock will not crow this day, until you three times deny that you know me" (Luke 22:34). He knows Peter's weakness, and He knows that the denials are coming, since it was predicted in Isaiah 53:12: "He poured out his soul to death, and was numbered with the transgressors; yet he bore the sin of many, and made intercession for the transgressors."

"Being numbered among the transgressors" and "pouring out his soul to death" did not indicate failure but prepared Christ for a "portion with the great" and the "strong." By citing Isaiah, Jesus was placing Peter's denials and His own suffering and death in light of His coming Resurrection from the dead and the redemption of the whole world. His suffering would overcome death and sin, but He must first undergo suffering due to the failure of His disciples. Jesus placed Peter's failure of faith and leadership into the long-prophesied plan of salvation, and He was able to summon Peter to "turn again" and become the leader who supports his brethren, the other Apostles.

This saying offers hope for the grace of repentance among those bishops and priests who have been involved in the scandals of the present era. This does not mean that child sex abusers should return to active ministry, but repentance can take various forms. Lives of penitence for one's own sins, for the victims, and for other sinners is a worthy way of life, even if public ministry is excluded. We will look at this more later in this book.

Jesus Washes the Apostles' Feet

St. John does not mention the institution of the Eucharist, but he does include the washing of the Apostles' feet, which is not mentioned in the Synoptic Gospels. It is difficult to understand the timing of these two events, both of which occurred during the Last Supper, so we will treat them as two distinct actions without concern for their temporal relationship. We want to see the meaning of Jesus' washing the Apostles' feet at the Last Supper in regard to their successors, the bishops and popes.

The foot washing is another action of the spiritual war between good and evil taking place at the Last Supper. On one side, Satan had already put the betrayal in Judas Iscariot's heart; on the other side, Jesus was fully aware of the Father's plan of salvation. Trusting that the Father had given all things to Him, He humbled Himself like a servant and washed the disciples' feet.

> And during supper, when the devil had already put it into the heart of Judas Iscariot, Simon's son, to betray him, Jesus, knowing that the Father had given all things into his hands, and that he had come from God and was going to God, rose from supper, laid aside his garments, and girded himself with a towel. Then he poured water into a basin, and began to wash the disciples' feet, and to wipe them with the towel with which he was girded. (John 13:2–5)

However, just as Peter had rejected Jesus' earlier teaching about suffering and the Cross, so he rejected the notion of Jesus washing his feet:

> He came to Simon Peter; and Peter said to him, "Lord, do you wash my feet?" Jesus answered him, "What I am doing you do not know now, but afterward you will understand." Peter said

to him, "You shall never wash my feet." Jesus answered him, "If I do not wash you, you have no part in me." (John 13:6–8)

Jesus' rebuff was gentler than it had been when Peter rejected the teaching on suffering and the Cross, but it was absolute. Refusing to accept Jesus as a servant who washes one's feet equals refusing any part in Jesus. At that point Peter insisted on a complete immersion into Jesus: "Lord, not my feet only but also my hands and my head!" (John 13:9). However, Jesus tempered that response with an assurance that Peter was already basically clean but this was not true of the betrayer (see John 13:10–11). By this statement Jesus continues to lay out the battle lines between good and evil as the conflict between the Kingdom of God and the kingdom of darkness comes to a head in Jesus' trials and Crucifixion.

Jesus explains to his Apostles that as He is truly "Teacher and Lord," yet washes their feet, so too the Apostles need to wash one another's feet (see John 13:12–17). This is the same lesson He taught after James and John sought positions of special honor:

"But it shall not be so among you; but whoever would be great among you must be your servant, and whoever would be first among you must be slave of all. For the Son of man also came not to be served but to serve, and to give his life as a ransom for many." (Mark 10:43–45)

Jesus directs His instruction to the one who is not clean in order to force the next stage of the confrontation between good and evil. First, He wants to single out the traitor from the rest of the Apostles, and He wants them to understand the treason within the context of the fulfillment of Old Testament prophecy and of the entire plan of salvation: "I am not speaking of you all; I know whom I have chosen; it is that the scripture may be fulfilled,

'He who ate my bread has lifted his heel against me'" (John 13:18). Here Jesus cites Psalm 41:9 to indicate that the traitor was predicted in Scripture: "Even my bosom friend in whom I trusted, who ate of my bread, has lifted his heel against me."

Of course, this implies that even the betrayal of the Messiah, like Peter's denials, has a place within God's plan of salvation, and therefore it will not and cannot prevent its fulfillment. The verse also indicates that Jesus truly considered Judas to be a "friend in whom I trusted," yet that trust was thoroughly betrayed. This statement appropriately situates the betrayal at the Last Supper, since Jesus' first mention of the betrayal came at the end of His discourse on the bread of life (see John 6:70–71).

Jesus next turns the Apostles' attention to the importance of believing that He is the Lord God ("I am"):

> "I tell you this now, before it takes place, that when it does take place you may believe that I am he. Truly, truly, I say to you, he who receives any one whom I send receives me; and he who receives me receives him who sent me." (John 13:19–20)

Both the fulfillment of the prophetic Psalm 41:9 and Jesus' knowledge of the suffering about to occur are proof of His divinity. The betrayal will not be a failure but proof that "I am." (The Greek reads "I am," without the word "he" in the text.) In Exodus 3:14 God tells Moses that His name is "I am." Here Jesus teaches the Apostles again that this is His identity, just as when He walked on the Sea of Galilee and said, "I am. Fear not!" (John 6:20). He repeats "I am," during the Last Supper to teach the Apostles what to believe about Him: Jesus is the same Lord God Who appeared to Moses in the burning bush in Exodus 3. If they believe, they will receive Him, and by receiving Him, they receive the Father Who sent Him.

Jesus tells the Apostles that He is "troubled in spirit" over the betrayal. The disciples do not comprehend, so Peter told the "beloved disciple" lying close to Jesus' breast to find out the identity of the traitor. Jesus indicates the traitor with a gesture: "It is he to whom I shall give this morsel when I have dipped it." He then gave the bread to Judas Iscariot (see John 13:22–26). Precisely at that point "Satan entered into him," and Jesus told him, "What you are going to do, do quickly" (John 13:27).

The other eleven Apostles reacted to Judas's departure, but they did not understand why Judas left their company. Some of them thought Jesus was telling Judas to buy what they needed for the feast or give something to the poor (see John 13:28–29). Perhaps this was because they were unwilling to connect Jesus' prediction of the betrayer with Judas's sudden departure from the supper. Even after Peter had asked John to find out the traitor's identity directly from Jesus, the sign of dipping the piece of bread in the dish with Jesus made no impact on anyone. The Apostles attributed good motives to Judas rather than lay the obvious accusation of treason at his feet, which would make them uncomfortable. They did not think clearly, they did not act, and Judas went out into the night to work his evil.

Significantly, Judas left in the night: "So, after receiving the morsel, he immediately went out; and it was night" (John 13:30). This is opposite to the time when Jesus performs the Father's work: "We must work the works of him who sent me, while it is day; night comes, when no one can work. As long as I am in the world, I am the light of the world" (John 9:4–5). At night, Satan can operate through Judas to lie about Jesus, betray Him with a kiss, and bring about His death. Jesus' trial before the Sanhedrin met illegally at night as well.

However, once Judas left the Upper Room, Jesus declared to the eleven who remained, "Now is the Son of man glorified, and in him God is glorified; if God is glorified in him, God will also glorify him in himself, and glorify him at once" (John

13:31–32). Judas's departure again signals Jesus to declare God's glorification and His own glory as a battle cry against the forces of Satan and darkness. "Glory" refers to God's power, which will be manifested by Jesus' acceptance of His suffering, death, Resurrection, and Ascension. Though suffering will begin with Judas's treasonous kiss in the darkness of Gethsemane, it will end in God's glorious victory in the Resurrection.

CHAPTER 4

GETHSEMANE BETRAYAL
AND ABANDONMENT

He was despised and rejected by men; a man of sorrows, and acquainted with grief; and as one from whom men hide their faces he was despised, and we esteemed him not. Surely he has borne our griefs and carried our sorrows; yet we esteemed him stricken, smitten by God, and afflicted. But he was wounded for our transgressions, he was bruised for our iniquities; upon him was the chastisement that made us whole, and with his stripes we are healed. (Isa. 53:3–5)

Isaiah prophesied that a suffering Servant of the Lord would redeem and heal humanity, not in spite of the suffering but because of it; the New Testament teaches that Jesus fulfilled this ministry. In a summary of Jesus' healing ministry Matthew 8:17 cites Isaiah 53:4: "This was to fulfil what was spoken by the prophet Isaiah, 'He took our infirmities and bore our diseases.'" Later, 1 Peter 2:24 cites Isaiah 53:5 to indicate the power of Christ's suffering both to redeem and heal the human race: "He himself bore our sins in his body on the tree, that we might die to sin and live to righteousness. 'By his wounds you have been healed.'"

This explains why the evangelists wrote more about Jesus' suffering and death than any other event in His public ministry. Jesus suffered like all of humanity, yet He gives far more than an example of heroic perseverance. Rather, His suffering has a power to redeem believers from sin and to heal those who connect their own pain and suffering to his.

Jesus invites His disciples to join Him in His suffering, making it a necessary aspect of following Him: "Whoever does not bear his own cross and come after me, cannot be my disciple" (Luke 14:27) and "If any man would come after me, let him deny himself and take up his cross daily and follow me." (Luke 9:23). Saint Paul also came to understand the importance of this doctrine: "And those who belong to Christ Jesus have crucified the flesh with its passions and desires" (Gal. 5:24) and "But far be it from me to glory except in the cross of our Lord Jesus Christ, by which the world has been crucified to me, and I to the world" (Gal. 6:14). St. Peter adds, "Since therefore Christ suffered in the flesh, arm yourselves with the same thought, for whoever has suffered in the flesh has ceased from sin, so as to live for the rest of the time in the flesh no longer by human passions but by the will of God" (1 Pet. 4:1).

Based on these teachings, disciples of Jesus Christ find power, meaning, and purpose in the sufferings of Jesus Christ as well as in their own pain, whether it is due to the accidents of life or to the suffering imposed on them by the sin of others. This does not preclude the possibility—indeed, the necessity—of doing all in one's power to end injustice and its consequences, as well as the suffering that simply comes from sickness, natural catastrophes, and other inevitable sources of human pain and grief. Still, until all suffering is ended, ultimately in heaven, those who endure its pain and agony can find meaning and power in it by considering the suffering and death of Jesus in faith, and then uniting their personal suffering with His. So powerful and important is this aspect of the Christian faith that St. Paul wrote: "Now I rejoice in my sufferings for your sake, and in my flesh I complete what is lacking in Christ's afflictions for the sake of his body, that is, the church (Col. 1:24).

In the context of the horrible scandal of sexual abuse of children, adolescents, and adults by members of the clergy, we will examine Christ's suffering in the next three chapters with a view to inviting victims to see themselves in Christ's sufferings. Victims typically suffer for years after the abuse, and their wounds are deep. We believe that they can relate their suffering to the various elements of Christ's Passion and death, and that His wounds are the sources of healing their pain. The wounds never go away completely, no more than scar tissue leaves the skin or healed broken bones look like the original bones. Still, healed bones are stronger than their original condition, and healed emotional and spiritual wounds can likewise become stronger than the original state.

The strength that results from Christ's healing will do more than merely aid victims to cope with life, their anger, and other forms of pain. Those who recognize their own biographies in Jesus Christ's pain will know Him as the Redeemer who brings them salvation. Some victims will even find the strength to bring healing to others who have suffered sexual abuse at the hands of family members, trusted professionals, and sex traffickers, who use their positions of power to abuse the vulnerable. Medical doctors, psychologists, and counselors are terrific helps in the healing process, but Christ's healing will have an even more profound effect on those who trust Him. For that reason we will examine each stage of Jesus' suffering and death.

Gethsemane: The Garden of the Apostles' Failures

From the Upper Room on the southwestern hill of Jerusalem, Jesus led the eleven Apostles to an olive grove on the lower slope of the Mount of Olives, east of the Kidron Valley and the walled city of Jerusalem. The place was named after an oil press (in Aramaic *geth* means "a press"; *seman* means "oil"). Matthew 26:36 and Mark 14:32 call the place Gethsemane, Luke calls it "the Mount of Olives" (Luke 22:39), and John simply mentions an unnamed "garden" across the Kidron Valley. Passover pilgrims were expected to spend the night in Jerusalem in order to fulfill their obligation to stay in the holy city for the feast, but due to the large numbers of people in the city, its limits were expanded to include the Mount of Olives so as to accommodate everyone. By staying in Gethsemane, Jesus was fulfilling the Law, but He was placing Himself in danger at the same time.

Jesus customarily stayed in that garden (see Luke 22:39), and He does so again. This contrasts with His efforts to keep secret the location of the Last Supper. That tactic prevented Judas Iscariot from knowing its location and betraying Jesus during that all-important meal. But after the Last Supper, Jesus made Himself vulnerable to discovery and arrest by the soldiers guided to Him by His treacherous disciple and newly ordained bishop, Judas Iscariot.

Jesus Prays in Gethsemane, and the Disciples Sleep

Upon arrival in the garden, Jesus first instructed the disciples, "Pray that you may not enter into temptation" (Luke 22:40). An interesting parallel to this request may be found in the Israelite feast of the day of Atonement (Yom Kippur), during which the high priest offered a bull for his personal sins and a goat for Israel's sins before entering the Holy of Holies to sprinkle the blood on the Ark of the Covenant. The whole night before the feast, the priest stayed awake to avoid inadvertent ritual pollution through a nocturnal emission. The younger priests remained awake with him, keeping him from falling asleep by "snapping their fingers" and reminding "my lord High Priest" to "walk on cold pavement" until he was wide awake (see Mishna, Tractate

Yoma 1:7). Here in Gethsemane, instead of the new priests of the New Covenant keeping Jesus the High Priest awake, He is the one to exhort them to watch against temptation by praying. He knows their weaknesses and is aware that they will fail the test, but His instruction is for the future when they will follow His advice and prayerfully keep watch in prayer as the antidote to temptation.

What is key to this episode is that Jesus "withdrew from them about a stone's throw" (Luke 22:41) and prayed. In the face of the coming betrayal, trials, torture, and death, Jesus turned to intimacy with His Father, the name with which each of His petitions begin: "Father, if you are willing, remove this cup from me; nevertheless not my will, but yours be done" (Luke 22:42; see also Matt. 26:39 and Mark 14:36). The underlying principle of His prayer extends from the Our Father, where He taught us to pray, "Thy will be done on earth as it is in heaven" (Matt. 6:10). Jesus expresses His own concerns about the coming suffering, but always returns to doing the Father's will, not His own based on fear of the pain about to be inflicted on Him.

Though Jesus entrusts Himself to the Father, He does not desire the "cup." Why did He speak of the cup? The "cup" refers to His suffering, as He explained to James and John in Mark 10:38 when He said, "Are you able to drink the cup that I drink, or to be baptized with the baptism with which I am baptized?" This image is rooted in the Old Testament image of the cup of suffering:

> For in the hand of the LORD there is a cup, with
> foaming wine, well mixed; and he will pour a
> draught from it, and all the wicked of the earth
> shall drain it down to the dregs. (Ps. 75:8)

> Rouse yourself, rouse yourself, stand up, O
> Jerusalem, you who have drunk at the hand of the

LORD the cup of his wrath, who have drunk to
the dregs the bowl of staggering. (Isa. 51:17)

Behold, I have taken from your hand the cup of staggering;
the bowl of my wrath you shall drink no more. (Isa. 51:22)

All three Synoptic writers emphasize the connection between Jesus' prayer and the image of suffering from Old Testament prophecy and the Psalms. They know that Jesus did not desire the approaching pain, but rather willingly accepted it from the Father as part of the necessary struggle between the Kingdom of God and the kingdom of darkness by which He will defeat sin and death.

Jesus' prayer may have included a consideration of the history of human sin, for which His suffering was the healing and His death was the redemption. Human history has been filled with violence, cruelty, the horrors of the wars large and small, and deception. He fully knew that sin would not end with modernity or with the increase of knowledge and wealth. He could contemplate the scientific, technological sophistication of the twentieth century and know that it would become the most violent, as 305 million people died in wars, genocides, and ideological purges, often at the hands of well-educated professionals. He knew of the enslavement of people He had created with freedom, including widespread slavery of the twenty-first century sex trade. He knew that Judas would betray Him, and that some bishops and priests through the ages would repeat Judas's treachery by seeking money, power, and self-gratification at the expense of "the least of his brothers and sisters"—the very people Jesus understood as His "brethren," whose suffering was taken on by Him as His own (see Matt. 25:40). This was His agony during prayer.

At this point, a heavenly response to His prayer arrived when "an angel appeared to him from heaven, strengthening him" (Luke 22:43). Jesus wanted such comfort and encouragement from His disciples, for whom, along with all other sinners, He was suffering. However, they were asleep instead of praying. The strength from the angel helped Him in His "agony," so "he prayed more fervently and his sweat became like drops of blood falling on the earth" (Luke 22:44). The strengthening presence of the angel did not remove Jesus' suffering, which was at this point interior, spiritual "agony" (in the Greek, *agonia*). This word was used in the Greek athletic stadium (called the *agon* or place of assembly), where the struggle to win the games was *agonia*. This word also applied to the struggle to win a lawsuit in court, and in many texts it refers to winning battles in war (see Herodotus; 2 Macc. 15:9; Josephus, 1, 426).

The last meaning connects well with Jesus in Gethsemane, as He is waging the greatest war against sin and death, God's two greatest enemies. Already the battle causes Him to sweat blood. This rare medical condition, hematidrosis, occurs when capillaries rupture near the sweat glands during extraordinary stress. This initial shedding of blood was the prelude to profuse bleeding at the pillar and on the cross, when His heart was pierced and emptied of His Precious Blood.

Many people who have been sexually and physically abused wait decades before revealing what happened to them. They experience a tremendous agony, alone in their pain. Typically they are tempted to blame themselves for the abuse; they feel anger toward the abuser for harming them and anger that their parents or Church leaders did not protect them; and they feel shame over having participated in the sexual acts, even though they may not have sought or desired this. They fear revealing their experiences, not being believed, and being blamed. These and other emotions churn in their hearts for years, driving them into isolation. Relationships with parents, spouses, children, and friends are affected, and they live in their own agony within the dark and often hidden world of a private Gethsemane in an emotional darkness.

Jesus is absolutely willing to enter their private Gethsemane with a depth of understanding from having spent a painful night in the original Gethsemane. They can weep with Him, sweat blood with Him, and agonize over the effects of the abuse. He will not force Himself into their private gardens of pain, but He is most willing to kneel next to them at their own rocks of agony over abuse. If they invite Jesus into this pain, He will love them there. He does not necessarily make the pain go away quickly, any more than the cup of pain passed away from Him. However, He suffers the agony with them, sweats blood for them, and weeps with them in the midst of their pain. He identifies with them as "the least of his brothers and sisters," and He will pray to the Father next to them, feeling a pain like theirs, having drunk a bitter cup of suffering.

I ask all of my suffering, betrayed brothers and sisters to invite Jesus into their personal gardens of agony so as to find a healing and comfort from Jesus, Who relates to them better than anyone else can.

Jesus Returns to the Sleeping Disciples

Jesus returned to His disciples, who were sleeping due to their "sorrow," and exhorted them again to pray to avoid temptation: "Why do you sleep? Rise and pray that you may not enter into temptation" (Luke 22:46; see also Matt. 26:40–46; Mark 14:37–42). The type of watchfulness Jesus considered necessary to avoid falling into temptation was a prayerful union with God. He Himself needed that type of prayer, and He taught that His disciples needed it too. However, the eleven Apostles gave into slumber instead of praying. Their sorrow exhausted them, and they did not ask for the virtue of hope to counteract the sorrow.

Many people still neglect or even avoid a serious prayer life. Some of them do so much activity that they make no time for prayer. Others are surrounded by so much noise that they cannot possibly hear God speak to them. These and any other excuses to avoid prayer have the same result: less sensitivity to God and an increased susceptibility to temptation. The failure of the Apostles to pray with Jesus was the lie behind their failure to stay with Jesus during the arrest.

In St. Matthew, Jesus includes a very important and well-known line in His admonition of the sleeping Apostles. Directly addressing Peter, He asked, "So, could you not watch with me one hour? Watch and pray that you may not enter into temptation; the spirit indeed is willing, but the flesh is weak" (Matt. 26:40–41).

Jesus' rebuke of Peter's inability to "watch with me one hour" indicates that prayer places the primary attention on the Person of Jesus. It is not a restful state of mind and certainly is not some state of nothingness or emptiness. Jesus is the central focus and content of our prayer, and it is through prayerful union with the Person of Christ that we find strength to overcome temptation. He reminds Peter, and all Christians, that the flesh is weak, even if the human spirit is willing to do what is right. Here, and in many other places in the New Testament, the flesh refers to those disordered drives and desires that lead to one's destruction if they are not brought into control and given direction.

Even though Peter and the others had been ordained bishops by Jesus Christ Himself, and although they had received His Body and Blood in the Holy Eucharist a few hours earlier, they had not yet overcome the weakness and self-destructive qualities of the flesh. They remained weak and in much need of prayer to center themselves on Jesus Christ. However, instead of praying, they fell asleep.

Though many factors have contributed to the increase of sexual abuse by priests from the mid-1970s to the 1990s, a decline in faithfulness to praying the Liturgy of the Hours and of prayer in general is one factor. For some, even the celebration of Mass has become a show or display rather than a personal and communal prayer. Some priests, and their people, considered it "Father So and So's Mass," because the priest did not celebrate it as Jesus' Mass.

An absence of prayer makes Christians, including priests and bishops, more susceptible to the various temptations that confront people in the present time, as it has in every era. Over the centuries, priests and religious have succumbed to the temptations and attractions of the secular world. Even monasteries and convents gave into the temptations to pursue monetary gain, acquisition of property, and sexual misconduct. In the eleventh century, the diocesan clergy began to live with common law wives and raise families in the rectories, fully in public view. Meanwhile, many of the monks engaged in homosexual behavior and pedophilia. Prayerful saints, like St. Peter Damian, came out of their hermitages and monasteries to exhort the priests and monks to repent of these sins and change their lives. Similarly, other saints in the late fifteenth and sixteenth centuries, such as St. Philip Neri and St. Ignatius Loyola, S.J., came from their own experiences of prayer and conversion to summon bishops and priests to holiness and prayerful reform.

Along with other elements of change, the present-day clergy must let Jesus Christ awaken them from a slumber that dulls their attentiveness to sexual temptation and attraction to material gain. The culture offers a constant barrage of these temptations radiating from the media. Serious prayer focused on the Person of Jesus Christ is the primary antidote to the material temptations around them. Allowing themselves to prayerfully reflect on the Gospels and engage Jesus in a lively prayer life offers the opportunity for self-recollection and ongoing examinations of conscience. These can keep them alert to the presence of the temptations that surround them.

Another area of prayer that is frequently neglected is the

commitment to praying the Liturgy of the Hours, which is the official prayer book of the Catholic Church, in accord with each of the rites of the Church. It is a common prayer by priests for the Church, interceding for the universal Church as well as for local and personal needs. In the early 1970s it became far too common for priests to neglect this liturgy, even though each deacon and priest promises the bishop at their ordinations to pray it every day until the end of their life. Failure to pray for the Church weakens both the priest, who does not keep the promise he made at ordination, and the Church, which needs prayer in this time of cultural and moral upheaval.

Finally, the Mass sometimes has become the occasion for the priest to perform rather than lead his people by praying the liturgy in word and action. Sometimes it is the performance of a mere duty that is part of the job description of a priest. Sometimes it is a dramatic performance that is more theatrical than prayerful. When the priest allows himself to be swept up by the Holy Spirit into personally praying the Mass, he leads the people in praying it as well. They either join him in the prayer or begin to search within themselves for the wellspring of prayer that they observe in the priest and desire for themselves.

Failure at these various levels of personal and communal prayer make the priest more susceptible to temptation and sin. That includes the temptations to spiritual and moral cowardice, as was true of the Apostles in Gethsemane, or temptations to material gain, such as was the case of Judas Iscariot, or sexual temptation, as has become all too common in our modern, sexually gluttonous society. In Gethsemane, Jesus summons us to pray; it is His antidote to temptation.

Judas Betrays Jesus

While Jesus was still speaking to warn the Apostles to pray, Judas Iscariot, "one of the twelve," led a crowd to arrest Jesus

(Luke 22:47). Judas had given them a sign, "The one I shall kiss is the man; seize him" (Matt. 26:48). He approached Jesus to kiss Him, which is not uncommon between men in the Middle East. However, it is usually a greeting for friends who have not seen each other in a while rather than for two men who just ate a meal together a couple hours earlier. This indicates that the premeditated corruption of a sign of friendship and love would become a sign of betrayal.

An interesting detail is that Judas greeted Jesus with the words, "Hail, Rabbi" (Matt. 26:49). Through this title Judas has reduced Jesus from the Messianic Son of Man, by which Jesus had described Himself and from being his "Lord," such as Peter had addressed Him (see Matt. 14:28; 17:4; 18:21). If Jesus were just one more rabbi, Judas could justify handing Him over to be tried by other rabbis. In St. Luke, Jesus challenges Judas with a question: "Judas, would you betray the Son of man with a kiss?" (Luke 22:48). Jesus had dipped bread in the dish with Judas at the Last Supper to make a last-ditch effort for restoring their relationship, but now Judas kisses Jesus as a signal to the crowd arresting Jesus, thereby using affection to betray Jesus.

As with Judas, the betrayal of Jesus by sex-offending bishops and priests is more easily justified in their minds if they have reduced Jesus' authority as their Lord and moral norm. Once a Christian begins to judge the truth of Jesus Christ and His Gospel by the norms of contemporary values, disobedience of the moral code that aids holiness of life becomes easy. Once a person distorts Christian values to vague abstractions, any action can be self-justified.

For instance, by placing primacy on love, but then redefining love in terms of contemporary confusion between lust and love, a person can justify strong sexual feelings as a loving act. This confusion prevents one from understanding the destructive nature of lust, particularly in abusive relationships by which a more powerful or authoritative person grooms and manipulates a victim into gratifying the strong person's desires of the corruptive flesh. Love is the highest of the three theological virtues (faith and hope being the other two); it is a gracious gift bestowed by God that elevates any natural love, such as family, romance or friendship, into a higher level of self-giving for the good of the loved one. Judas's deceptive and treasonous kiss is the proper image for the sexual abuse of minors and of adults by bishops and priests. Like Judas, they are the minority of the clergy, but like Judas, they remain in the Church doing horrible damage to individuals and to the Church as a whole.

Furthermore, Judas's kiss is an appropriate symbol for the evil deeds of those modern priests who have distorted sexuality. Human sexuality is meant for the procreation of children, but it is also a great expression of human love. Abusers, however, have snatched personal pleasure from children, adolescents, and adults in destructive relationships that call to mind the "wicked steward" who abuses the other servants, and "eats and drinks with the drunken," with no concern that his master will return unexpectedly and "punish" (i.e., cut him in two pieces) him "and put him with the hypocrites" where "men will weep and gnash their teeth" (Matt. 24:49–51).

Similarly, abusers do not consider the judgment of the sheep and the goats (see Matt. 25:31ff), by which their treatment of the "least of the brethren" is accounted as being done to Christ. In that light, the sexual abuse by bishops and priests is as much a betrayal of Christ as was Judas's kiss. Whatever the priest abusers have done to their victims, they did to Jesus Christ, according to His accounting. Just as we lament Judas's kiss, so we are shocked by the evil committed by clergy sexual abusers.

Certainly Judas was not seeking personal pleasure from kissing Jesus, but rather was using the kiss merely to mark Jesus for arrest and thereby earn his thirty pieces of silver. He was also currying the Sanhedrin's favor, since they were the religious power in Jerusalem. He no longer believed that following Jesus would offer him the power, prestige, or wealth that the Sanhedrin and its leaders could offer him. This kind of motive also has been a stumbling block for many priests. Instead of seeking to serve Jesus Christ and His people as they deserve, in humility and total generosity, some priests foolishly seek position, power, and status through their role in the Church. They would find more of it in politics and business, but some of them may consider that too difficult and risky a route. Status in the Church may entail less effort and be less hazardous than secular success, so they take it as an easy way. That is as foolish and fleeting as Judas's efforts and ought to never be part of a priest's calculation in the ministry.

Peter Takes Up the Sword

The other disciples proposed, "Lord, shall we strike with the sword?" Before He could answer, "one of them struck the slave of the high priest and cut off his right ear" (Luke 22:49–50). St. John identified the one who used the sword as Simon Peter and the name of the high priest's slave as Malchus (John 18:10). This makes sense, since Peter, James, and John were the three who had accompanied Jesus about a "stone's throw" away from the other eight (Luke 22:41).

Jesus took control of the situation and responded in three ways. First, He put an end to the attempt to use armed resistance by giving a principle: "No more of this!" "Put your sword back into its place; for all who take the sword will perish by the sword" (Luke 22:51; Matt. 26:52; John 18:11). Second, Jesus "touched his ear and healed" Malchus (Luke 22:51). Third, He set these events in the context of God's redemptive plan: "Shall I not drink the cup which the Father has given me?" (John 18:11). This refers to removing the cup of suffering mentioned in His prayer (see Matt. 26:39; Mark 14:36; Luke 22:42) and in the question He posed to James and John: "Are you able to drink the cup that I drink, or to be baptized with the baptism with which I am baptized?" (Mark 10:22; Matt. 20:22). When suffering with Jesus was a theoretical notion, accompanied by the possibility of sitting on His right and left, James and John were ready to accept the cup of pain with Him. When Peter, James, and John witnessed Jesus' transfiguration, they were ready to build three tents, one each for Jesus, Moses, and Elijah (see Mark 9:5; Matt. 17:4; Luke 9:33). Here, Jesus offers them the Father's plan to "drink the cup which the Father has given me," but they tried their own plan with a sword.

Matthew 26:51–55 recorded Jesus' critique of both the Apostles' lack of understanding and of the arresting crowd's hypocrisy. When He said, "Put your sword back into its place" (Matt. 26:52a), He gave three reasons against using violence. First, "All who take the sword will perish by the sword" (i.e., the violent will die through violence). Second, Jesus already has more powerful angels at His disposal. "Do you think that I cannot appeal to my Father, and he will at once send me more than twelve legions of angels?" (Matt. 26:23). In other words, He is both the Son of God the Father, who could receive anything He asks of the Father, and the Son of Man, who has angels at His disposal. Jesus knew He had received power over His life and death from the Father:

> "For this reason the Father loves me, because I lay down my life, that I may take it again. No one takes it from me, but I lay it down of my own accord. I have power to lay it down, and I have power to take it again; this charge I have received from my Father." (John 10:17–18)

That power explains why Jesus could walk through the crowds that wanted to kill Him on various occasions: after His criticism of a lack of faith among the people of Nazareth (Luke 4:29-30); and when He claimed to be the Lord God (John 8:59; John 10:39). However, now, in Gethsemane, it was time to lay down His life for the life of the world, and the Apostles' feeble attempts to prevent His death by striking off the ear of the high priest's servant was an action outside of the Father's will. The Apostles' sleepiness during Jesus' prayer prevented them from understanding that this was the "hour" for Jesus to "drink the cup," and their futile actions could not stop God's plan.

Third, the arrest fulfills Scripture: "But how then should the scriptures be fulfilled, that it must be so?" (Matt. 26:54). This means that each step of the way, from the Last Supper to the Crucifixion, death, and burial, was predicted in earlier Scriptures and will not be prevented. Rather, they will be elements of suffering that God uses to redeem sinners from sin and death.

Jesus Addresses the Crowd That Came to Arrest Him

Jesus then turned to the crowd led by Judas that had come to arrest Him in the secret of the night:

> "Have you come out as against a robber, with swords and clubs to capture me? Day after day I sat in the temple teaching, and you did not seize me. But all this has taken place, that the scriptures of the prophets might be fulfilled." (Matt. 26:55–56; see also Luke 22:52-53; Mark 14:48-49)

He opens with a rhetorical question about treating Him as if He were a robber, even though He had been very accessible to the leaders and their Temple officers during the previous five days. This question points out their cowardice in arresting Him at night, and their hypocrisy by not making it a public act. Their treachery in the darkness of night is a fulfillment of both His prediction about these events and of the prophets' teachings.

At the Last Supper He had told the Apostles, "You will all fall away because of me this night; for it is written, 'I will strike the shepherd, and the sheep of the flock will be scattered'" (Matt. 26:31), citing the prophet Zechariah: "Awake, O sword, against my shepherd, against the man who stands next to me," says the LORD of hosts. "Strike the shepherd, that the sheep may be scattered; I will turn my hand against the little ones" (Zech. 13:7).

At the moment of His arrest, these words were fulfilled as the eleven Apostles forsook Him and fled (see Matt. 26:56).

St. John brings out a very interesting element of this encounter with the arresting crowd that is not found in the other evangelists. Jesus stepped forward to confront His assailants, and in so doing, He frightens them with a claim to being divine:

> Then Jesus, knowing all that was to befall him, came forward and said to them, "Whom do you seek?" They answered him, "Jesus of Nazareth." Jesus said to them, "I am." Judas, who betrayed him, was standing with them. When he said to them, "I am," they drew back and fell to the ground. (John 18:4–6)

While many English translations read "I am he," the word *he* is not in the Greek text. This is the name of the Lord God in Exodus 3:14, and therefore Jesus is claiming to be the Lord God at His arrest. In the face of this, the crowd falls backward to the ground. Jesus then confronted them a second time with a view to letting the disciples go free: "Again he asked them, 'Whom do you seek?' And they said, 'Jesus of Nazareth.' Jesus answered, 'I told you that I am; so, if you seek me, let these men go'" (John 18:7–8).

Even as they come to arrest Jesus in the secret darkness of the garden, they implicitly recognize the reality of His claim to be God, even if it is with the same fear experienced by the devils—"Even the demons believe—and shudder" (Jas. 2:19).

St. John adds his own editorial comment that Jesus is fulfilling

His own words spoken at the Last Supper: "This was to fulfil the word which he had spoken, 'Of those whom you gave me I lost not one'" (John 18:9), a reference to Jesus' final prayer: "While I was with them, I kept them in thy name, which thou hast given me; I have guarded them, and none of them is lost but the son of perdition, that the scripture might be fulfilled" (John 17:12). This also shows the fulfillment of the prophetic statement regarding Judas found in Psalm 41:9, discussed in the preceding chapter on the Last Supper.

Flight of the Apostles

"Then all the disciples forsook him and fled" (Matt. 26:56). The eleven Apostles forsake Jesus in the face of His statement that the arrest and His imminent death are fulfilling the Scripture. They were willing to direct the way of redemption in accord with their own wits, such as fighting the crowd with the sword, but they could not stand by Jesus if it meant accompanying Him in His acceptance of suffering and pain. They run and hide behind locked doors for the next couple of days, leaving Jesus to suffer and die. Only two of the Apostles will hover around the edge of Jesus' Passion. One of them will deny knowing Him, and only the "beloved disciple" will approach the Cross and stay to the end.

These events are very relevant to the present situation regarding sexual scandals by contemporary priests. We can remind ourselves that the first twelve bishops merely hours prior had been ordained by Jesus' word and received their first Holy Communion. Now, during a time of agonizing prayer, one bishop betrays Jesus with a kiss in order to get thirty pieces of silver, and the other eleven bishops run away in the face of Jesus' danger, fearing for themselves.

These Apostles are models both for the minority of perpetrators who sexually abuse children (3 percent of the total number of priests have committed these crimes) and for the weakness and cowardice of some bishops in addressing these sins. Of course, there are many cases when the bishops and superiors were unaware of the crimes. Sometimes they believed that psychological help could rectify an offender. However, sometimes the cover-up of horribly evil, even violent acts, were kept hidden.

Each bishop or religious superior who has covered up any cases of sexual abuse must examine their conscience before Jesus Christ Himself and face the full truth of their own motivations and failures. This is not an examination of excuses by which they can be exonerated in a courtroom, but a thorough moral examination of conscience so as to give a proper account to the Judge of all, who knows all and will summon all to take full responsibility for each and every action, thought, and sin of omission. It is also an examination of conscience that can help the Church deal with correcting these evils. The people of God can deal with honesty, but not with excuses and falsehood.

In conclusion, "the band of soldiers and their captain and the officers of the Jews seized Jesus and bound him" (John 18:12). This leads to the next stage of a series of trials that conclude with Jesus' torment and death.

CHAPTER 5

---∞∞∞---

THE TRIAL OF THE JUDGE OF ALL

The clergy sexual abuse crisis in the Catholic Church has become a hot topic because the news media has extensively covered the arrests and trials of alleged perpetrators of these crimes. The bishops who aggressively tackled the problem rarely made headlines; they were simply doing what is expected of them. Bishops who failed to understand the crisis or who neglected to address complaints of abuse were investigated, sometimes indicted and put on trial, as were the actual perpetrators of the abuse.

Another aspect of prosecuting abusers and those who neglected to prevent the abuse is that the victims are required to testify in public, thereby reliving the pain of their past. Their families suffer alongside them, reopening old wounds and at times discovering for the first time what happened to their beloved relative or friend.

Finally, some priests and bishops have been falsely accused of abuse or neglect. They, too, get removed from the priestly ministry they love and cherish. In some cases, even when they are exonerated, they are not permitted to return to their priestly service. Their hearts are broken and they are tempted to become bitter, suffering as they are pushed aside.

The role of police investigations, arrests, trials, and media coverage is an important component of the present suffering in the clergy abuse crisis. Therefore, it's important for us to examine our Lord's own experiences at His four trials—at the house of Annas, at Caiaphas's house, Herod's palace, and Pilate's Praetorium. As we enter these events in our imagination and connect the present suffering to that of Jesus Christ, we can discover the redemptive element of our present suffering, unite it with that of Jesus Christ, and then become part of the healing of our Church and of the rest of the world enduring similar pain.

Introduction to the Trials of Jesus

The crowd of soldiers arrested Jesus in Gethsemane to bring Him to the courts of the retired high priest, Annas, and then present Him to the high priest Caiaphas in order to try and condemn Him. The great irony here is that the Lord, eternal High Priest, and Judge of all humanity, is being put on trial by both the former and the present high priests. As a result of their condemnation, Jesus will be lifted up on the Cross as both the Lamb of God Who is sacrificed for the sins of the world (see John 1:29) and as the one true and eternal High Priest Who offers Himself. The acts of two high priests of the Old Covenant will establish Jesus as the High Priest of the new and everlasting covenant Who is seated in the heavenly Holy of Holies at the right hand of the Father for all eternity (see Hebrews 5—10). Annas and Caiaphas's very attempts to preserve their power and position will lead to their actual undoing.

In AD 6, the Roman Procurator Quirinius deposed Joazar as high priest and in his place appointed Annas (called "Ananus" by Josephus), son of Seth (Josephus, Jewish Antiquities xviii, 26). Annas ben Seth was the father of five other high priests— Eleazar, who succeeded him from AD 16–17, Jonathan, who succeeded Caiaphas from AD 36–37, Theophilus from AD

37–41, Matthias from AD 42–43, and eighteen years later, Annas II from AD 61–62. Annas's son-in-law was Joseph Caiaphas, who was high priest between his sons Eleazar and Jonathan, ruling throughout the procuratorship of Pontius Pilate from AD 18 to 36. Annas was the grandfather of Matthias, son of Theophilus, who was high priest from AD 65 to 68, the period when the Jewish Revolt against Rome broke out (AD 66–72). The fact that he and his sons ran the high priesthood for about forty-five years indicates the tremendous influence he had and explains why Jesus was first brought to him for the initial examination of the charges against Him.

Jesus in the Court of Annas the High Priest

St. John sets the scene by describing how the crowd "led him to Annas; for he was the father-in-law of Caiaphas, who was high priest that year" (John 18:13), and was the leader "who had given counsel to the Jews that it was expedient that one man should die for the people" (John 18:14). He reminds the reader that Caiaphas had said that Jesus should "die for the people" so that "the whole nation should not perish," a decision considered prophetic (see John 11:49–52).

Peter's Denials of Jesus

Before the trials actually began, each evangelist introduces the fulfillment of Jesus' prophecy of Peter's three denials of Jesus (see Matt. 26:33–35; Mark 14:29–31; Luke 22:33–34; John 13:37–38). St. Mark and St. Luke simply mention the house of the high priest, without naming him. St. Matthew wrote that the soldiers "led him to Caiaphas the high priest, where the scribes and the elders had gathered" (Matt. 26:57–58), but he does not mention the precise location. St. John offers more details, as on other occasions, writing that "another disciple" was known to the high priest and was able to convince the maid at the door to allow Peter into Annas's courtyard (see John 18:15–16). The implication is that John was the "other disciple" and is therefore the source of the details that explain how Peter entered Annas's well-guarded courtyard, as well as the importance of the maid at the door. All four Gospels mention the maid who is the first to question Peter and evoke his first denial of knowing Jesus. "The maid who kept the door said to Peter, 'Are not you also one of this man's disciples?' He said, 'I am not'" (John 18:17; see also Matt. 26:69–70; Mark 14:66–67; Luke 22:56–57).

Despite his protestation to Jesus that he would never deny Him and would die for Him, Peter wilts in cowardice in the presence of the maid who is in charge of the door. Then Peter joined the soldiers and servants to warm himself near a fire (see Mark 14:67; Luke 22:55; John 18:18; Matt. 26:69), but only St. John adds that it was a "charcoal fire," the first of two mentions of a charcoal fire in the Bible (see John 18:18). The significance of the other charcoal fire will become apparent in Chapter 7.

Annas the High Priest Questions Jesus

St. John turns the attention away from Peter to Annas' questions "about his disciples and his teaching" (John 18:19). Jesus answered:

> "I have spoken openly to the world; I have always taught in synagogues and in the temple, where all Jews come together; I have said nothing secretly. Why do you ask me? Ask those who have heard me, what I said to them; they know what I said." (John 18:20)

St. John had presented Jesus' open teaching in the synagogues and Temple throughout his Gospel, particularly in chapters 5 through 10. Jesus had openly engaged the leaders through challenges about the truth of His message and the falsehood or partial truths of their lives, yet they did not arrest Him out of fear for the crowds, whose instinct of faith stirred them to accept His teaching as truth.

Annas's line of questioning and Jesus' answers are relevant to the sexual scandals in the contemporary Church, whether the evils of pedophilia, homosexual or heterosexual relationships, pornography addictions, or other misbehavior in the sexual realm. It is certainly true that temptations from the natural appetites for sex, possessions, status, food, drink, and other forms of overindulgence have a power and energy of their own. Certainly, all human beings are called to the natural cardinal virtue of temperance, by which one has self-control over the appetites through a reasonable understanding of the proper role of sexuality, food, drink, and so on in human life.

On a deeper level, Christians understand the natural virtue of temperance within a set of higher vocations from God. People called by God to Holy Matrimony need to restrain themselves sexually from fornication and adultery, as well as any abusive actions toward one's spouse. Those called to religious life and the priesthood freely give up the natural good of marriage and sexual expression "for the sake of the Kingdom of God" (Matt. 19:12). Sexual restraint and temperance belong to the holiness of life to which the Lord God calls each person, whether in marriage or freely accepted celibacy under religious vows before God. Those who maintain the proper chastity of marriage or priestly or religious vows are rewarded by God with eternal life; those who die while refusing to be chaste will be condemned by the Lord as unfaithful servants.

In recent decades, some theologians have questioned and denied Jesus Christ's teachings about marriage, celibacy, and sexual morality in general because they accept the changing norms from contemporary culture. Since the sexual revolution of the late 1960s, marriage has been treated as unnecessary in the culture, so that not only are the majority of American adults in the early twenty-first century unmarried, but more than 50 percent of all children are born to unmarried people. Birth control and abortion are seen as important positive values, marriage has been redefined to include couples of the same gender, and gender itself is presented to be as malleable as silly putty either through "sex change" operations or through simple declarations of a new identity.

In response to this, some theologians, followed by the clergy they teach in seminaries, reject the teachings of Christ in favor of these modern innovations. They are like the Sadducee party of the high priests. They adapted to Greek culture when the Seleucid king Antiochus III conquered Judea in 198 BC (see 1 Macc. 1) and later adapted to Roman culture, despite Pompey's initial persecution when he took control of Jerusalem in 63 BC. They followed the ancient Israelite temptation to adapt to the surrounding culture, as when they worshiped Baal and other Canaanite gods. That same temptation exists among Christians, who find it too hard to reject prevailing cultural trends when they contradict the teachings of Jesus Christ and His Church.

The willingness to at first tolerate some of the cultural values commonly leads to accepting them and even promoting them. If super wealthy members of the present secular culture can find Catholics who willingly take money in order to become pro-abortion Catholics for "choice," and if bishops can prevent their priests from participating in open opposition to abortion or even from preaching against abortion, then there will certainly be theologians, priests, bishops, and cardinals who tolerate and promote illicit sexual unions among the clergy. Some of these clergymen will manipulate weaker people to engage in these illicit sexual unions, in part because they no longer have a theological basis for opposing these sins, and they become capable of justifying any behavior at all.

An officer hit Jesus for answering Annas's question, but Jesus responded, "If I have spoken wrongly, bear witness to the wrong; but if I have spoken rightly, why do you strike me?" Annas then sent Jesus to Caiaphas (see John 18:21–24). This is parallel to abusive clergy who reject the truth of Jesus' teaching but possess no capacity to offer reasonable explanations for their behavior. They resort to raw power to get their way, whether by intimidating their sexual and financial victims or those who stand in favor of Jesus Christ's teachings. These men are ecclesiastical bullies, who would do well to see themselves in the light of Annas and his soldier who tried to intimidate Jesus into silence but failed. On the other hand, those clergy and laity who teach Jesus' Gospel day after day can look to Jesus as He answers the bully forthrightly and humbly, confidently knowing that they will be exonerated by God's glory.

Peter's Second and Third Denials of Jesus

The attention turns away from Jesus and back to Peter as he is challenged a second time for being one of Jesus' disciples. While standing "on the porch" of the courtyard (Matt. 26:71), "warming himself" at the charcoal fire (John 18:25) and keeping a low profile, a second bystander accuses Peter of being a disciple of Jesus. With greater force, he "again denied it with an oath" (Matt. 26:72; John 18:25). At this point Peter broke the Eighth Commandment, falsely swearing an oath to deny his knowledge of Jesus.

His third denial comes after someone insisted that he was with Jesus, since he was clearly a Galilean and not someone from among the Judaean bystanders: "Certainly you are also one of them, for your accent betrays you" (Matt. 26:73; see also Mark 14:70–71; Luke 22:59). Even more vehemently Peter denies knowing Jesus, swearing and invoking "a curse on himself." With the words of his self-imprecation on his lips, "immediately the cock crowed" (Matt. 26:74; Mark 14:72; Luke 22:60; John 18:26–27), thereby fulfilling Jesus' precise prediction.

Each Gospel points out that at this moment Peter remembered Jesus' words that Peter would betray Him before the cock crowed. St. Luke includes a poignant detail:

> And the Lord turned and looked at Peter. And Peter remembered the word of the Lord, how he had said to him, "Before the cock crows today, you will deny me three times." And he went out and wept bitterly. (Luke 22:61–62; see also 12:9; Matt. 26:75)

Jesus' direct gaze at the leader of the Apostles brought His words to the forefront of Peter's consciousness. He had adamantly sworn that he would die with Jesus. Yet in the midst of the challenge, he was unable to be firmly loyal to Jesus. At this point he left the high priest's courtyard to weep bitterly over his sin of denying Jesus before men.

Priests and bishops who have broken the promises of celibacy they made at their ordination Mass and religious who have broken their vows of chastity would do well to look at their failures through the lens of St. Peter's failure to keep his word. Whether these sins were committed with a woman, a man, a child, an adolescent, or alone, they all add up to varying levels of failing to keep one's word to God and the Church.

Just as Peter is no longer centered on Jesus but instead focuses on his fear, so also is it common that those clergy and religious who fail to keep their oath of chastity for the sake of the Kingdom of God have turned their attention to their own loneliness, the promise of pleasure with another person, or perhaps even love and being loved by an individual.

Likewise, when Jesus takes the initiative to turn His attention to the sinner, and the sinner looks back at Him, then a way of sorrow for the deed, repentance, and conversion opens up. Grief for the evil deed itself, for the scandal caused to another, and for the other effects of the sin may take time in order to be fully integrated by the offender. Weeping over having fallen short of Jesus' expectations, over the harm done to oneself, and the harm done to the persons with whom or against whom one has sinned is a first and essential step in reconciliation. The arrogant who refuse to admit to their wrongdoing will miss it; the humble who repent will find it and grow.

The Soldiers' First Mockery of Jesus

Mockery of Jesus is repeated throughout His trials and Crucifixion. Typically, people who have the upper hand in society demonstrate their power by mocking and ridiculing the weak or the opponents who come under their control. Frequently people attack their moral superiors as a defense against trying to improve their own immoral behavior along the lines of their opponent's integrity. This may explain the mockery by the soldiers, both Jewish and Roman, throughout Jesus' Passion. With prisoners under their control for a brief time, they had the chance to display their superiority. Furthermore, five days earlier in the Temple, they had been unable to prevent Jesus from entering the Temple and driving out the money-changers. Six months earlier they had tried to arrest Him on the Feast of Tabernacles, but they were overwhelmed by His teaching and got into trouble with the leaders of the Sanhedrin (see John 7:32, 44–49). Now they did not fear Jesus or the crowds, so they "mocked him and beat him" and blindfolded Him, saying, "Prophesy! Who is it that struck you?" (Luke 22:63–65; see also Mark 14:65; John 18:22).

The phenomenon of mockery is, sadly, just as common in modern society as in antiquity. Mockery seeks its target's vulnerabilities, such as the failure of most people to attain the perfect ideals of manhood or womanhood. Among boys, this typically translates into mockery of any sensitive or effeminate qualities or any homosexual elements that might be betrayed.

Harshness or masculine behaviors in girls evoke similar ridicule. While Jesus Christ suffered through the mockery He received with silent strength, many humans are crushed by it or become isolated. They retreat into relationships with like-minded people or with those who might protect them. Yet even when people seek refuge from rejection and mockery, they are vulnerable to sexual or physical abuse.

Since Jesus was mocked and bullied, He can meet victims at the point of their pain. He achieved a victory over the soldiers by His silent endurance and His offering up ofHimself for His victimizers. His prayer on the Cross must have begun at the very beginning of their torment: "Father, forgive them; for they know not what they do" (Luke 23:34). By entering into the experience of being mocked by bullies, Jesus knows exactly what it is like and can relate well to the bullied. At this point He wins a grace, a spiritual power to overcome mockery and bullying for every victim. Victims of bullying can meet Christ in His silent response to mockery and in such a meditation speak to Him of their own experience. They can listen to Him as He responds to their stories, and His wounded heart can become a source that heals the loneliness and pain—whether physical or emotional—that bullies inflict.

Jesus' Trial Before the Sanhedrin

The trial moved to the house of "Caiaphas the high priest, where the scribes and the elders had gathered" for a meeting of the Sanhedrin, or Jewish council, and Peter cowered in the courtyard (Matt. 26:57–58). Caiaphas and the other chief priests had the greatest political clout with the Romans. The Pharisees were the pious laypeople, represented by the scribes (their intellectuals) and the elders. In the initial stage of the trial, these various parties "sought false testimony against Jesus" because they wanted to "put him to death" rather than find the truth. They found "many false witnesses," but as is the case with liars, their testimony did not agree. Jewish law requires two witnesses who can testify to the same statements (see Num. 35:30; Deut. 17:6; 19:15). Only after a string of deceivers spoke up could they find two men who agreed to say, "This fellow said, 'I am able to destroy the temple of God, and to build it in three days" (Matt. 26:61). Of course, Jesus had not said this. A rather different saying is found in John: "Destroy this temple, and in three days I will raise it up" (John 2:19). Jesus did not say that He would destroy the temple; He said that if others destroyed the temple, He would raise it up, but He had not threatened the temple. Further, St. John explained that He spoke of the "temple of his body" (John 2:21), not the temple building.

Throughout the modern sexual scandal in the Church, false accusations directed at a variety of individuals have been a further evil component. Particularly in the early years of the scandal, but even in its later development, far too many young victims have not been heeded, trusted, or believed. Sometimes their parents refused to accept their stories because they had put so much confidence in the priests. Sometimes church officials did not believe them and rejected their witness. Sometimes they even came to doubt themselves. All too often, people who tried to report abuse, whether parents, teachers, friends, and even other clergy, were not believed. Too many of the perpetrators were trying to cover their own tracks, and sometimes bishops and priests who were their friends helped them instead of the victims, as the records later demonstrated.

In addition, cases of false accusations have been made against priests and bishops over the years — often when lawsuits became very lucrative or a priest was disliked for some reason. Completely innocent clergy have been removed from their ministry, and even after they were exonerated, they were forbidden to celebrate the sacraments publicly and preach the Gospel they love due to a cloud of suspicion that clung to them after falsehoods had been spoken about them.

Sexual misconduct inflicts horrible suffering on its victims, but the pain is aggravated by false witness and deception. People have a right to the truth, and throughout all levels of the sexual scandal, this right has been violated, just as it had been violated in the trial of Jesus Christ. All victims of lies and falsehood under oath can discover a new level of integrity by standing next to Jesus, who is the Truth personified (see John 14:6), as He listened to the lies spoken against Him under oath during His trial. The priests and Pharisees searched for false witnesses, and Jesus had to listen to the variety of lies spoken about him. Through it all, they confirmed His teaching given six months earlier at the Feast of Tabernacles:

> "You are of your father the devil, and your will is to do your
> father's desires. He was a murderer from the beginning, and
> has nothing to do with the truth, because there is no truth in
> him. When he lies, he speaks according to his own nature, for
> he is a liar and the father of lies. But, because I tell the truth,
> you do not believe me." (John 8:44–45)

Still, no matter how much sway falsehood has for a time, the truth is more powerful. Whether it is discovered in this life or not, it will be proclaimed with the full force before the whole world by the same Lord Jesus "who will come again to judge the living and the dead" at the end of time.

Jesus' Silence

The failure of the false witnesses to convict Jesus led to Caiaphas taking control of the trial by speaking directly to Jesus, Who had remained silent through it all. First, he demanded that Jesus answer the charges: "Have you no answer to make? What is it that these men testify against you?" (Matt. 26:62). If Jesus remained silent, it would be logical to construe that He was actually guilty, since the Law reads: "If any one sins in that he hears a public adjuration to testify and though he is a witness, whether he has seen or come to know the matter, yet does not speak, he shall bear his iniquity" (Lev. 5:1).

However, a yet deeper reality was taking place, based on Isaiah's prophecy in chapter 53 about the "Suffering Servant" who would save all people from their sins without speaking: "He was oppressed, and he was afflicted, yet he opened not his mouth; like a lamb that is led to the slaughter, and like a sheep that before its shearers is dumb, so he opened not his mouth" (Isa. 53:7). Jesus is the "Lamb of God who takes away the sins of the world," identified by St. John the Baptist (see John 1:29). He will be a silent sacrifice for sin, without any noisy talk.

Jesus' silence relates to the experience of the abused in two ways. Victims were often silent when the abuser first violated them, because they were in a state of shock. They were silenced by the violation of their innocence, by being used for an adult's pleasure, and by the shock of a priest or bishop being inappropriately sexual. Second, they frequently remained silent for many years after the abuse because their shock made them unable to speak about it. Young people struggle to integrate their own sexuality, and abuse by an adult retards that integration further. Often victims blame themselves and are ashamed to speak of the deeds done to them. They fear that no one will believe them, so they do not want to open up the issue. They often do not know whom they can trust with such a horrendous secret.

The silent Jesus, the sacrificial Victim Who "opened not his mouth," can reach out to the victims of abuse during their silence. Sometimes their regret at being silent about their experience makes them feel another type of guilt; in such cases, let them spend time with Jesus Who was silent as He heard the false accusations. Let the victims speak to Him about their silence and then listen to him speak to their hearts.

Jesus Answers His Accusers with the Truth

Stumped by Jesus' silence, Caiaphas solemnly demanded that He answer a completely different question: "I adjure you by the living God, tell us if you are the Christ, the Son of God" (Matt. 26:63). His question echoes Simon Peter's confession of faith, "You are the Christ, the Son of the living God" (Matt. 16:18), who then stood silently in Caiaphas' courtyard. His silence came not from strength, as it did from Jesus, but from cowardice. While Peter's faith had been a grace from God, the origin of Caiaphas's knowledge of Jesus' titles remains a mystery. We will see that this question will have no bearing on the charges made by the chief priests when they bring Jesus before Pilate. It is simply a way to get a conviction according to Jewish Law.

Jesus finally responded, but with a view forward to the end of the world: "You have said so. But I tell you, hereafter you will see the Son of man seated at the right hand of Power, and coming on the clouds of heaven" (Matt. 26:64). He accepted the truth of Caiaphas's statement that He is the Christ, the Son of the living God—"You have said so." Caiaphas had adjured Him most solemnly, and Jesus speaks only the truth, so He admits to His identity, just as He had when Simon Peter had made the same profession. However, He does not accept it on Caiaphas' terms, but in terms of God's eternal plan, which determines that the Son of God is also the Son of man who will judge the whole world with full divine authority. He is the fulfillment of Daniel's vision of the Messiah, the "Son of man" who rules an eternal kingdom of all people:

> I saw in the night visions, and behold, with the clouds of
> heaven there came one like a son of man, and he came to the
> Ancient of Days and was presented before him. And to him
> was given dominion and glory and kingdom, that all peoples,

nations, and languages should serve him; his dominion is an everlasting dominion, which shall not pass away, and his kingdom one that shall not be destroyed. (Dan. 7:13–14)

Jesus included a reference to a messianic psalm: "The LORD says to my lord: 'Sit at my right hand, till I make your enemies your footstool'" (Ps. 110:1). While Caiaphas had a certain authority to judge Jesus, Jesus looked straight at him and stated that He had the authority of God to judge every nation and people, including Caiaphas.

Jesus' claim here brings us back to a point He frequently made in His parables about the inevitable coexistence of sinners and the righteous within the Church: Throughout history they will coexist, but one day Jesus will give a true and righteous verdict on each and every one. The weeds and the bad fish will be gathered by the angels and thrown into the fire; the wheat and the good fish will be gathered into barns. The foolish virgins will be locked out of the wedding feast, and the goats will be prevented from entering the Father's kingdom.

This true and morally righteous judgment is too often forgotten or even denied by unrepentant abusers who will be condemned for their sins at the coming of Jesus Christ. They push away thoughts about the ultimate results of their sinful abuse and refuse to consider its effects on their victims or even on their willing partners. They do not care that the victims of sexual abuse experience guilt that cripples their capacity to enter loving, committed relationships with future spouses. The victims' sexual identity becomes confused, and they often find it difficult to perceive other people or themselves as anything more than mere objects or tools of sensual gratification. These effects commonly last far beyond adolescence and even into old age if shame and embarrassment prevent the victim from speaking about these tensions so as to integrate and resolve them. For these deeds will the abusers stand shamefacedly before their Judge, the Son of Man.

The High Priest's Verdict

Once he heard Jesus' word, "the high priest tore his robes," which was an ancient demonstration of extreme grief (see, for example, Gen. 37:29; 44:13; Jer. 41:5). It was part of the judicial process for condemning a blasphemer, as stated in the Mishna (Sanhedrin 7): "They that judge a blasphemer, first ask the witnesses, and bid him speak out plainly what he has heard; and when he speaks it, the judges standing on their feet rend their garments, and do not sew them up again." Caiaphas followed this sign with his verdict and a demand to the Sanhedrin for a sentence: "'He has uttered blasphemy. Why do we still need witnesses? You have now heard his blasphemy. What is your judgment?' They answered, 'He deserves death'" (Matt. 26:65–66).

A legal procedure problem in this trial is explained by the Mishna (Sanhedrin 4:1): "In civil cases the whole body of the court may defend or accuse, while in criminal cases all of them may acquit, but the whole body must not accuse." This principle was intended to assure fairness to the accused. After a unanimous verdict to condemn a criminal, the final decision had to be postponed in order to search for other witnesses so as to prevent a miscarriage of justice, particularly in a death sentence case. This principle was not followed in Jesus' trial, since it had already been decided that He had to die.

The priests and elders convicted Jesus of blasphemy after He had claimed to fulfill Daniel's prophecies. Giving Him the death penalty would rid them of the problem posed by Jesus' actions and words. Ironically, they helped fulfill the Scriptures that had prophesied God's way to save the world. The Old Testament will be cited throughout Jesus' sufferings as the actions of the Sanhedrin, Pilate, the soldiers, and the crowds fulfill the words spoken centuries earlier by the prophets. God's plan will progress, despite the plans of mere mortals.

The Soldiers and the Sanhedrin Mock Jesus a Second Time

The Sanhedrin believed that Jesus was in their control, so they began to abuse Him physically and verbally. "They spat in his face, and struck him; and some slapped him" (Matt. 26:67). These priests and elders had a sacred charge to administer justice based on religious and moral principles; however, they misused their position and trust by abusing a condemned man. Even if their verdict had been correct, the punishment would have been execution, not torment of a bound, helpless criminal. Yet their actions fulfilled prophecies made 570 years earlier about Israel's Savior becoming a "suffering servant:

> "I gave my back to the smiters, and my cheeks
> to those who pulled out the beard; I hid not my
> face from shame and spitting." (Isa. 50:6)

> "He was despised and rejected by men; a man of
> sorrows, and acquainted with grief; and as one
> from whom men hide their faces he was despised,
> and we esteemed him not." (Isa. 53:3)

Ironically, they demanded, "Prophesy to us, you Christ! Who is it that struck you?" (Matt. 26:68). They did not know that He had already prophesied their behavior three different times as He made His way to Jerusalem (see Matt. 16:21; 17:22–23; 20:17–19), and at this moment they fulfilled both His prophecies and the ancient prophecies about Him.

Jewish law did not allow trials to take place at night; they were supposed to be public so they could be based on true evidence and correct judicial procedure. In a possible attempt to keep the letter of the law while contravening its purpose, the actual condemnation to death was decreed the following morning (see Matt. 27:1–10), when they reached an official decision.

Once the officials formally declared the death penalty, they led Jesus to Pilate. In so doing, the chief priests and elders fulfilled Jesus' prophecy in His third prediction of the Passion:

> "Behold, we are going up to Jerusalem; and the Son of man will be delivered to the chief priests and scribes, and they will condemn him to death, and deliver him to the Gentiles to be mocked and scourged and crucified, and he will be raised on the third day." (Matt. 20:18–19)

This points out Jesus' ability to prophesy, something they had mocked in Matthew 26:68. They also contradicted their earlier stated plans not to arrest Jesus during the Passover celebrations. Jesus shows Himself to be far more in charge of events than the apparent circumstances would indicate.

Judas Commits Suicide

In an ironic contrast to the Sanhedrin's decision to condemn Jesus on false charges, Judas rendered a true verdict on Jesus and regretted his acts of betrayal (see Matt. 27:3–4). In accord with Mishna (Sanhedrin 4), his testimony should have been admitted before the court to exonerate Jesus on that next day. Jewish legal practice was concerned that new witnesses might arise to exonerate an accused person, so verdicts of condemnation were not supposed to be made on the day of the trial. However, in Jesus' case, the Sanhedrin's decision had nothing to do with the evidence, just as Judas's decision to betray Jesus had nothing to do with the truth—as evidenced by Judas's direct denial of being the traitor: "It is not I, Rabbi" (Matt. 26:25).

Identifying Judas as "his betrayer" is a term derived from the verb used in Matthew 27:2 for the phrase "delivered him" (*paredokan*) to Pilate. This is a verbal connection that hints at the symbiotic relationship between the Sanhedrin and Judas. The Sanhedrin betrayed its own principles of justice in court procedures by condemning Jesus with false witnesses and incorrect procedure; Judas betrayed Jesus with a kiss for monetary gain. While the motives of the scribes, Pharisees, and Sadducees to seek Jesus' death had gradually developed since the beginning of Jesus' successful healings, exorcisms, and teachings in Galilee, Judas's motives for betraying Jesus to the Sanhedrin are not explicitly stated, other than his love of money (see John 12:5–6; Matt. 26:15). He became a prime example of Paul's teaching of the truly evil desire for money that causes some Christians to depart from the truth of the faith: "For the love of money is the root of all evils; it is through this craving that some have wandered away from the faith and pierced their hearts with many pangs" (1 Tim. 6:10).

However, nothing is ever said about rejecting some teaching or other, nor is there mention of any particular envy on the part of the other disciples, or of feelings that Jesus had slighted him, or any other motive for betraying Jesus. The absence of such motives may help explain why Judas came to realize that his betrayal had gone too far: the condemnation of Jesus to death is more than he bargained for, and he apparently considers it too much. He is capable of fully recognizing that Jesus is innocent and that his betrayal is a sin: "I have sinned in betraying innocent blood" (Matt. 27:3).

While the *Revised Standard Version* suggests that Judas "repented," a better translation would be "regretted," which properly translates the word *metameletheis*, whereas "repented" would properly translate *metanoeo*. Matthew uses the verb *metamelomai* to indicate the profound contrast between Peter's tearful repentance (Matthew 26:75) and Judas's mere regret that led to his suicide.

The chief priests in the Temple responded curtly and cynically to Judas, "What is that to us? See to it yourself" (Matt. 27:4). If the leaders of the Sanhedrin had been authentically concerned with justice, they would have immediately called for a new trial, as the Mishna requires. Furthermore, had the priests reopened the case, Judas, along with the others who had testified falsely during the trial, could have been executed as false witnesses in a capital crime case. It would have also become an indictment of the priests in regard to their incorrect procedures. Instead, they simply order Judas to take care of his own sin of false testimony. Tragically, it is precisely his attempt to take care of the problem of sin through his own efforts that reduces him to mere remorse and regret rather than an authentic repentance that flows from God's grace.

Over the years, priests and bishops involved in the sexual scandals of past decades can find themselves exemplified both by Judas and by the leaders of the Sanhedrin. A number of priests who committed these crimes realized, like Judas, that they had betrayed young people by robbing them of their innocence. They were swept into an evil crime by the feelings of the moment, a loosening of their moral code during a strong temptation, and a self-centered fall into being controlled by their passions.

In fact, the great majority of perpetrators of these crimes committed them only once—but like Judas, once too many. They regretted their sin and kept themselves from doing it again. However, the young person whose innocence they took remained harmed by the act, as is the standard experience of young victims, whether of homosexual or heterosexual acts. While the adult perpetrators hope that the matter has gone away, in fact it is not addressed by the young person until later in life, when its harmful effects appear in their marriages or raise other issues. When the now-older victim realizes the impact of the earlier sexual experience, he confronts the adult and opens up cases that are at times decades old.

However, like the leaders of the Sanhedrin who refused to take any responsibility for their deceptions and evil decisions, some priests and bishops deny that they did anything wrong. They may claim that their sexual encounters were not abusive, that they were consensual, that the young person initiated it, or that it was to the young person's advantage. They try to deceive their accusers, sometimes even themselves, and certainly try to deceive God Himself. Their commitment to their own advantages, pleasures, vaguely and falsely "good" intentions, and present place in society and the Church make them cavalier with the facts and the deeper truth of their deeds.

Such an attitude is more commonly found among that minority of clergy sexual abusers who are repeat offenders. The frequent repetition of this sin, or any other sin, makes it possible to quash the conscience, not unlike the sociopath who feels no empathy for his victims and in his unshakeable self-confidence can justify anything he does. This can be particularly true of those who know enough theology or canon law to invent a justification of anything—not unlike those civil lawyers who find ways to justify the corrupt acts of politicians or the evil deeds of wealthy syndicate criminals.

The antidote to legalistic manipulation is to understand the truth of the moral principles embedded in the law and make a commitment to implement them. The moral principles are available to our conscience from the natural law and from God's revelation. God is Himself the authority behind these moral principles, and He will judge each person according to the norm of His truth, not by some legalistic manipulation of the facts. Contradicting or misapplying the moral values underlying the law in order to achieve one's own purposes will not be tolerated by God when He judges each person.

Remembering that judgment and preparing for it with integrity of life is the proper antidote.

Judas apparently became disgusted with the thirty pieces of silver and with himself. He threw the thirty pieces of silver into the temple in order to symbolize that the chief priests bore the responsibility for condemning Jesus. He then "departed; and hanged himself" (Matt. 27:5).

Of the Gospels, only Matthew mentions Judas's suicide. St. Luke wrote the other report of Judas's death in Acts 1:18–20, though with a few different details. His suicide tragically fulfilled Jesus' words at the Last Supper: "The Son of man goes as it is written of him, but woe to that man by whom the Son of man is betrayed! It would have been better for that man if he had not been born" (Matt. 26:24).

Judas's suicide is the prime indicator that his regret over betraying Jesus was not true repentance. He did not believe that he could be forgiven, and by killing himself, he turned that thought into a self-fulfilling prophecy. He could not accept himself, and he believed that his betrayal made it impossible for God to ever accept him again. He committed the sin of despair and made self-destruction his future. He stands in contrast to Simon Peter, who saw Jesus gazing at him after his third denial. Peter, like Judas, departed from the scene, but Peter bitterly wept penitential tears, while Judas hung himself, making himself incapable of any weeping.

This relates to some painfully sad situations in the present sex scandal crisis, in which some victims and the perpetrators of the crimes have committed suicide. In these cases, neither victims nor perpetrators could face the shame and embarrassment. As is commonly the case, too many victims blame themselves for allowing the perpetrator to talk them into the sexual acts, even though they were often tricked into it through clever processes of grooming or forced by other pressures and even sometimes through violence.

A few priests have committed suicide once they were accused, apparently unable to cope with the shame, the prospect of a trial and conviction, or punishment. Even though they had heard many confessions and presumably had been merciful and compassionate to sinners in their ministry, they somehow seem to fail to recognize the possibility of their own repentance, reconciliation with God and their victims, and redemption.

Of course, both victims and perpetrators would face many painful consequences as a result of the past deeds, but they could come to see that even their suffering can be part of their healing. That is the power of Christ's sufferings — not only to win the forgiveness of sin, but also to give meaning to human suffering by spiritually uniting one's pain with His, an idea that will be developed in the next chapter. The key is to focus on Jesus Christ during times of guilt and suffering, as did Peter after his third denial, instead of turning merely to one's personal resources, which leave a guilty person empty and hollow to the point of despair.

The chief priests could not accept the thirty pieces of silver that Judas had thrown at them: "It is not lawful to put them into the treasury, since they are blood money" (Matt. 27:6). This may be a reference to a law in Deuteronomy: "You shall not bring the hire of a harlot, or the wages of a dog, into the house of the Lord your God in payment for any vow; for both of these are an abomination to the Lord your God" (Deut. 23:18). Though this is not precisely the situation here, their legal decision proves the point Jesus had made in Matthew 23:23–24:

> "Woe to you, scribes and Pharisees, hypocrites! for you tithe mint and dill and cumin, and have neglected the weightier matters of the law, justice and mercy and faith; these you ought to have done, without neglecting the others. You blind guides, straining out a gnat and swallowing a camel!"

The chief priests are concerned that Judas's "blood money" would bring ritual pollution into the temple, while they had perpetrated injustice in the Sanhedrin's condemnation of an innocent man through false witnesses.

It is important to reflect on the immense seriousness of the moral, religious, and civil laws that have been broken by the clergy perpetrators of sexual abuse against the young. First, they sinned against the Sixth and Ninth Commandments by engaging in illicit sexual acts outside of marriage, breaking their freely taken vows of chastity and solemn promises of celibacy.

Second, too many bishops and superiors of religious orders have covered up these crimes against young people. In about one hundred cases, they moved the accused to other countries, and in even more cases, to other parishes within the very country or even the diocese in which the offense took place. Far too often, the offenders committed the same crimes against boys and in 20 percent of the cases against girls, causing great harm to even more victims.

Third, when accusations were made against some bishops and cardinals, and it became commonly known that they were targeting seminarians, it was not addressed forthrightly but covered up with well-known secrets.

The chief priests "took counsel" and decided to use the thirty pieces of silver to buy a burial plot for strangers, "called the Field of Blood to this day" (Matt. 27:8). Today a small Greek Orthodox monastery commemorates this site, southeast of the Old City of Jerusalem where the Kidron and Gehenna valleys meet. Even this event fulfills an Old Testament prophecy:

> "And they took the thirty pieces of silver, the price of him on whom a price had been set by some of the sons of Israel, and they gave them for the potter's field, as the Lord directed me." (Matt. 27:9–10)

Though St. Matthew attributes it to Jeremiah, we find the words in Zechariah:

> Then I said to them, "If it seems right to you, give me my wages; but if not, keep them." And they weighed out as my wages thirty shekels of silver. Then the Lord said to me, "Cast it into the treasury"—the lordly price at which I was paid off by them. So I took the thirty shekels of silver and cast them into the treasury in the house of the Lord." (Zech. 11:12–13)

A number of explanations have been proposed to reconcile this discrepancy. The most probable opinion seems to be that the name of the prophet was originally omitted by the Evangelist, and that the name of Jeremiah was added by some later copyist. Evidence is that it is omitted in two twelfth-century Syriac manuscripts, a later Persic, two Itala, and some other Latin copies. Also, it is common for Matthew to omit the name of the prophet when he quotes them (see Matt. 1:22; 2:5,15; 13:35; 21:4). Jeremiah may have been mentioned because this passage alludes to two passages that mention buying a field in that prophet's writings: Jeremiah 19:1–13 and Jeremiah 32:7.

Buying the Field of Blood with the silver coins given to Judas painfully brings to mind the amounts of money by which victims and their families were paid off to keep silent about the abuse perpetrated by priests and bishops. On one hand, it is right and just to compensate the victims for treatment of their pain and ongoing psychological struggle regarding the abuse that they had endured. On the other hand, the punitive damages that are owed to the victims ought to be paid by the perpetrators of the crimes, not taken from Church funds. The people of God generously donate money, property, time, and love to the Church because in general the Church is very conscientious about making sure that these resources get to the people who need them. However, they do not donate money in order to finance payoffs for crimes committed by the clergy.

In effect, these payoffs take away from the direct service to the poor and from education and other worthy apostolates. While the Church ought to be willing to provide medical and psychological care for the victims of abuse, the perpetrators of the crimes ought to be made fully responsible for the punitive damages imposed because of their crimes. Building schools and churches, supplying aid to the poor and the unborn, and funding the various evangelization and catechetical ministries and services ought not be deflected to pay punitive damages. If the clergy knew ahead of time that they would be held responsible for any punitive damages, they would be more likely to refrain from such abuse. This is particularly the case since 2002, when clergy and church workers began being trained to report any abuse to the police, as well as to ecclesial authorities.

Jesus' Trials Before the Political Leaders

While the Sanhedrin condemned Jesus to death, they sought the authority of the Roman procurator to take charge of the actual execution. For that reason "the whole company of them arose, and brought him before Pilate" (Luke 23:1). Their accusations against Jesus are rather different from the charges they had made against Him in the Sanhedrin: "We found this man perverting our nation, and forbidding us to give tribute to Caesar, and saying that he himself is Christ a king" (Luke 23:2). In the Sanhedrin they had asked, "Are you the Son of God, then?" (Luke 22:70), which concerned Jesus' religious claims to be the Messiah. Here the leaders of the Sanhedrin interpret Jesus' claim to be "Christ" as a claim to political kingship. They add the false accusation that Jesus had spoken against paying taxes to Caesar. What He had said when the Pharisees and Herodian party attempted to entrap Him was "render to Caesar the things that are Caesar's, and to God the things that are God's" (Luke 20:25). Since the leaders had changed the venue to a Roman court, they adapted their false accusations to political issues that might worry the empire's representative rather than address the religious concerns of the Sanhedrin. They were willing to do anything necessary to destroy Jesus.

Too often the sex abuse crisis has become an occasion of politicizing the accusations. For example, since 81 percent of the minors abused by priests were adolescent males, some people have emphasized that this is a homosexual issue. In addition, research by the *Los Angeles Times* indicates that sexual abuse cases against boys increased as the number of homosexual seminarians and priests increased in the 1970s.

However, others refuse to blame homosexuality as such because the majority of homosexual priests have not abused minors, and many of the abusers self-identify as heterosexual. The meaning of the social data is obviously complex, and conservative and liberal political agendas take up the issue, with people on both sides failing to integrate the available information when it is inconvenient. All of the relevant information about sexual abuse still needs analysis and reflection by competent folks.

Until that point, the issue must be brought back to the spiritual concerns of the priesthood and the Church's proper care of people vulnerable to sexual exploitation. Whom are the priests serving? Are they committing themselves to serving Jesus Christ, acting in the Person of Christ (in *Person Christi*), or are they serving themselves and their appetites, particularly their sexual appetites? Are their vows taken before God, with an absolute commitment to live a chaste and holy life of service to God and His Church, or have they come to be served (see Matt. 20:28; Mark 10:45)? How do priests serve young people? How do they protect all people from predation, especially those who are vulnerable due to their youth, physical, emotional or mental disabilities? Such concerns, rather than politically correct or other political issues, need to be at the forefront.

Jesus Before Pilate

Given the seriousness of the politicized charges against Jesus, Pilate asked Him, "Are you the King of the Jews?" To this Jesus answered as He had answered the Sanhedrin, "You have said so" (Luke 22:3; see also 22:70). Pilate sees through the obvious falsity of the charge and answered the chief priests and the crowds, saying, "I find no crime in this man" (Luke 23:4).

St. John develops this part of the trial scene, showing how Jesus, the true King of Israel, is judged by Pilate and rejected by His own people. Pilate called Jesus away from the crowd for a more private conversation inside the Praetorium. When Pilate asked Him if He was "the King of the Jews," Jesus responded with a question for Pilate: "Do you say this of your own accord, or did others say it to you about me?" (John 18:34). Pilate identifies the Jews as the source of the accusation and simply wants Jesus to explain what He had done to evoke such accusations. As is typical in John's Gospel, Jesus' dialogue invites Pilate to deeper levels of meaning, if he is open to pursuing them.

> "My kingship is not of this world; if my kingship were of this world, my servants would fight, that I might not be handed over to the Jews; but my kingship is not from the world." Pilate said to him, "So you are a king?" Jesus answered, "You say that I am a king. For this I was born, and for this I have come into the world, to bear witness to the truth. Every one who is of the truth hears my voice." (John 18:36–37)

However, Pilate's own cynicism about the existence and identity of truth brings it to an end: "Pilate said to him, 'What is truth?' After he had said this, he went out to the Jews again, and told them, 'I find no crime in him'" (John 18:38).

Jesus Before Herod and His Third Experience of Mockery

The same people insist on Jesus being a dangerous insurgent, saying, "He stirs up the people, teaching throughout all Judea, from Galilee even to this place" (Luke 23:5). Yet with their mention of His Galilean origins, they give Pilate a way out of putting Jesus on trial: Jesus the Galilean belongs to Herod's jurisdiction, so Pilate "sent him over to Herod, who was himself in Jerusalem at that time" (Luke 23:7).

After Herod the Great died in 4 BC, his kingdom was divided among his sons, who were given the title of "tetrarch"—that is, ruler of a fourth of the kingdom. Herod Antipas was the tetrarch of Galilee and Perea, though he was also called the "king" (Mark 6:14, 26). As such, any claims that Jesus is a king would affect Herod Antipas more than it would Pilate; therefore, Pilate sent Jesus to be questioned by Herod Antipas.

When Jesus came to his Jerusalem residence, Herod "was very glad, for he had long desired to see him, because he had heard about him, and he was hoping to see some sign done by him" (Luke 23:8). This desire to see Jesus goes back to Luke 9:7–9, when he had heard of Jesus' miracles and preaching. However, when Jesus neither answered Herod's questions nor performed some miracle, Herod and his soldiers turned against Jesus, treating Him with contempt and mockingly "arraying him in gorgeous apparel" before sending Him back to Pilate—gestures that helped Herod and Pilate overcome their previous enmity and become friends (see Luke 23:9–12).

Jesus' Second Trial Before Pilate

When Herod returned Jesus to Pilate's custody, Pilate confronted the priests and leaders with the fact that they had falsely accused Jesus of political charges for fomenting insurrection among the people:

> "You brought me this man as one who was perverting the people; and after examining him before you, behold, I did not find this man guilty of any of your charges against him; neither did Herod, for he sent him back to us. Behold, nothing deserving death has been done by him; I will therefore chastise him and release him." (Luke 23:13–16)

Yet, even though Pilate knows that Jesus is innocent of any crime, he still offers to "chastise" Him—that is, to scourge Him—before releasing Him.

St. Matthew does not mention Jesus' appearance before Herod, but he does describe the second stage of Jesus' trial before Pilate in greater detail than St. Luke. He describes how the chief priests and elders insert themselves into the discussion with further accusations while Jesus remains silent (see Matt. 27:12). The actual accusations are not stated explicitly, but from Pilate's words, we can infer they concerned some form of threat to Roman political power.

Jesus' silence must be understood in the context of a prophesy in Isaiah's fourth Servant Song: "He was oppressed, and he was afflicted, yet he opened not his mouth; like a lamb that is led to the slaughter, and like a sheep that before its shearers is dumb, so he opened not his mouth" (Isa. 53:7).

Jesus' silence was not that of a guilty person who is incapable of refuting the charges against him. Rather, His silence belonged to the faithful Servant of the Lord who was fully aware that His suffering belonged to the redemption of the world, including the very people who were anxiously working to kill Him. Further, His silence flowed from the strength of a man who recognized the incapacity of His hearers to either recognize or accept the truth, such as in Psalm 38, where the innocent man stood before treacherous accusers:

Those who seek my life lay their snares, those who seek my hurt speak of ruin, and meditate treachery all the day long. But I am like a deaf man, I do not hear, like a dumb man who does not open his mouth. Yea, I am like a man who does not hear, and in whose mouth are no rebukes. (Ps. 38:12–14)

Pilate tried to get Jesus to respond to the accusations: "Do you not hear how many things they testify against you?" (Matt. 27:13). But Jesus remained steadfastly silent, evoking amazement from the governor. Pilate's wonderment at Jesus' silence made him yet more reluctant to execute Him.

At this point we learn of his custom of releasing a prisoner of the crowd's choosing at the feast of Passover (see Matt. 27:15–16; Mark 15:6; Luke 23:17; John 18:39). At the same time, the evangelists mention the notorious prisoner Barabbas, "who had committed murder in the insurrection" (Mark 15:7) and was a "robber" (John 18:40). One irony is that Barabbas is an Aramaic word meaning "son of the father," while Jesus Christ is the true Son of God the Father. Another irony is that the adjective describing this prisoner is *episemos*, meaning either "notorious" or "famous." This may indicate the different attitudes toward Barabbas, who was notorious to the Romans but famous to the Jews.

Pilate offered the crowd the choice between Barabbas and Jesus, well aware that "it was out of envy that they had delivered him up" (Matt. 27: 18). Precisely at this point, Pilate's wife sent him a warning message: "Have nothing to do with that righteous man, for I have suffered much over him today in a dream" (Matt. 27:19). This is the sixth dream by which God revealed His will (see also Matt. 1:20; 2:12, 13, 19, 20), but it is the only dream that is not obeyed. The other five dreams all served to save Jesus' life. Pilate failed to do so.

The chief priests stir up the people to choose Barabbas rather than Jesus, despite Pilate's attempts to sway them to take Jesus (see Matt. 27:20–21; Mark 15:10–11; Luke 23:18–20; John 18:39–40). With Jesus still in custody, Pilate foolishly asked the crowd what to do with Jesus, and their response was to demand His Crucifixion. Pilate tried to reason with them, pleading that they identify the evil Jesus had done (see Matt. 27:22–23), but they offer no justification for their demand; they simply repeat the demand more loudly and insistently.

Pilate was responsible for dispensing justice in the name of the Roman Empire. However, in the face of the unjust demands to kill Jesus, Whom Pilate had found innocent, and the preference to save the murderous Barabbas, whom Pilate had found guilty, he capitulates to the mob. He feared a riot and handed Jesus over to the crowd, denying responsibility by washing his hands in front of everyone, saying, "I am innocent of this man's blood; see to it yourselves." The people accepted the responsibility and said, "His blood be on us and on our children!" (Matt. 27:24–25). This fulfills Jesus' words in Matthew 21:42–43:

> Jesus said to them, "Have you never read in the scriptures: 'The very stone which the builders rejected has become the head of the corner; this was the Lord's doing, and it is marvelous in our eyes'? Therefore I tell you, the kingdom of God will be taken away from you and given to a nation producing the fruits of it."

Jesus Is Scourged and Crowned During His Fourth Experience of Being Mocked

After releasing Barabbas, Pilate had the innocent Jesus scourged by his soldiers, as all four Gospels describe (see Matt. 27:26; Mark 15:15; Luke 23:16, 22; John 19:1). However, after the scourging, the Gospels also concur that the soldiers took it upon their own initiative to make a crown of thorns, put it on His head, mockingly call to Him, "Hail, King of the Jews!" and beat Him (see Matt. 27:27–31; Mark 15:17–20; John 19:2–3; in Luke 23:11 Herod's soldiers mock Jesus, but there is no mention of Pilate's soldiers doing so).

St. John describes how Pilate paraded Jesus in these first torments as proof of Jesus' innocence: "'See, I am bringing him out to you, that you may know that I find no crime in him.' So Jesus came out, wearing the crown of thorns and the purple robe. Pilate said to them, 'Behold the man!'" (John 19:4–5).

Rather than evoking compassion, the chief priests and officers cried out, "Crucify him, crucify him!" Pilate tried to induce the Jewish leaders to take full responsibility, saying "Take him yourselves and crucify him, for I find no crime in him." The Jewish leaders insisted that Jesus had broken Jewish law: "We have a law, and by that law he ought to die, because he has made himself the Son of God" (John 19:6–7).

Becoming yet more frightened, Pilate returned Jesus inside the Praetorium for another private conversation, demanding an explanation: "Where are you from?" Jesus remained silent, and Pilate became more agitated and insisted on his power over Jesus: "You will not speak to me? Do you not know that I have power to release you, and power to crucify you?" However, Jesus spoke as the one in actual control of the situation when He explained, "You would have no power over me unless it had been given you from above; therefore he who delivered me to you has the greater sin" (John 19:8–11).

Finally, Pilate—absolutely convinced of Jesus' innocence—sought to release Him. About to lose their gambit to have Jesus crucified by the Roman procurator, the Jews cried out, "If you release this man, you are not Caesar's friend; every one who makes himself a king sets himself against Caesar." Pilate brought Jesus out of the Praetorium and sat down on his judgment seat, presenting Jesus to the public with the words, "Behold your King!" They reacted violently, "Away with him, away with him, crucify him!" When Pilate said, "Shall I crucify your King?" the chief priests answered, "We have no king but Caesar." At that point Pilate handed Jesus over to them to be crucified (see John 19:12–16). The Judge of all the world was condemned after much torment and then led out to be killed.

CHAPTER 6

———∞∞———

JESUS' WAY OF THE CROSS

As we begin to examine Jesus' Way of the Cross, let us first recall His words to the Apostles about the necessity of following Him along this way. He first taught this when he instructed the Apostles about their first mission trip: "Who does not take his cross and follow me is not worthy of me" (Matt. 10:38). He repeated the instruction after Peter had rebuked Him for predicting his suffering, death, and Resurrection (see Matt. 16:21–23). He addressed all of the disciples with these words: "If any man would come after me, let him deny himself and take up his cross and follow me" (Matt. 16:24; see also Mark 8:34).

Jesus did not tell His disciples to go suffer for Him, but He tells them it is necessary to "come after" Him in denying oneself and taking up the cross to "follow" Him. For this reason Hebrews accurately describes Jesus as the "pioneer of salvation":

But we see Jesus, who for a little while was made lower than the angels, crowned with glory and honor because of the suffering of death, so that by the grace of God he might taste death for every one. For it was fitting that he, for whom and by whom all things exist, in bringing many sons to glory, should make the pioneer of their salvation perfect through suffering. (Heb. 2:9–10)

Let us run with perseverance the race that is set before us, looking to Jesus the pioneer and perfecter of our faith, who for the joy that was set before him endured the cross, despising the shame, and is seated at the right hand of the throne of God. Consider him who endured from sinners such hostility against himself, so that you may not grow weary or fainthearted. (Heb. 12:1–3)

Every Christian needs frequent reminders that Jesus Christ makes suffering an essential component of being a disciple. For that reason Catholics over many centuries have had a strong devotion to the Stations of the Cross. This also explains the great detail and extensive writing about the Passion and death of Christ in each of the Gospels; it is the longest episode in the first three Gospels, and only in John does the Last Supper Discourse (see John 13—17) exceed the Passion narrative in length.

At this time of suffering in the Church due to the decades-long sexual abuse scandal, Jesus' Way of the Cross is a way to further understand the suffering and experience of those who have been abused, their family, friends, and relatives, the Church community, and the great majority of clergy and religious who did not commit these crimes. Not only will Christ's sufferings offer a perspective on their own pain, but each person can unite their pain with Christ's suffering.

The wounds suffered by His Crucifixion and death bring healing and make us whole (see Isa. 53:3–5). We unite our pain with His in our prayers, such as the Morning Offering and most especially in the Mass, which is the unbloody representation of his death on the Cross. Holy Communion is not only the reception of His Body and Blood in the Blessed Sacrament. It is also our own choice to unite our sufferings with

His at the Offertory of Mass so that our gift of our personal pain may be consecrated with the bread and wine and joined with His death on the Cross during the Consecration of Mass. This communion with Jesus' pain also brings a deep healing to all who enter into it.

The Gospel Way of the Cross

Matthew, Mark, and John treat Jesus' Way of the Cross very succinctly, but Luke offers more details. All three synoptic writers mention that Jesus left the Praetorium carrying His Cross, but Simon from Cyrene (in present-day Libya) was forced to help Jesus carry the Cross (see Matt. 27:32; Mark 15:21; Luke 23:26). All four Gospels mention that this journey ended at the "place of the skull," or Golgotha in Aramaic (see Matt. 27:33; Mark 15:22; Luke 23:33; John 19:17). No other events along the way interest the evangelists, except for St. Luke.

St. Luke, who frequently includes episodes about women, describes how "a great multitude of the people" followed Jesus, including some "women who bewailed and lamented him" (Luke 23:27). To these compassionate women, Jesus spoke:

> "Daughters of Jerusalem, do not weep for me, but weep for yourselves and for your children. For behold, the days are coming when they will say, 'Blessed are the barren, and the wombs that never bore, and the breasts that never gave suck!' Then they will begin to say to the mountains, 'Fall on us'; and to the hills, 'Cover us.' For if they do this when the wood is green, what will happen when it is dry?" (Luke 23:28–31)

Amazingly, as these women seek to comfort Jesus, He turns the situation around to warn them of the even greater dangers in store for them and their children because the city had rejected Jesus as the Messiah. Earlier He had warned His disciples about the coming destruction of Jerusalem because it had rejected Him as it had rejected the prophets before Him:

> "O Jerusalem, Jerusalem, killing the prophets and stoning those who are sent to you! How often would I have gathered your children together as a hen gathers her brood under her wings, and you would not! Behold, your house is forsaken. And I tell you, you will not see me until you say, 'Blessed is he who comes in the name of the Lord!'" (Luke 13:34–35; see also Matt. 23:37–39)

Now He shows more concern for the welfare of these compassionate women and their children in regard to the coming destruction of Jerusalem than He does for His own welfare in the present moment.

Jesus had similarly warned His disciples about the coming destruction of Jerusalem: "Alas for those who are with child and for those who give suck in those days! For great distress shall be upon the earth and wrath upon this people" (Luke 21:23; see also Matt. 24:19; Mark 13:17). These warnings about the dangers of the final days of Jerusalem and of the world draw upon the Old Testament prophets, who also described that people would beg for the mountains to cover them for protection at the end of time (see Hos. 10:8; Is. 2:19–22), and they prepare for the prophecies in the Book of Revelation (see Rev. 6:15–16).

The conversation between the "daughters of Jerusalem" and Jesus is pertinent to the present situation of the priest sexual abuse scandal in a number of ways. First, the women's compassion for Jesus points to the need to console those who are suffering in the present crisis. Most importantly, this applies to the victims of the abuse, whether small children, adolescents, abused adults, including the disabled, nuns, vulnerable seminarians, clergy and laity, as well as their shocked families. Other members of the Church who are scandalized by these crimes also need consolation:

priests who have been falsely accused of crimes and the clergy who never engaged in these crimes and yet are tarred with the same brush. We can console each other, but most poignantly, the suffering Lord Jesus, carrying His Cross to Golgotha, best consoles because He undergoes these pains on account of the sins of some of His priests. He personally knows the intensity of pain and can encounter others in their deepest hurt.

Every Christian can face the pain that the abuse scandal imposes on them when they do so with Jesus. Then, like Him, we can meet other sufferers from our own experience of pain and console them as fellow sufferers. No one need exaggerate his or her own pain, nor diminish the pain of anyone else. Rather, together we join Jesus Christ and discover the power of suffering to redeem everyone in the Church who is presently suffering. St. Paul proclaimed this most poignantly in Colossians: "Now I rejoice in my sufferings for your sake, and in my flesh I complete what is lacking in Christ's afflictions for the sake of his body, that is, the church" (Col. 1:24). Each of us can gain wisdom and insight into the suffering of other people from the things we undergo, and we can lovingly console them as Jesus did.

Another aspect of Jesus' consoling words to the "daughters of Jerusalem" is His wider historical perspective on His present sufferings and their future suffering. Similarly, the present abuse scandal needs a wider historical perspective. For this reason, the faithful in the Church must look at the previous periods of priest scandals, such as the horrible papacies of the tenth and early eleventh centuries — the widespread homosexual abuse in the monasteries of those days and the widespread open concubinage by diocesan clergy. Then we must look to the lives of the great reforming saints who corrected that period of abuse — Sts. Peter Damian, Pope Gregory VII, and others who worked hard at reform, even to the point of having their lives threatened. Likewise, the widespread sexual misconduct of clergy in the fifteenth and early sixteenth centuries was transformed by reforming saints, including St. Ignatius Loyola, St. Peter Neri, and St. Charles Borromeo, who was shot in the back by a priest who rejected his reform program (the bullets were absorbed into the fabric of the bishop's cope and he survived).

Perspective can also be gained from the many studies about widespread sexual abuse in modern culture. They indicate that between 3 and 4 percent of priests have abused children and adolescents, while 9.4 percent of public school teachers and administrators abuse the children in their care, and a high percentage of children are abused in their own homes. Society as a whole must gain perspective on the causes of abuse and the means of prevention, as well as study the ways to end the trafficking and enslavement of people, which is particularly aimed at their sexual exploitation. Just as Jesus wanted the "daughters of Jerusalem" to see sin within their culture as the cause of coming pain and destruction, so also we need to teach and warn our culture about the evils of sexual abuse and misconduct of all kinds so as to avert such a high level of interior societal corruption that may bring about the destruction of the whole society.

Jesus Is Crucified and Dies

The Gospels agree that once they came to the place called the Skull (in Aramaic, Golgotha; in Latin, Calvary), Jesus was crucified with two criminals, "one on the right and one on the left" (Luke 23:33; see also Matt. 27:33, 38; Mark 15:22, 27; John 19:17–18). The Gospels include important details about the events and words of Jesus as He is dying, and these offer extremely rich material for meditation on the abuse crisis.

Jesus Rejects the Wine Mixed with Gall

Matthew and Mark say that the soldiers offered Jesus an initial drink of wine "mixed with gall" (Matt. 27:34) or "myrrh" (Mark

15:23). This act by the soldiers combined mercy, since this mixture was a painkiller, and mockery, since it was a bitter taste given to someone already suffering excruciating pain. On another level, their act fulfilled a Scripture: "They gave me poison for food, and for my thirst they gave me vinegar to drink" (Ps. 69:21). However, Jesus refused to drink it so that He could fully embrace the pain of the crucifixion.

In a society that continues to reap the bitter fruit of the drug revolution of the mid-twentieth century, it is important that Jesus refused to take something that would have dulled His pain at least for a while. He won the grace and power to reject using a drug, such as enslaves many modern people.

Sadly, many victims of sexual abuse, including the abuse by clergy, have used drugs to deaden the pain caused by the sexual abuse, by the betrayal from clergy and religious they had trusted, and by the failure of others to protect them from the abuse. While never denying their pain, they need to know that alcohol and drug abuse can only increase their suffering, in both the short run and the long run. Instead, they can meet Jesus Christ at this point of His suffering on the cross by prayerfully imagining His refusal of the pain-killing wine even as He hangs above the crowd, pierced with nails in His hands and feet, struggling to breathe. Those who have been abused can unite their suffering to Jesus' pain spiritually. If they have a problem with drugs or alcohol, they can join Jesus in rejecting the substance they are abusing that abuses them in turn. When they feel too weak to say no to the drug, they can ask Jesus for the power of His refusal and find a new freedom in Him.

Understandably, many who have been abused also enter into habits of sexual sin, which is typically compulsive and at times even abusive of others. Whether it is compulsive sexual contact with other people, compulsive self-abuse, or pornography addictions, they, too, can meet Jesus Christ at this moment of refusing a drink meant to ease His pain. He can strengthen them to turn away from illicit and compulsive sexual actions so as to enter a new level of integrating sexuality into the whole of their lives in a positive and healthy way.

Jesus Is Stripped and Hung on the Cross

None of the Gospels describe the very act of crucifying Jesus but simply state that the soldiers "crucified him." The ancients were well enough acquainted with this punishment, since it was normally carried out in very public places. However, the gruesome details of that deed can be derived from reading the details contained within the Gospels. For instance, the only mention of the use of nails in crucifying Jesus came from the Apostle Thomas, who demanded to see and touch the mark of the nails in the risen Jesus as the only authentic evidence he would accept (see John 20:25).

Another detail is that the soldiers had stripped Jesus of His clothing before nailing Him to the cross. The evidence is found in all four Gospels that after Jesus was hung on the Cross, they "divided his garments among them by casting lots" (see Matt. 27:35; Mark 15:24; Luke 23:24). St. John gives the most detail, saying that the soldiers "took his garments and made four parts, one for each soldier," but they left His tunic in one piece because it "was without seam, woven from top to bottom" (John 19:23). Therefore they decided not to tear it, but to draw lots to see who would get it. In so doing, they took a role in fulfilling another verse from the Psalms: "They divide my garments among them, and for my raiment they cast lots" (Ps. 22:18). Of course, the Roman soldiers, being foreign pagans, would not have known this text, but they became instruments of its fulfillment anyway, simply by following their own greed.

Those who have been sexually abused can meet Jesus Christ in this part of His suffering. They, too, have been stripped of their clothing in various degrees. Their personal sense of modesty was violated by clergy who used them for visual or tactile pleasure, and the act of being used is typically recalled with shame and regret, anger and betrayal. In some cases, their pictures have been kept in computer files and even posted on the internet by the abusers, adding to a public humiliation that cannot be erased.

These victims can contemplate Jesus' own experience of being stripped and speak to Him as people who have experienced a humiliation that parallels His. They can allow the Lord to speak to their hearts about the act of being stripped, forced, or seduced into an unwanted experience that still causes confusion and shame. When such pictures have been publicly distributed, it is possible to see a parallel to Jesus hanging on the cross next to a city gate as the soldiers divided His garments among themselves. Jesus shares their powerlessness to stop this robbery of personal innocence and dignity, as He watched the distribution of the clothes His Blessed Mother, standing nearby, made for Him. His powerlessness and public humiliation can be a source of healing the effects of the victims' shame because it is almighty God Who has "emptied himself, taking the form of a servant, being born in the likeness of men ... and became obedient unto death, even death on a cross" (Phil. 2:7–8). Jesus' humiliation has a power to heal both because He is both the infinite God and a fellow sufferer.

"Counted Among the Transgressors"

The four Gospels agree that Jesus was crucified between two criminals, "one on the right and one on the left" (Matt. 27:38; see also Mark 15:27; Luke 23:33; John 19:18). This was understood as a fulfillment of Isaiah's description of the suffering Servant of the Lord: "He poured out his soul to death, and was numbered with the transgressors; yet he bore the sin of many, and made intercession for the transgressors" (Isa. 53:12). Jesus makes reference to the fulfillment of that prophecy in the Upper Room: "For I tell you that this scripture must be fulfilled in me, 'And he was reckoned with transgressors'" (Luke 22:37).

Passers-by would think that Jesus deserved His death since He was crucified along with two criminals. Similarly, some people think the victims of sexual abuse may well be just as guilty as their abusers because they may have invited the sexual aggression. Why did they not fight off the abuser? Perhaps they are not victims but are people who deserve as much opprobrium as the abusers.

In addition, the victims often blame themselves for the abuse and hold guilt inside of themselves with a strong feeling of shame at having been part of the sexual acts. They may have felt a certain pleasure as part of the sexual experience, even while they felt entrapped by unwanted exploitation. This confusion of emotions requires serious counsel in order to sort through its various strands, but contemplating Jesus' experience of victimhood as He hung upon the cross stripped of His clothes is a spiritual aid to further integration of the experience of abuse.

A number of priests and religious have been falsely accused of sexual abuse and have been lumped with the guilty. Some people suspect that "where there is smoke there is fire." What else have they done? Perhaps they were not really guilty on this account, but something else lurks in the background. Some of those who were even proven to be innocent still have been kept from active priestly ministry, a course of action that thereby places them among the guilty in the eyes of casual observers.

In prayer, these innocent people can bring themselves to identify with Jesus as He hangs crucified between two criminals. At that moment "he was numbered among the transgressors" and shared in the general condemnation that the passing crowds expressed against all three of them. Likewise do the victims of the sexual abuse scandal find themselves "numbered among transgressors." Some of these innocent victims may want to speak to Jesus as He hangs on the Cross; some may want to imagine themselves hanging on a cross near Him. In a prayer of the imagination, they may want to speak to Jesus about the rejection, isolation, and shame they feel. What might Jesus say in return? What would the victim hear Jesus say to them? His words will not be the superficialities of those who merely observe and judge the victim from a distance, but instead He will speak directly to the heart, knowing its depths, and speaking the full truth that each one needs to hear.

At the same time, those abusers who are actually guilty may also place themselves in this scene. They, too, are hanging on their own crosses, though they hang there as people who have legitimately been found guilty of a crime. They may find it helpful to identify with one of the two thieves on the other crosses, asking themselves with which thief they most closely identify at this point in their lives. They can either demand to be set free from their suffering as a way to demonstrate that Jesus is the Messiah, or they can use this experience of painful shame and embarrassment to examine their consciences in a decision to repent and seek His mercy. We will look at this choice more closely below.

Jesus Forgives the People Crucifying Him

Jesus spoke a number of times from the Cross, statements which are traditionally known as His "Seven Last Words." The first statement is a prayer to His heavenly Father: "Father, forgive them; for they know not what they do" (Luke 23:34). He sought no revenge against those who falsely accused Him, condemned Him, and insisted on His execution. He utters no threats against them, nor does He curse them. He does not blame Himself or anyone else. Rather, He prays that the Father forgive them all. In this way, He lives the Sermon on the Mount: "Love your enemies and pray for those who persecute you" (Matt. 5:44). Had Judas Iscariot believed Jesus' message, he would have been able to hear the same plea for his forgiveness, since he, too, would have been included in this prayer. Peter did come to experience it for himself, as would the rest of the eleven Apostles.

Jesus exemplified the prayer He had taught His disciples, though with an important difference. He had taught them to ask the Father for the forgiveness of their sins in proportion to the manner in which we forgive others: "Forgive us our sins, for we ourselves forgive every one who is indebted to us" (Luke 11:4). "And forgive us our debts, as we also have forgiven our debtors" (Matt. 6:12). Jesus' intercession for His killers to receive the Father's forgiveness for this sin anchors in painful reality His earlier instructions to His disciples on their need to forgive:

> "For if you forgive men their trespasses, your
> heavenly Father also will forgive you; but if you do
> not forgive men their trespasses, neither will your
> Father forgive your trespasses." (Matt. 6:12–15)

> "And whenever you stand praying, forgive, if you have
> anything against any one; so that your Father also who is
> in heaven may forgive you your trespasses." (Mark 11:25)

> "Take heed to yourselves; if your brother sins, rebuke
> him, and if he repents, forgive him." (Luke 17:3)

Yet Jesus was not asking for forgiveness, since He had committed no wrong. He was asking the Father to forgive those who unjustly tortured and killed Him. Without having prayed this way on the Cross, Jesus' instructions would be reduced to mere pious platitudes. However, this prayer for forgiveness comes from a man Who was unjustly nailed to a cross, with the jeers and mockery of His killers still ringing in His ears. In this light, His teaching has an authority and power to induce His disciples to imitate Him. That was the case for the first Christian martyr—the first of more than 70 million—St. Stephen the deacon, who was killed by being stoned to death outside Jerusalem (see Acts 7: 59–60).

This prayer was a continuation of the ministry of forgiveness that Jesus had shown to the paralytic who had been lowered through a roof: "Take heart, my son; your sins are forgiven" (Matt. 9:2; see also Mark 2:5; Luke 5:20). He also shows the impact of His words at the Last Supper: "This is my blood of the covenant, which is poured out for many for the forgiveness of sins" (Matt. 26:28). He prayed while He shed His blood on the Cross, making clear that He does so for the forgiveness of all sins, including those of the people who bore false witness against Him and crucified Him.

These words for forgiveness from the Cross deepen our understanding of St. Paul's teaching about the Eucharist, "For as often as you eat this bread and drink the cup, you proclaim the Lord's death until he comes" (1 Cor. 11:26). These words also reach forward to the night of the Resurrection, when He empowered the Apostles to forgive or to retain sins: "If you forgive the sins of any, they are forgiven; if you retain the sins of any, they are retained" (John 20:23).

For me or anyone else to tell the victims of sexual abuse to "just forgive" their abusers would be superficial, especially if their childhood and youth had been interrupted, if not destroyed, by it. No one ought to short-circuit a victim's need to process their anger, pain, and shame. Rather, let them come to the Cross themselves and meet Jesus in His suffering and allow their pain to join with His. Those who suffer deeply share a communion of mutual understanding to which other people have little access. That is one reason that veterans of battle say little to noncombatants about the trauma of war but speak to each other with understanding, even if they fought in different wars. They can tear up or even weep over horrible memories and lost war buddies and comprehend each other, frequently without words.

It is precisely to this kind of communion of suffering shared with Jesus on the Cross that I invite the victims of sexual abuse. They may not necessarily say much, but they can silently grieve their pain, the injustice committed against their innocence, and the corrupt handling of their situation by those who should have protected them. Only within that communion of pain can they hear Jesus pronounce his prayer, "Father, forgive them, they know not what they do." They may hear His words of forgiveness being directed to themselves; they may hear it addressed to those who harmed and even tortured them. At some point, they may be able to speak those same words themselves in a prayer for their abusers. However, to avoid a superficial statement of mere words, they can simply be with Jesus, feel their own pain alongside Him, and let His suffering bring them healing before they say this word of forgiveness themselves.

The Fifth Experience of Mockery as Jesus Hung on the Cross

As Jesus hung above the onlookers, four distinct groups of people mock Him for His failure to save Himself. Golgotha stands just outside a gate on the west side of Jerusalem, the threshold of which can still be seen inside the Russian Orthodox Church of St. Alexander. People passed through that gate the whole time Jesus hung dying—local residents, merchants, and pilgrims entering the city to celebrate Passover, some of them bringing their Passover lambs to be sacrificed in the temple on the east side of the city. St. Matthew notes that "those who passed by derided him, wagging their heads." They said out loud, "You who would destroy the temple and build it in three days, save yourself! If you are the Son of God, come down from the cross" (Matt. 27:39–40; see also Mark 15:29–30).

The chief priests of the Sadducee party and the scribes and

elders of the Pharisee party also taunted Him with exhortations to save Himself:

> "He saved others; he cannot save himself. He is the King of Israel; let him come down now from the cross, and we will believe in him. He trusts in God; let God deliver him now, if he desires him; for he said, 'I am the Son of God.'" (Matt. 27:42–43; see also Mark 15:31–32; Luke 23:35)

Neither the passers-by nor the leaders spoke directly to Jesus, but rather to the crowd in general. They used the taunts to justify themselves to one another. The Roman soldiers, who crucified the three men and stood guard until they died, joined in the mockery even as they offered Him some of their own sour wine, the regular drink of soldiers. They based their ridicule on the titulus they had nailed above His head on the Cross, saying to Him, "If you are the King of the Jews, save yourself!" (Luke 23:37). Unlike the other taunters, they actually spoke directly to Jesus. The fourth group consisted of the two criminals who were crucified on either side of Him. While the other groups mocked Him, these men "reproached" Him (see Matt. 27:44; Mark 15:32).

Such taunts were understood by the evangelists and the Church throughout history as the fulfillment of Old Testament prophecies. Already in the soldiers' scourging of Jesus and the division of His clothing, we saw the fulfillment of verses in Psalm 22. That is also true of the mockery: "All who see me mock at me, they make mouths at me, they wag their heads; He committed his cause to the LORD; let him deliver him, let him rescue him, for he delights in him!" (Ps. 22:7). This passage and Psalm 109:25 are written from the perspective of the one who is suffering and acknowledging what others are saying and doing about him. A much later book is the Wisdom of Solomon, the composition of a Jewish sage who primarily wrote about the importance of wisdom and the folly of paganism. It contains a passage that resonates precisely with the description of those who mocked Jesus:

> He professes to have knowledge of God, and calls himself a child of the Lord. He became to us a reproof of our thoughts; the very sight of him is a burden to us, because his manner of life is unlike that of others, and his ways are strange. We are considered by him as something base, and he avoids our ways as unclean; he calls the last end of the righteous happy, and boasts that God is his Father. Let us see if his words are true, and let us test what will happen at the end of his life; for if the righteous man is God's son, he will help him, and will deliver him from the hand of his adversaries. Let us test him with insult and torture, that we may find out how gentle he is, and make trial of his forbearance. Let us condemn him to a shameful death, for, according to what he says, he will be protected. (Wisdom 2:13–20)

The presence of these passages shows both the prophetic nature of the Old Testament as well as the universality of mockery and taunting of vulnerable people.

Mockery sadly belongs to the experience of many victims of sexual abuse, who were mocked by schoolmates for having hung out with a priest, and then were mocked for having been seduced by him. One small-town man was ridiculed by other men in town who claimed to have known for years that the priest had been abusing boys. While that may have been an implicit admission that some of them were among his victims, it was equally an admission that they had done nothing to confront the offender. Then, when a victim did confront the situation and have the priest removed from ministry, the other men mocked him for being a victim!

Sometimes victims are mocked for having believed the Catholic Faith in the first place. They still want to receive Christ in Holy Communion, yet they are enraged by what a priest did to them. They know that Catholicism teaches that any sex outside of marriage is sinful, and they know that the abusive priests had failed to live Catholic moral teaching. Yet they also know that the priest used his position of trust and religious authority as a means of seducing victims and keeping them silent. They feel very foolish for having trusted a priest who should have been present to serve and help them, not take advantage of them. In many ways the mockery they receive from others concurs with their own feelings of being fools.

The suffering can prayerfully contemplate Jesus Christ on the Cross, enduring those who used mockery for self-justification and to garner support from the crowd. As they hear the mockery of the soldiers and the two criminals against Jesus, they may recall their own experiences of being ridiculed. The taunts from the past and imagined mockery may run through their memories and imagination, but Jesus' experience of the same has a power to heal them, partly because He suffers just like them but mostly because His wounds heal us in many ways. He is God, and therefore outside of time, so He can enter the pain of being mocked in the present time. He so identifies with the victims that "whatever they do to the least of my brothers and sisters, they do to me" (Matt. 25:40, 45), and whatever the crucifiers did to Him now heals everyone who approach Him in faith.

Jesus' Sixth Experience of Mockery and a Conversion

St. Luke looks more closely at the two criminals' mockery of Jesus through the lens of a tradition he had learned, probably while staying in Jerusalem from AD 58–59 during St. Paul's imprisonment in Caesarea Maritima. He attributes the mockery to one who "railed" at Jesus saying, "Are you not the Christ?

Save yourself and us!" However, the other criminal rebuked him, saying, "Do you not fear God, since you are under the same sentence of condemnation? And we indeed justly; for we are receiving the due reward of our deeds; but this man has done nothing wrong." Having rebuked the taunter, he said, "Jesus, remember me when you come into your kingdom," to which Jesus responded, "Truly, I say to you, today you will be with me in Paradise" (Luke 23:39–43).

As mentioned above, priest abusers can identify with the two criminals who were crucified with Jesus. They often suffer a great deal, especially after they get caught. They lose their reputations, their priesthood, their jobs, and, for those convicted criminally, they usually lose their freedom by imprisonment. Some of the incarcerated get beaten and even murdered, since a large percentage of prison inmates have been sexually abused and do not feel much restraint in regard to taking out their pent-up anger on sex abusers who end up in prison with them.

In light of the two criminals crucified with Jesus, the priest perpetrators of sexual abuse, along with all other abusive persons, have to make a choice. They can mockingly call for Jesus to save them by extricating them from the punishment they deserve, or they can own up to their responsibility and guilt and turn to Jesus for forgiveness and ultimate redemption. The so-called "good thief" did not ask to be extricated from his punishment; he recognized it as his just desserts for the evil he had done. Instead, he humbly petitioned Jesus to simply remember him in His kingdom. The good thief had come to believe the message of Jesus' kingship, and because of his humble, repentant faith, the Church has named him a saint: St. Dismas, the good thief.

A Mother's Love

In contrast to the mockery, Jesus' mother and one Apostle, the beloved John, and two other women, both named Mary, stood at the Cross in faithful silence to comfort Him. All three Synoptic Gospels identify these women as those who had "followed Jesus from Galilee" and had ministered to Him. Though no words are attributed to them, they remained with Him to the end and became faithful witnesses of His death and burial.

St. John highlights Jesus' mother at the Cross, along with other details that show the Crucifixion to be the unraveling of the fall into Original Sin. For instance, "in the place where he was crucified there was a garden" (John 19:41), a fact that was confirmed by excavations below the floor of the Holy Sepulcher Church in the late 1920s. Jesus, the New Adam hanging on the Cross (see 1 Cor. 15:2, 45; Rom. 5:14ff), which is the new tree of eternal life, spoke to His mother, whom He addresses as "Woman." Significantly, Eve was simply called "Woman" before she sinned, and only after the Fall is she referred to as Eve. In this garden in Jerusalem, the woman standing at the Cross is the "New Eve" who had been conceived "full of grace" and without original sin, like the first Woman, yet who never disobeyed any of God's commandments.

Jesus Christ is the New Adam who recognizes the importance of the New Eve standing near the Cross, His tree of life. Seeing her and His beloved disciple, He said, "Woman, behold, your son!" To the disciple He said, "Behold, your mother!" (John 19:26–27). With these words began the mutual entrustment of every "beloved disciple" to His mother's love, and of her to every "beloved disciple." As the New Adam, Jesus undoes the sin of the first Adam and its subsequent punishment of death, thereby beginning a "new creation" (2 Cor. 5:17). However, He includes His mother as a gift bestowed from the Cross upon beloved disciples, who are the "rest of her offspring" (Rev. 12:17). We will discuss the Blessed Mother's role in the last chapter of this book.

The "beloved disciple" had been at the Last Supper (see John 13:23), stood at the Cross (see John 19:26–27), entered Jesus' empty tomb (see John 20:2ff), and witnessed Jesus' Resurrection appearance at the Sea of Galilee (see John 21:7, 20). He was the only newly ordained bishop to stay with Jesus to the end, like Jesus' mother and the other holy women. At the Cross he distinguished himself by his love of Jesus, which overcame his fear of death, and by his acceptance of Jesus' mother into his home, allowing her to be his mother and himself to be her son.

His faithful love of Jesus, despite his cowardice in Gethsemane, is an essential component for the correction and sanctification of the clergy in every age, including the present. Every bishop and priest can benefit from John's fidelity at the Cross. In this period after the liturgical fads of removing crucifixes and tabernacles from churches, bishops and priests do well to spend time before the Blessed Sacrament, as if they were praying in Gethsemane with Jesus, or contemplating the crucifix on or near the altar. These devotions can help make priests more like St. John, who stayed with Jesus even when the majority of his fellow bishops had abandoned, denied, or betrayed the Lord. Such fidelity sustains a priest and pleases God until the majority comes around, such as happened on the Sunday of the Resurrection.

The Time of Jesus' Death

The Gospels do not mention specific dates or times of the day for most events in Christ's public ministry, but the Crucifixion is an exception. All four mention the importance of "the sixth hour"—that is, noon. The date was the Friday before Passover, as Mark and Luke state when explaining the need to bury Jesus quickly in a nearby tomb: "And when evening had come, since it was the day of Preparation, that is, the day before the Sabbath" (Mark 15:42; see also Luke 23:54). St. John mentions the "day of Preparation of the Passover" three times: during the trial with Pilate (see John 19:14), to explain the need to hasten the death of the three crucified men in order to removed them from their crosses before the solemn Sabbath of the Passover (see John 19:31), and at the burial (see John 19:42). However, St. Matthew identifies the date in a different context, namely, the "next day, that is, after the day of Preparation," when the chief priests and the Pharisees asked Pilate to post a guard at Jesus' tomb to prevent the disciples from stealing the body (see Matt. 27:62).

The significance of the Crucifixion taking place on a Friday is linked to God's creation of the first man and woman on the "sixth day" (Gen. 1:31), which is Friday in Jewish accounting of days. Some of the Eastern Fathers of the Church identify Friday as the day of the first sin, not long after the creation of man and woman. Therefore it was appropriate for the redemption of fallen humanity to be accomplished on the sixth day. Also, Christ "rested" in the tomb on the Sabbath, but He rose on Sunday to begin a "new creation" (2 Cor. 5:17).

Finally, the connection between Passover and Jesus' death helps characterize death and resurrection as a new passing over from death to life as well as a liberation from slavery to sin. Israel celebrated that the angel of death had passed over their houses during the tenth plague against the Egyptians, when their firstborn sons were killed (see Exodus 12). At the same time, the Israelites left their enslavement in Egypt, "that house of bondage" (Ex. 13:3; 20:2).

The time of Jesus hanging on the Cross is also specified. The three synoptics describe a darkness that began around noon and lasted until 3:00 p.m., the time of Jesus' death: "Now from the sixth hour there was darkness over all the land until the ninth hour" (Matt. 27:45; see also Mark 15:33; Luke 23:44). St. John identifies noon as the time of Pilate's presentation of Jesus after the scourging and crowning of thorns: "Now it was the day of Preparation of the Passover; it was about the sixth hour. He said to the Jews, 'Behold your King!'" (John 19:14). Part of the significance of the identification of the time of the Crucifixion is that on the other side of Jerusalem, the priests were slaughtering the Passover lambs. Thousands of priests were killing the 200,000 lambs brought by Jerusalemites and pilgrims for the feast. Meanwhile, on the west side of the city, Jesus Christ, "the lamb of God who takes away the sin of the world!" (John 1:29), was being slain at the request and with the oversight of the high priest and other priests.

Jesus' Three Final Statements

Death is the second most important moment of a human being's existence, conception being the most important. A person's existence begins at conception, but no one has the capacity to decide the time, origin, or manner of his or her conception—except for the Son of God, the Word Who became flesh and dwelt among us (see John 1:14).

On the other hand, death is the moment at which one is defined for all eternity. Throughout life we are like clay that is molded by the society and world around us, by our own desires, by Satan, or by the Lord God. At death, that clay is fired in the kiln of separating the soul and body, and after that it cannot be shaped anymore. The purification of Purgatory is like the potter filing off rough spots from a fired vessel, but he does not reshape the vessel. The soul remains for all eternity, either as God's workmanship shaped into His own image and likeness, or as a misshapen, even hideous vessel shaped by self-will, the world, and/or the devil.

Due to the importance of death in defining a person for all eternity, the living seek to remember the last words of a dying person. For instance, St. Thomas More told his executioner, "Pray for me, as I will for thee, that we may merrily meet in heaven." Similarly, the Lord's disciples remembered His last words as He hung on the Cross. So important have these final words been to Christians throughout the centuries that a special service, the

Tre Horae, is often held in Catholic churches on Good Friday from noon to 3:00 p.m. to meditate on the "Seven Last Words of Christ." Having already looked at the first three above, we will consider the last four statements of Jesus' final moments.

Jesus Reaches Out to the Atheists

At the ninth hour Jesus cried with a loud voice, "Eloi, Eloi, lama sabachthani?" which means, "My God, my God, why have you forsaken me?" (Mark 15:34; Matt. 27:46). Very close to death, Jesus summoned the remainder of His strength and cried loudly the opening verse of Psalm 22 for all to hear. Earlier we saw that Psalm 22:16–18 was understood prophetically even as pagan Roman soldiers fulfilled it in three ways. They scourged Him (see Ps. 22:17); they nailed Jesus to the Cross (see Ps. 22:16); and they drew lots for His clothing (see Ps. 22:18). Approaching death, Jesus drew attention to the opening of Psalm 22 to show all Jews, including His disciples, that the events of His death fulfilled those Scriptures.

That psalm is also a prayer directed to God by a man enduring tremendous pain. The entire opening invocation asks God to explain why He has abandoned the sufferer:

> My God, my God, why have you forsaken me? Why are you
> so far from helping me, from the words of my groaning? O my
> God, I cry by day, but you do not answer; and by night, but find
> no rest." (Ps. 22:1–2)

Amazingly, the person who feels totally abandoned by God still addresses God personally about being so far away from His torment. Jesus on the Cross makes this petition His own, thereby uniting Himself to all other people who experience apparent total abandonment by God.

This same prayer corresponds well to the situation of the

11,000 victims of Catholic clergy sexual abuse, along with all other victims of pain and abuse in history. Human history is filled with horrific suffering, whether due to the forces of nature, or to the torment and death flowing from human malice. No one gains higher moral status by pitting the suffering of one group against another, except perhaps perpetrators of evil who want to turn public attention away from their own evildoing. Instead, "crying loudly" with Jesus in His moment of being forsaken, we unite our own moments of abandonment with Him as He, God made flesh, asks God, "Why am I suffering?"

Yet precisely because He is infinite God made flesh, He can make room for the cries of every Jew in the concentration camps, the prisoners of the Soviet gulag, the genocides of Congo, Biafra, Rwanda, and elsewhere, the slaves past and present, the poor, and the sexually abused. Everyone who trusts in God and yet feels absolutely abandoned in horrible suffering can pray with Jesus, "My God, my God, why have you forsaken me?" It tears a person apart, but it is at some points in life the only honest way to pray. Yet it remains a prayer to God, and it keeps one in authentic communication with Him.

In that light, Psalm 22 then affirms confidence in God because He has helped Israel in past history:

> Yet you are holy, enthroned on the praises of Israel.
>
> In you our fathers trusted; they trusted, and you delivered them.
>
> To you they cried, and were saved; in you they trusted, and were not disappointed. (Ps. 22:3–5)

The psalmist bases his confidence in the Lord on His past help for Israel, such as the Exodus from Egypt, teaching suffering people to recall past consolations during experiences of desolation. An important antidote to despair is the proclamation that the Lord is "holy, enthroned on the praises of Israel" (Ps. 22:3). Therefore, in the midst of the suffering, and even for the suffering itself, we praise God. We do not praise Him in spite of the problems and evil but instead for them, remembering in that moment that He is enthroned in those praises. The psalmist recognized this fact of the spiritual life even as he continued to describe his misery:

> But I am a worm, and no man; scorned by men, and despised by the people.
>
> All who see me mock at me, they make mouths at me, they wag their heads;
>
> "He committed his cause to the Lord; let him deliver him, let him rescue him, for he delights in him!" (Ps. 22:6–8)

The psalmist then makes a second act of confidence, based on remembering God's protection from his infancy in the care of his mother: "Yet you are he who took me from the womb; you kept me safe upon my mother's breasts. Upon you was I cast from my birth, and since my mother bore me you have been my God" (Ps. 22:9–10).

Who can bring these verses to mind without considering Jesus' words to His blessed mother, the "Woman" standing at the Cross, whom He had just placed in the care of His "beloved disciple"? It also brings to mind Simeon's prophecy to Blessed Mary that her heart would be pierced so that the inner thoughts of many might be revealed (see Luke 2:35).

Following this ebb and flow of lament and confidence, the psalmist makes a petition: "Be not far from me, for trouble is near and there is none to help" (Ps. 22:11). Though the psalm opened an expression of despair, this verse demonstrates that no one who cries out to God during an experience of abandonment can actually despair. Rather, the honest description of the petitioner's actual state, without pretense of denial of the pain, is the authentic basis of faith in the real God. The authenticity flows from the humility to express profound neediness, as is seen when the psalmist resumes the description of his suffering (see Ps. 22:12–18), much of which was actually happening to Jesus at the moment He made this psalm prayer His own. Even in these depths of pain He could pray:

> But you, O Lord, be not far off! O you my help, hasten to my aid! Deliver my soul from the sword, my life from the power of the dog! Save me from the mouth of the lion, my afflicted soul from the horns of the wild oxen! (Ps. 22:19–21)

Though the enemies are as violent and vicious as animals, He can ask for deliverance from danger at their hands and then conclude the whole psalm with a hymn of thanksgiving for the help God will give (see Ps. 22:22–26) and a hymn of praise that the Lord will have dominion over the whole world (see Ps. 22:27–31).

However, praying this psalm does not help everyone to perceive Jesus' suffering in its light, since "some of the bystanders hearing it said, 'Behold, he is calling Elijah.' One ran and, filling a sponge full of vinegar, put it on a reed and gave it to him to drink, saying, 'Wait, let us see whether Elijah will come to take him down.'" (Mark 15:35-36; see also Matt. 27:47-49). Their inability to understand His actual words turns the prayer during abandonment into a failure to be saved by Elijah, the prophet whom Jews expected to come to Israel during Passover. When Elijah did not appear to help Jesus, the crowd perceived still another level of Jesus' failure.

Jesus Approaches Death with Thirst

Both Matthew and Mark state that Jesus cried aloud just before

He died, however neither gives the content of that cry. Both St. John and St. Luke give the words of Jesus' final cry, and these have very deep meaning, as with His other final words.

"After this Jesus, knowing that all was now finished, said (to fulfil the scripture), 'I thirst'" (John 19:28). St. John shows Jesus fulfilling Psalm 69:21, cited above: "They gave me poison for food, and for my thirst they gave me vinegar to drink." However, instead of the offer of a pain killer originating with those who were crucifying Him as part of their profession, Jesus enters the final stage of dying with the words, "I thirst." Those nearby the Cross understood this as merely physical thirst from dehydration, so "they put a sponge full of the vinegar on hyssop and held it to his mouth" (John 19:29). What a response — a bit of vinegar soaked in a sponge offered to the lips of the one Who changed 180 gallons of water into the best wine ever!

Venerable Archbishop Fulton J. Sheen understood this more deeply as Jesus' thirst for humanity. Our Lord often expressed this "thirst," this desire for people to come to Him for redemption, healing, and infinite divine love (see Matt. 23:37; Luke 13:34; John 17:24).

The question then becomes, "How do I respond to Jesus' thirst for souls?" Do I perceive Him as thirsting for my soul in order to devour or destroy me? Do I understand that He thirsts for people to come to Him so that He might satisfy their deepest desires, thirsts, and hungers for the infinite, unconditional love of God? Is He seeking me in order to accomplish His own devious plans, or does He desire to nourish me with the Holy Spirit, Who springs forth from His heart like a never-ending spring of water?

Sadly, so many of the young people who experienced physical and sexual abuse by priests had been looking for the love promised by Christ. They had a thirst for a love that was greater than what they had known. Some were children in orphanages whose parents had died or had abandoned them or had become incapable of caring for their children due to illness, drug abuse, and other circumstances. Some had been physically abused in their homes by parents, relatives, or others. They sought protection and the love of Jesus Christ for them in their great vulnerability. Most children who suffered abuse lived with their families in the normal life of the parishes. Many of them looked to their priests and teachers as the representatives of Jesus Christ to whom they entrusted themselves for spiritual growth and friendship during the various crises of maturing through childhood and adolescence. They wanted a guide and friend with whom they could speak of anything so as to find some compassionate understanding and the wisdom to work through it all.

In His thirst for these souls, the Lord had raised up priests and other religious to receive and care for them. He gave them a mission to evangelize, catechize, instruct, care for, and befriend these souls. However, in about 11,000 cases, these apostles' thirst for love had turned into the vinegar of selfish desire, often rooted in their own past pain, abuse, and narcissistic self-indulgence. These priests and religious no longer centered on Jesus' words, "I thirst" as He hung dying on the Cross; they no longer saw that these young people were the "least of my brethren," and they did not always realize that the misery and horror they committed against their innocence was in fact equally done to Jesus Himself.

Instead of perceiving the thirst of Jesus that leads humans to God's infinite love, they drew others to feed their personal gratification. They became overwhelmed by their own needs and devoured the innocence of children and harmed them for life. In this process, they made Jesus' desire for their souls appear to these children as dangerous and destructive, thereby driving them away from God, His authentic love, the Church, the sacraments, and other people.

The antidote is, in part, is to turn back to the dying words of Jesus and hear Him speak again to each of our hearts. Whether someone is a victim of abuse, a family member or friend, the lay faithful who are outraged by the scandal, the priests who experience more isolation from people because of the abuse by other priests, or an abuser himself, all are called by Jesus' dying words on the Cross, "I thirst." He thirsts for each of us to approach Him and discover that He will not give us vinegar, nor will he devour and destroy us, but instead He will give us the water of eternal life. He will place a light burden and easy yoke upon us, but only because He is pulling the yoke alongside each of us and is helping to carry the load. We can choose to let His thirst for our souls become the greatest quenching of our own thirst for infinite love.

Jesus "received the vinegar" and declared, "It is finished," before He "gave up his spirit" (John 19:30). This is the second of four occasions in Scripture when the phrase "It is finished" appears.

To better understand the relevance of the first use of the phrase, recall the prologue at the beginning of John's Gospel that prepares the reader to understand an insider's perspective on Jesus as the Word Who "became flesh and dwelt among us" (John 1:14). This prologue begins by describing Jesus as the Word Who is God, through Whom all creation was made: "In the beginning was the Word, and the Word was with God, and the Word was God. He was in the beginning with God; all things were made through him, and without him was not anything made that was made" (John 1:1–3). Jesus' role in creation helps us link the words "It is finished" with the first time this phrase is used in Scripture—namely, at the Creation that came into being through the Word: "Thus the heavens and the earth were finished, and all the host of them" (Gen. 2:1).

The third occasion is when a seventh angel pours the seventh bowl of God's wrath into the air once the demonic spirits had gathered the leaders of the world at Armageddon for the final battle with God the Almighty. As he does so, a voice spoke from God's throne in the heavenly temple and announced, "It is done!" (Rev. 16:13–17).

The fourth occasion is also in the Book of Revelation, when the voice of the one seated on the throne again spoke, though this time only to those who had entered the new and heavenly Jerusalem: "Behold, I make all things new.... Write this, for these words are trustworthy and true.... It is done! I am the Alpha and the Omega, the beginning and the end. To the thirsty I will give from the fountain of the water of life without payment" (Rev. 21:5–6).

The announcement of completion is stated these four times: at the beginning of Creation, on the Cross as Jesus dies, and at the end of the world, when the evil are gathered for destruction and the righteous are gathered for salvation. Clearly, at the Creation and at the end of time, it refers to what God has accomplished in regard to creation, particularly to humanity. This is also the case when Jesus says "It is finished" on the Cross: the great work of human redemption has been accomplished as Jesus experiences the full brunt of human evil and its consequence, death. While the rest of us experience death as the wages of our sins, Jesus approaches it as the wages for the sins of the rest of humanity. Yet He is fully aware that His death will become the turning point in the ultimate defeat of sin and death, so before He exhales for the last time, He can breathe out the words, "It is finished," the words spoken on the Friday of the first week of Creation. However, on the Friday of this Holy Week, the last step in the start of the new creation of humanity "is finished" as Jesus dies and moves to the Sabbath rest in a tomb.

Jesus Commends Himself to the Father

Finally, Jesus' last sentence is addressed to His Father as He shouts loudly one last time: "Father, into your hands I commit my spirit!" (Luke 23:46). Jesus' words are once again a citation of a Psalm, namely Psalm 31:5. The whole Psalm is an individual lament in the face of enemies who are attacking the psalmist as he seeks God's protection. It opens with a plea for refuge and deliverance: "In you O Lord, do I seek refuge; let me never be put to shame; in your righteousness deliver me!" (Ps. 31:1). This is followed by confessions of faith and trust in the Lord: "Yea, you are my rock and my fortress; for your name's sake lead me and guide me" (Ps. 31:3), and "Into your hand I commit my spirit; you have redeemed me, O Lord, faithful God" (Ps. 31:5). When citing Psalm 22:1, Jesus spoke out the great lamentation, "My God, my God, why have you forsaken me?" Now, in citing Psalm 31, He remains completely focused on God, but He cries aloud His absolute confidence, not simply in "the Lord," but in the very Father whose will He agreed to do as He prayed in Gethsemane. He made that commitment while sweating blood; now He reissues His commitment as "he breathed his last" (Luke 23:46).

Seven Reactions to Jesus' Death

First: Nature

Just as Jesus was about to take His last breath, the sun ceased its light and the land became dark. "There was darkness over the whole land until the ninth hour, while the sun's light failed" (Luke 23:44). Once He died, "the earth shook, and the rocks were split" (Matt. 27:51). Everyone who visits Mount Calvary cannot help but notice that it is a crag of limestone with a large crack that has split it into two parts.

Second: The Underworld

Next, the underworld responded after the earthquake: "The tombs also were opened, and many bodies of the saints who had fallen asleep were raised, and coming out of the tombs after his resurrection they went into the holy city and appeared to many" (Matt. 27:52). St. Peter explained the background of this phenomenon:

> For Christ also died for sins once for all, the righteous for the unrighteous, that he might bring us to God, being put to death in the flesh but made alive in the spirit; in which he went and preached to the spirits in prison, who formerly did not obey, when God's patience waited in the days of Noah, during the building of the ark, in which a few, that is, eight persons, were saved through water. (1 Peter 3:18–20)

Jesus descended among the dead from ages past. These were the souls who had died before His saving death occurred. However, He preached to all of them so that they could hear the good news of salvation and accept the salvation He had accomplished on the Cross. These were the many good people who were born subject to Original Sin and therefore could not enter the glory of heaven. In fact, heaven was closed to everyone until Jesus' redemptive suffering and death opened its gates.

Third: God Responded

On the east side of Jerusalem, the Israelite priests were finishing their task of killing the Passover lambs—about 200,000 of them, according to Josephus. They had to finish these sacrifices before 3:00 p.m. so the people could complete the preparation and roasting of these lambs before sundown. This highlights the significance of Jesus Christ, "the Lamb of God who takes away the sin of the world" (John 1:29), Who died at the moment of the last Passover lambs in the temple.

Within that context we read that "the curtain of the temple was torn in two, from top to bottom" (Mark 15:38; see also Matt. 27:51; Luke 23:45). This veil was made of blue, purple, and scarlet wool intertwined (see Ex. 26:31; 36:35), and it required three hundred men to move it.

An allusion to the tearing of the veil was made in a comment attributed to Rabbi Johanan ben Zakkai in the Talmud. Yoma

9 mentions that forty years before the Temple was destroyed, the door of the Temple opened by itself. Since the Temple was destroyed in August AD 70, he is apparently referring to the splitting of the curtain of the Temple in the year Jesus died.

The significance of the curtain being torn from the top down is that it was an act of God. Had it been a human action, it would have been from the bottom up. This is therefore another sign that the Old Covenant was over and a New Covenant in Christ's Blood has begun. A new Lamb of God is the Passover sacrifice; the death of God the Son on the Cross becomes a new atonement for sins that replaces the sprinkling of the blood of bulls and goats.

> For if the sprinkling of defiled persons with the blood of goats and bulls and with the ashes of a heifer sanctifies for the purification of the flesh, how much more shall the blood of Christ, who through the eternal Spirit offered himself without blemish to God, purify your conscience from dead works to serve the living God. Therefore he is the mediator of a new covenant, so that those who are called may receive the promised eternal inheritance, since a death has occurred which redeems them from the transgressions under the first covenant. (Heb. 9:13–15; see also Heb. 10:4–10)

Fourth: The Roman Centurion Proclaims Jesus Divine

After Jesus died, the Roman centurion and the other soldiers guarding Him were awestruck by the phenomena of nature that had responded to Jesus' death. "When the centurion and those who were with him, keeping watch over Jesus, saw the earthquake and what took place, they were filled with awe, and said, 'Truly this was the Son of God!'" (Matt. 27:54; see also Mark 15:34–39; Luke 23:47).

This statement ought to be linked to the various occasions

when the demons had announced that Jesus was the Son of God (see Matt. 8:29; Mark 1:24; 3:11; 5:7; Luke 4:34, 41; 8:28), as well as to His miracles and Peter's correct confession that Jesus is the Christ, the Son of the living God (see Matt. 16:16; 14:33; Mark 8:29; Luke 9:20). Jesus always ordered the demons, the healed people, and the disciples to be silent and tell no one of His identity. The two times that people openly state that Jesus is the Son of God without being silenced are the high priest's question during His trial (see Mark 14:61; Matt. 26:63) and the centurion's statement after Jesus died.

This teaches us that the essence of Jesus' redemption is His death on the Cross, not the exorcisms or healings. As important as they had been for the individuals who received them, they still did not reach the depth of meaning for the redemption.

Fifth: The Multitudes Lament

After having enthusiastically mocked Jesus, the same crowds were obscured by the darkening of the sun and shaken by the earthquake. They experienced the fear of God and began to feel sorrow for what they had done and witnessed (see Luke 23:48).

Sixth: Jesus' Followers Watch

Jesus' few faithful disciples stood looking from a distance, bearing witness to all that happened so that they could become proper witnesses of it: "And all his acquaintances and the women who had followed him from Galilee stood at a distance and saw these things" (Luke 23:49).

Seventh: The Centurion Pierces His Side

The soldiers broke the legs of the two thieves, who were still alive, but they pierced the side of Jesus, Who had already died:

> So the soldiers came and broke the legs of the first, and of the

other who had been crucified with him; but when they came to
Jesus and saw that he was already dead, they did not break his
legs. But one of the soldiers pierced his side with a spear, and at
once there came out blood and water. He who saw it has borne
witness—his testimony is true, and he knows that he tells the
truth—that you also may believe. For these things took place
that the scripture might be fulfilled, "Not a bone of him shall
be broken." And again another scripture says, "They shall look
on him whom they have pierced." (John 19:32–37)

Jesus' Burial

Various people took down the body of Jesus and prepared Him
for burial. Joseph of Arimathea (a town west of Jerusalem) was
a wealthy member of the Jerusalem Sanhedrin who looked for
the coming of the kingdom of God and had been taught by
Jesus, though secretly out of fear of the other Jews (see Mt. 27:57
Luke 23:50–51; John 19:38; Mark 15:43). As a disciple, he had a
personal interest in giving Jesus a proper burial, so he overcame his
fear and boldly went to Pilate to ask to take charge of Jesus' body.

Nicodemus, another member of the Sanhedrin, had met Jesus
by night (see John 19:39; 3:1–2) and had weakly tried to defend
Him before the Sanhedrin six months earlier (see John 7:50–53).
He helped Joseph care for Jesus' body.

Some women followers, who had accompanied Him from
Galilee, were present: Mary Magdalene; Mary, the mother of
James and Joses; and Salome (Matt. 27:56; Mark 15:40, 47), who
is also identified as the wife of Clopas and sister of Jesus' Mother
Mary (John 19:25); and Mary, the Mother of Jesus.

These people prepared Christ's dead body for burial on the
Passover Preparation Day, "the day before the Sabbath"—i.e., a
Friday. They had to finish before sundown, since such work was
not permitted on the Sabbath. When Joseph of Arimathea asked
Pilate for Jesus' body, Pilate was amazed that Jesus was already

dead. He summoned the centurion to ascertain if indeed that was the case, and only then did he release the corpse (see Mark 15:44–45).

After getting Pilate's permission to bury Jesus, Joseph of Arimathea bought a linen to wrap His body (see Mark 15:46), and Nicodemus brought a hundred-pound mixture of myrrh and aloes for the body in accord with Jewish burial custom. They placed Jesus' body in Joseph's tomb. The women paid close attention to the burial place before returning to the city to prepare more spices to complete the hasty burial process done before the Sabbath sunset. Then "they rested according to the commandment" (see Luke 23:55–56). They planned to return to complete the burial customs, but a great shock would confront them on that third day, and they would be summoned to new levels of faith, reconciliation, and a new mission.

CHAPTER 7

―――∞∞∞―――

THE RISEN CHRIST RECONCILES, RESTORES, AND EMPOWERS HIS DISCIPLES

"Christ is risen! Truly He is risen!" Christians in the Eastern Churches, Catholic and Orthodox alike, announce this to one another as a greeting throughout the Week of the Resurrection. Serious fasting and abstinence prepare their hearts for such rejoicing, as does a long history of suffering. Eastern Christians bore the brunt of the worst wave of martyrdom in history—the twentieth century's atheistic and nationalistic persecution during which 40 million Christians were martyred amid the 305 million people killed in war, genocide, and political extermination. These Eastern Christians in the former Soviet Union, Communist China, and their allies lost tens of millions of their brothers and sisters—bishops, priests, nuns, the lay faithful alike. In the twenty-first century, the persecution of Eastern Christians continues in the onslaught of terrorist attacks. The terrorists actually kill more Muslims than non-Muslims, but Christians and Jews also get singled out for attack by agents of hatred and terror.

This widespread suffering and persecution by Christians, especially in the East, strengthens their enthusiastic shouts of

"Christ is risen! Truly He is risen!" Faith in the Risen Christ steels the souls of those who fermented raisins so their ordained cell mates throughout the Gulag could unite their pain with that of Christ crucified by offering it in the Divine Liturgy. Holy Communion brought them peace. Middle Eastern Christians offer exultant shouts to the Risen Lord, despite churches being bombed during the liturgies, men and women being crucified, and children being abducted, sold into slavery, or killed in front of their parents.

The Resurrection is not an abstract idea; it is a concrete historical event described in all four Gospels. Remembering and celebrating the power of Christ's triumph over death is a source of hope that strengthens martyrs and every other type of sufferer. Of course, this includes the victims of the modern sexual revolution, among whom are those who endured sexual abuse, such as those harmed by clergy and religious.

Christians have drawn great strength from the Risen Lord, and martyrs in particular amaze their persecutors by enduring suffering and death with hope and even interior peace. The victims of sexual abuse carry a distinctive pain because of the very sensitive and vulnerable sexual aspect of their lives that has been deeply wounded, and because the pain was inflicted by people they trusted to love and care for them. However, like the martyrs, many of them discover in Jesus' Resurrection a hope that heals the spiritual, psychological, social, and physical dimensions of their lives.

The witnesses to the Risen Christ include the holy women who had stood near the Cross during His execution, disciples who were on the periphery of His circle, the Apostles who had run and hidden to avoid suffering and death, and Peter who had denied Him. Jesus addressed each one uniquely, just as He continues to meet Christians throughout history, including the victims and perpetrators of sexual abuse. Jesus also equipped each person with the spiritual gifts needed to be His messengers throughout the whole world. Therefore, contemporary Christians can approach Jesus with their various needs for healing and transformation, as well as for empowerment to evangelize the world.

We will examine the various accounts of the Resurrection according to the times in which they occurred—early morning, mid-morning, afternoon, and evening on the first Easter—through the later appearances in Jerusalem and Galilee. The Resurrection of Jesus Christ is an infinite mystery, so its depths will continue to intrigue the redeemed for all eternity as they contemplate it with God's light and clarity in heaven. For the purposes of this study, three points will be made. First, each appearance of the Risen Christ is a conversion experience that shows the difficulty but necessity of faith that His Resurrection is true. Second, Jesus teaches His disciples the need for ever deeper instruction on the meaning of His life and ministry, His death, Resurrection, and Ascension. Third, He commissions the witnesses of His Resurrection to spread His Gospel to the whole world.

The Day of the Resurrection

The four evangelists describe different events after Jesus rose from the dead, from the early morning through the evening of the "first day of the week," though none of them describes the actual moment of the Resurrection. Each episode draws attention to the disciples' response and their interactions with the Risen Lord. Consistently, the disciples did not expect Jesus' Resurrection, and each of them had to come to the belief that He truly had risen from the dead. Some of them had difficulty accepting it even when they saw Him. In addition to the disciples' conversion from doubt to faith, Jesus gave them a variety of missions.

In our own time, this period of the priest abuse scandals also requires a deeper conversion to faith in Jesus, the power of His saving death, and the hope of His glorious Resurrection from the dead. The whole Church, from the hierarchy to the laity, needs new encounters with Jesus so as to be reconciled for a lack of faith in Him, for neglecting their responsibility, and for allowing scandal to drive people from the practice of the faith and receiving the sacraments, Reconcilation and Holy Communion in particular. Meeting the Risen Lord Jesus will also entail a renewal of mission for each person whom He encounters. Openness to accepting His mission will push each Christian from the sidelines to the forefront of addressing the faithlessness and immorality of contemporary society, exactly as was true of the first-century Apostles and disciples.

We will move through the various appearances of Jesus as they occurred during that momentous first day of the week. Let us prayerfully allow the Risen Lord to confront whatever is lacking in our faith so that we, too, can be more deeply reconciled to Him and to the missions He gives us in this present age.

Early Morning on the First Day of the Week: The Tomb, the Angels, and the First Appearances of Jesus

In the early morning, predawn darkness on the "first day of the week," which we call Sunday, St. Matthew mentions that two of the women that had witnessed Jesus' burial went to His tomb (see Matt. 28:1): Mary Magdalene and "the other Mary," the mother of Jesus' "brothers" James and Joses (see Matt. 27:55–56). He omits the "mother of the sons of Zebedee" who had also stood at the Cross, but Mark mentions "Salome," who is apparently that very woman (see Mark 16:1).

These women had "bought spices, so that they might go and anoint him" (Mark 16:1; see also Luke 24:1), thereby completing the process of Jesus' burial. The importance of this detail is that the women had not gone to the tomb expecting to see the Risen Lord Jesus; they went there expecting to find His corpse, and the tomb sealed by a heavy stone (see Mark 16:2).

Upon the women's arrival, earth and heaven responded. First, "there was a great earthquake," which calls to mind the earthquake that occurred when Jesus died on the Cross (see Matt. 27:51). Second, "an angel of the Lord descended from heaven and came and rolled back the stone, and sat upon it" (Matt. 28:2). The angel looked "like lightning, and his raiment white as snow, causing the guards to tremble and become "like dead men" (Matt. 28:23–24). Note the ironic reversal of the soldiers becoming like dead men, while the Son of Man is no longer dead. However, they did not see Jesus at that point because the stone was rolled back—not to let Jesus out of the tomb; He could accomplish that on His own. Rather, it was moved to let the women into the tomb as witnesses to Jesus' absence. When they entered the tomb, "they saw a young man sitting on the right side, dressed in a white robe; and they were amazed" (Mark 16:5), but "they did not find the body" they had expected to anoint (Luke 24:3). Luke describes the women's interior reactions as being "perplexed about this" when "two men stood by them in dazzling apparel" and "they were frightened and bowed their faces to the ground" (Luke 24:4–5).

The women were unable to analyze and clarify the situation, so an angel explained it to them. As is typical of meetings with angels, the opening words were "Be not afraid" (Matt. 28:5). Inside the tomb the angel explained the reason: "I know that you seek Jesus who was crucified. He is not here; for he has risen, as he said. Come, see the place where he lay" (Matt. 28:5–6; Mark 16:6). In Luke the angel uses more rhetorical forms:

> "Why do you seek the living among the dead? Remember how he told you, while he was still in Galilee, that the Son of man must be delivered into the hands of sinful men, and be crucified, and on the third day rise." (Luke 24:5–7)

Since none of the Gospels describes Jesus' act of rising,

the angel's description of Jesus and invitation to see the place where He lay served as an announcement. The great irony is that the angel commanded the women not to fear because they were seeking Jesus, while the soldiers guarding the tomb were terrified to the point of death because they failed to keep Jesus inside His tomb (see Matt. 28:4).

The angel then instructed these women to go quickly and announce Jesus' Resurrection to His disciples and then meet Jesus in Galilee (see Matt. 28:7). This instruction confirmed Christ's words at the Last Supper: "But after I am raised up, I will go before you to Galilee" (Matt. 26:32; see also Mark 14:28).

St. Luke describes the women as having "remembered his words," that is, His predictions of His coming death and Resurrection. While the women had remained at the Cross and burial out of love of Jesus, and they returned to the tomb to anoint His corpse out of love, now they were becoming open to faith in Him. Remembering Jesus' predictions of His coming suffering, death, and Resurrection in the light of the angel's words about His actual rising from the dead is the beginning of their conversion to faith in the Resurrection as literally true. With this first ray of faith, they returned from the tomb and "told all this to the eleven and to all the rest" of the disciples, who do not yet have faith: "These words seemed to them an idle tale, and they did not believe them" (Luke 24:8–11).

St. John singles out Mary Magdalen as having come to the tomb, though her first words imply the presence of the other women: "We do not know where they have laid him." The scenes bring to mind the love of the woman in the Song of Songs, who searches for her beloved:

Upon my bed by night I sought him whom my soul loves; I sought him, but found him not; I called him, but he gave no answer. I will rise now and go about the city, in the streets and in the squares; I will seek him whom my soul loves. I sought him, but found him not. The watchmen found me, as they went about in the city. "Have you seen him whom my soul loves?" Scarcely had I passed them, when I found him whom my soul loves. I held him, and would not let him go until I had brought him into my mother's house, and into the chamber of her that conceived me." (Song of Songs 3:1–4)

Mary Magdalen sought Jesus out of great love for Him, while the Apostles remained hiding in the Upper Room out of fear for their lives. Once Mary saw the stone rolled away, she ran to tell Simon Peter and the "beloved disciple" that "they have taken the Lord out of the tomb, and we do not know where they have laid him" (John 20:1–2). She did not believe in the Resurrection yet, but rather assumed that someone had stolen Jesus' dead body. Peter and John ran toward the tomb, where they saw Jesus' burial cloths neatly folded and lying there. The "beloved disciple," who, like the women, had remained at the Cross out of love for Jesus, also began a conversion to faith: he "saw and believed; for as yet they did not know the Scripture, that he must rise from the dead" (John 20:6). Another reference to this event is found in Luke 24:12: "Peter ran to the tomb and peering saw the cloth alone, and he went by himself amazed at what had happened."

While Peter and John returned to the others, Mary Magdalen remained at the tomb, weeping. She had come to the tomb full of grief, expecting to shed the normal tears of mourning the dead Jesus, but then she finds a second loss—Jesus' body is missing. She assumes that someone has stolen the body and perhaps done something unseemly with it. At this point "she stooped to look into the tomb," where "she saw two angels in white, sitting where the body of Jesus had lain." They asked her, "Woman, why are you weeping?" (John 20:11–13). The presence of two angels makes their testimony more legally binding, since the Law requires "two or three witnesses" (see Deut. 17:6; 19:15). She answered, "Because they have taken away my Lord, and I do not know where they have laid him." Amazingly, she is so focused on the absence of Jesus' body that she ignores the fact that she is speaking to two angels.

Only when she turns from the empty tomb does she see Jesus standing next to her. He must have appeared in an ordinary way, since she easily assumed He was the gardener, yet "she did not know that it was Jesus" (John 20:14). She may have failed to recognize Him because she still did not expect Jesus to be raised from the dead. Also, she remained focused on her original mission of caring for His corpse.

Like the angels, Jesus took the initiative to speak. "Woman, why are you weeping? Whom do you seek?" She replied, "Sir, if you have carried him away, tell me where you have laid him, and I will take him away" (John 20:15). She was able to recognize Jesus when He spoke her name: "Mary." She immediately called him "Rabboni!" (which means Teacher). Jesus responds by giving her two commands and a message: "Jesus said to her, 'Do not hold me, for I have not yet ascended to the Father; but go to my brethren and say to them, I am ascending to my Father and your Father, to my God and your God'" (John 20:1).

He first commands her not to touch Him. In Matthew, the women "came up and took hold of his feet and worshiped him" (Matthew 28:9), implying that they clung to Him. Jesus' command to Mary is that she not "cling" to Him because He still has a mission. Jesus' second command is to proclaim her faith in the Resurrection. Of course, she cannot fulfill that mission if she continues clinging to Jesus.

Mary's love motivated her to fulfill her mission. She went to the disciples to announce the Lord's message to her: "I am ascending to my Father and your Father, to my God and your God." This time she didn't tell the Apostles about the empty tomb, but instead proclaimed Jesus' Resurrection: "I have seen the Lord!" Then she told them the rest of Jesus' message about His coming Ascension to the Father (see John 20:18).

The Guards Inform the Chief Priests About the Risen Christ

St. Matthew, differently than St. John, tells how the women as a group "ran to tell his disciples" that they had seen Jesus and He had greeted them. Following His instructions—"Do not be afraid; go and tell my brethren to go to Galilee, and there they will see me"—they fulfill their mission and tell the Apostles Jesus' message (Matt. 28:8-10).

In contrast, the soldiers guarding the tomb went to the chief priests to inform them about "all that had taken place." The priests and elders "took counsel" and chose to give the guards "a sum of money" and their own instructions: "Tell people, 'His disciples came by night and stole him away while we were asleep.' And if this comes to the governor's ears, we will satisfy him and keep you out of trouble" (Matt. 28:11–14).

These choices show how sin tends to harden the sinner's heart and then easily leads to further sin. All of these people—the chief priests, the elders, and the soldiers—had taken part in the arrest and false conviction of Jesus. They had paid Judas Iscariot to betray Jesus, and the soldiers followed him to the garden of Gethsemane, where their signal was Judas's deceptive kiss. The priests and elders had paid for a number of false witnesses and then they interrogated Jesus. Soldiers repeatedly mocked, slapped and spit on Him, imprisoned Him, and led Him to Pilate's court. There, the priests and elders made new false accusations against Jesus in order to show that Jesus had broken Roman law so that He could be crucified. One act of bearing false witness led to another, until finally, when the soldiers truthfully testified that Jesus was risen, their previous sins, plus the Sanhedrin's sins, induced them to yet another false testimony, along with bribery.

The soldiers accepted the bribe and "spread" that story to the Jews of the evangelist's own day (see Matt. 28:15), thereby continuing the contrast between truth and falsehood after the Resurrection. Along these lines, in the Acts of the Apostles, the chief priests and elders will arrest Jesus' Apostles frequently for preaching about His death and Resurrection. Never once do they offer to walk to the tomb and demonstrate that Jesus was still dead. In fact, they never deny His Resurrection in any of the Apostles' trials; they simply order the Apostles to be quiet about Jesus and speak no more about Him. This is the opposite of what the angels and the Risen Jesus had commanded, and the Apostles will have a very basic choice to make at that point.

We might keep this scene in mind when considering the cover-ups of abusive priests, religious, and bishops. Far too often the grave sin of false testimony has been committed, and in some cases the victims and their families were paid money to keep quiet. Sometimes bishops and other leaders used their authority to seduce seminarians and then bribe them with gifts, favors, and ecclesial promotions, or even issue threats against them if they told the truth about a prelate's sins.

Yet another parallel can be seen among those Catholics who deny the validity and importance of God's commandments. Beginning in the late 1960s, it came to be seen as "prophetic" to stand against the institutional Church by criticizing a legalistic approach to God's law. So, a "bold and prophetic" priest, nun, or teacher might tell people that it is not mortally sinful to miss Mass on Sunday. Further, if a boy and a girl love each other, sexual expression is not a sin because it is loving. So on it went into a variety of issues (except for racism, violence, and a few other sins). Of course, it became easy for the same clerics to excuse their own sins, including abusive sexual contact with minors or vulnerable adults.

In contrast, faithful Catholics should consider the commands of the angels and the Risen Lord Jesus to proclaim His Resurrection and to teach all nations "to observe all that I have commanded you" (Matt. 28:20). Like the women who came to Jesus' empty tomb, we receive that same mission to be faithful witnesses to Jesus' life, saving death, and glorious Resurrection and to share His teachings.

The Afternoon of the Resurrection: The Lord Jesus Walks to Emmaus

During His final journey to Jerusalem, Jesus had promised His disciples that "where two or three are gathered in my name, there am I in the midst of them" (Matt. 18:20). St. Luke is the only evangelist who describes the presence of Jesus with two disciples leaving Jerusalem for "a village named Emmaus, about seven miles" away (Luke 24:13–14). One disciple was named "Cleopas," who may well be the Clopas mentioned in John 19:25, the husband of the Mary identified as a "sister" of Jesus' Mother. Clopas is a Semitic name (found in Aramaic in the city of Palmyra), and Cleopas is a Greek name meaning "the father's glory." Having both a Semitic and a Greek name was a common practice among Jews—e.g., Thomas is Didymus (the Aramaic and Greek words for "twin") and Saul is Paul. Cleopas' unnamed companion was later identified by St. Hegesippus as Cleopas' son Simeon, who later became the bishop of Jerusalem after the martyrdom of his brother, St. James, also known as the brother of Jesus. St. Hegesippus wrote in his *Hypomnemata* ("Memoranda") how St. Jude's grandsons had told him that Cleopas/Clopas was the brother of St. Joseph, Jesus' foster father, and therefore James, Joses, Simeon, and others were known as His "brothers and sisters." If Hegesippus is correct, Jesus therefore met His own relatives on the road to Emmaus. "Their eyes were kept from recognizing him" (Luke 24:16), a passive expression that indicates God prevented them from recognizing Jesus through mere physical sight. As with Mary Magdalen, who "did not know that it was Jesus" (John 20:14), neither did Jesus' relatives recognize Him.

Apparently these two traveling companions were pious Jews who had come to celebrate Passover in the Holy City, in addition to being disciples of Jesus. Once the Sabbath was over, they began to walk home, since such a long journey was prohibited on the Sabbath. Their conversation was about the things that had happened to Jesus on Friday and on the reports of the women who had gone to Jesus' tomb. Yet they were walking away from the scene and leaving the community of disciples back in Jerusalem.

In this, Clopas and his companion well represent the many fine Catholics who are shocked and perplexed, scandalized, and even filled with doubt after the sex abuse scandal. They walk away from the Church, the community of believers who remain after the scandal, and from the sacraments. Cleopas may have discussed the meaning of Jesus' suffering and death, the Apostles' failure to remain faithful and responsible, or even his own failure to defend Jesus, believe in Him more deeply, or stand by Him at the Cross, as Mary, his wife, had done. Perhaps he considered Jesus to be a failure, along with His new community of Apostles and disciples.

So also do painful thoughts of the Church's corruption and failure fill the minds of many contemporary Catholics. They are scandalized by the failure of the bishops to root out sexual abuse and financial mismanagement or, in some cases, crimes. Yet they love the truth of Jesus Christ and of the Church He established, and they desire to defend that truth and live it better than some of the priests and bishops. They are furious about the pain imposed on the victims, especially since many of them are fathers of children. They blame the sinful clerics, Vatican II, the vernacular liturgy, or the failure to heed the messages from Fatima, Akita, and other visions of the Blessed Mother. They seem to walk away, like Cleopas, yet they hopefully still care enough to discuss reform of the Church.

Fruitfully we can note that the Risen Lord Jesus walked on the same road to Emmaus, away from the Holy City where He had been falsely accused, crucified and buried, and where eleven of His cowardly Apostles continued to hide in the locked Upper Room. He walked that road away in order to accompany the two disciples who were discussing their grief, pain, and the reports of events that did not yet add up for them. All of those Catholics who are in the process of walking away from the Church today because of the scandal can likewise be alert to Jesus' desire to accompany them on their journey.

On the road to Emmaus, Jesus took the initiative by asking the two disciples, "What is this conversation which you are holding with each other as you walk?" With sadness, Cleopas answered with his own question, "Are you the only visitor to Jerusalem who does not know the things that have happened there in these days?" When Jesus "played dumb" by asking "What things?" Cleopas explained how Jesus of Nazareth, "a prophet mighty in deed and word before God and all the people," had been crucified. They "had hoped that he was the one to redeem Israel," and on this third day since His death, some women had reported a "vision of angels, who said that he was alive," as had others, "but him they did not see" (Luke 24:17–24).

Like those faithful Catholics presently discussing the various scandals of the modern Church, Cleopas was well informed about the key events of the preceding two days. He was capable of knowing certain events, but they evoked sadness because he had no way to connect them in a meaningful way. The inability to find meaning in his pain and suffering may also have been one of the blocks in recognizing Jesus as He walked next to him.

Jesus' first response was to rebuke the two disciples. "O foolish men, and slow of heart to believe all that the prophets have spoken! Was it not necessary that the Christ should suffer these things and enter into his glory?" (Luke 24:25–26). They had failed to understand the Scriptural prophecies about the Messiah, just as Peter and John inside the empty tomb had failed to "know the scripture, that he must rise from the dead" (John 20:9). Furthermore, Jesus had taught His disciples that He would suffer, die, and rise, but they failed to understand those words too. Therefore, Jesus proceeded to explain how He had fulfilled Scripture, "beginning with Moses and all the prophets he interpreted to them in all the Scriptures the things concerning himself" (Luke 24:27).

As the three approached Emmaus, Cleopas and his companion "urged" Jesus to remain with them for the evening and their meal at the end of the day (see Luke 24:28–29), not unlike Abraham and Lot did for their angelic visitors (see Gen. 18:1-5; 19:1-3). During their meal, again at his own initiative, Jesus "took the bread and blessed, and broke it, and gave it to them." Only at that point "their eyes were opened and they recognized him; and he vanished out of their sight" (Luke 24:30–31).

Jesus' exposition of Scripture caused their hearts to burn within them (see Luke 24:32), in contrast to Jesus' initial rebuke that they were "foolish" and "slow of heart to believe" (see Luke 24:25). The two disciples had been profoundly hurt by the abuse and death of Jesus. Particularly since they were Middle Eastern men, they felt both a strong obligation to protect their Teacher and relative as well as shame that they were too weak to save Him from death. Though they had begun the conversation with Jesus with great sadness in their hearts, after understanding God's plan throughout history to redeem the world through the Messiah's suffering, death, and Resurrection, they found fire within their hearts. The stirring of faith within their hearts as they recognized the fulfillment of Scripture in Jesus Christ's suffering and death transformed their sadness into great joy and enthusiasm.

The shock of priests and bishops abusing children and teenagers has caused tremendous sadness, grief, and anger throughout the Church. Such understandable outrage has caused many people to walk away from the Church. However, just as Jesus' dialogue on the road inflamed the two disciples' hearts with a recognition of the truth about Him, similarly, in the present crisis, a burning excitement about the truth of Jesus will purify the grief, anger, and disappointment Catholics feel in regard to sinful bishops and priests and their bishops who failed to assert proper authority in cleaning up the corruption. That purification can turn mere human sadness and grief into the blessed mourning that is assured of God's ultimate comfort (see Matt. 5:4). It will transform anger and rage into the righteous anger that does not lead to sin, but rather motivates wise action that reforms the evils.

That flame, which is ultimately a gift of the Holy Spirit present within the heart to evoke saving faith, hope, and love, will help disillusioned Catholics recognize Jesus' presence in the breaking of the bread. Though we may try remove ourselves from the Church, let us never cease hearing Jesus speak the truth of Sacred Scripture to inflame our hearts and recognize Him in the most Holy and Blessed Sacrament. There we will find His peace and eternal life.

Evening of the Resurrection: The Risen Lord Jesus Appears in the Upper Room

Though the Risen Lord Jesus had not given the two disciples in Emmaus any instructions, they returned to Jerusalem and the Apostles in the Upper Room. Everyone present shared their stories of seeing the Risen Jesus.

Precisely at that point, "Jesus himself stood among them." Despite their proclamation, "The Lord has risen indeed," they assumed they were seeing a ghost. They perceived the Risen

Jesus through the lenses of their own assumptions, and they were "terrified" and "afraid."

However, Jesus rejected their explanation, denied being a ghost, and offered His own evidence. First, He let them see and touch His hands and feet. When they still "disbelieved for joy"—an interesting parallel to Gethsemane where they were "asleep from grief" (Luke 22:45)—Jesus then ate "broiled fish," proving His Resurrection, since ghosts cannot eat (see Luke 24:36–43).

Faith in the reality of Jesus' Resurrection did not come easily to the Apostles. The miracles, including three resuscitations from the dead (Jairus's daughter, the son of the widow of Nain, and Lazarus), and the exorcisms they had witnessed, had at various moments evoked some faith that He was "the Son of God" (Matt. 14:33). However, as the Risen Jesus appeared among them, they had trouble believing that He was truly human. A ghost was less than fully human; living flesh and blood is completely human. Perhaps, too, their faith was made more difficult by the guilt they experienced for having failed Him.

But, until He could convince them that the same human who had died on the Cross was now standing and speaking to them, the next part of His message to them would be without effect. For that reason He let them see and touch His hands and feet, and He ate the fish that they had already broiled, showing that He shared their food and therefore their humanity. Furthermore, when Jesus showed His hands and feet to the Apostles as proof, they could know that it was truly Jesus because the nail mark wounds were glorified.

The Apostles' struggle to believe in Jesus' Resurrection, even as He stood before their eyes, opens another concern of the present crisis in the Church—a crisis of Catholic faith. First, we must be very clear that the sexual abusers have by no means been limited either to the progressive or to the traditional sides of the Church; men adamantly professing the Church's teaching have contradicted it by sexually abusing minors, and progressives professing justice to the helpless have done the same. This is a human failure to integrate all aspects of one's faith and moral behavior common to all sinners on various levels.

Yet compromising the fullness of the Catholic faith has been a factor in giving the clergy mental reservations and psychological permission to avoid taking the doctrinal and moral demands of Catholicism seriously. Often enough, professors taught seminarians preparing for the priesthood that the dogmas of the Church were negotiable in modern times so as to enable contemporary people to live a Christian life without "mythic" doctrines standing in the way of a commitment to the Church's mission to help the poor find justice.

For example, when I was a seminarian in the 1970s, one professor told our class that he had "crossed his fingers" when he took the oath against modernism required of him before he started teaching in the seminary. Another, a well-known New Testament professor at the time, argued at dinner that we had to get rid of the doctrine of Jesus' virgin birth because modern families cannot relate to a virginal mother, a celibate foster father, and a divine Son. Besides refuting his patently false claims that the Gospel texts did not identify Jesus' mother as a virgin, I pointed out that no family in history was ever composed of a virginal mother; that was pretty much the point of the Angel Gabriel's announcement.

Other professors denied the truth of Jesus' Resurrection. One said, "If they found Jesus' body, it would not change my faith." Rejection of the authority of the Church, the infallibility of the Pope, transubstantiation in the Eucharist, and other doctrines were part of the education program back then, which in turn weakened the moral commitment of those who accepted it.

Of course, these same professors often looked to other sources of authority on which to base their ideas. In the 1960s and 1970s, authority was granted to social sciences, such as psychology and sociology, and to existentialist trends in philosophy. When both philosophy and psychology overlapped in writers such as Carl Rogers, Abraham Maslow, Eric Ericson, and others, all the better. One temptation of that period was to judge religious truth, or the usefulness and authenticity of the Bible, or moral theology on the basis of psychology or philosophy. For instance, R. Bultmann rejected the Resurrection and Jesus' miracles as myths because they were not compatible with the necessity of anxiety as humans face the inevitability of death in Heidegger's philosophy of authentic faith.

Furthermore, since some schools of modern psychology believed that sexual expression and freedom were positive goods necessary for human development, moral theology had to accept sexual behaviors more neutrally, without judgment or condemnation, despite the centuries of the Church's rejection of these behaviors. Priests, religious, and laity taught their students that masturbation was normal development and therefore not sinful. Sexual relations before marriage could be morally acceptable if the couple really loved each other.

During this period a large number of priests and religious left those vocations to marry—often enough to marry each other. By the mid-1970s, it was common to hear of men leaving seminaries or the priestly ministry in order to enter same-sex relationships. Though one cannot blame every act of sexual abuse of children on this new ideology, it certainly forms a factor in the background of people's experience. While cases of sexual misconduct existed in the 1950s and early 1960s, the John Jay Institute studies clearly indicate an increase in it from the late 1960s into the 1980s. Then, as the legal cases and convictions mounted, along with greater care by the bishops to train priests in child protection and general sexual abstinence, the rate of misconduct cases declined significantly. False moral teaching harmed people's consciences, and correcting these errors, even if out of fear of punishment, corrected consciences. The same is true of theological teaching, which provides the basis for Catholic morality. Clearer teaching about Jesus makes a positive impact on understanding the context of spiritual and moral behavior.

Having proven to the assembled disciples that He was truly alive and not a ghost, Jesus' next move was to teach them the same lessons about fulfilling the Old Testament that He had given to the two disciples on the road to Emmaus: "These are my words which I spoke to you, while I was still with you, that everything written about me in the law of Moses and the prophets and the psalms must be fulfilled" (Luke 24:44). He "opened their minds to understand the scriptures" concerning five issues. First, the Christ had to suffer; second, He had to "rise from the dead" on the third day; third, "repentance and forgiveness of sins should be preached in his name to all nations, beginning from Jerusalem;" fourth, the disciples are "witnesses of these things;" and fifth, they will receive "the promise of my Father" and be "clothed with power from on high" (Luke 24:45–49). Jesus commissioned them to share this message with the world, just as He had commissioned the women at the tomb, especially Mary Magdalen, to tell the Good News to the Apostles. That evening witnessed the Apostles' commission to bring Jesus' good news to all the world.

Jesus' instruction about understanding the Old Testament in light of His death and Resurrection served to correct the Apostles' cowardice. They had abandoned Him in Gethsemane to save their own lives, despite earlier protestations of willingness to die with Him. They continued to hide in the Upper Room, locking the doors out of fear for their lives and safety, a fear that made love impossible (see 1 John 4:18). Throughout the day of the Resurrection they were consumed with "unbelief and hardness of heart, because they had not believed those who saw him after he had risen" (Mark 16:14). That same evening Jesus lovingly corrected them by explaining His ministry, suffering, death, and Resurrection by means of the expanse of salvation history revealed in the Old Testament.

Along with the many human aids to moral correction and emotional, psychological, and intellectual maturity, Jesus' revelation to the human heart helps correct its moral problems. Jesus' authoritative instruction on the fullness of salvation inspires people with the purpose God has for human existence, giving them the most basic reasons to live morality and holiness. His message about His fulfillment of the Old Testament prophecies also restored the Apostles' commission to proclaim the Gospel of salvation to the world: "repentance and forgiveness of sins should be preached in his name to all nations, beginning from Jerusalem" (Luke 24:47).

Contemporary bishops, priests, and laity can also be restored to continue this apostolic service, which will motivate Catholics to move beyond their own locked and shuttered upper rooms, wherein internal squabbles paralyze them from evangelizing. Christ desires them to believe from the depths of their hearts the truth of His ministry, death, and Resurrection so that He can send them into the wider world to win every person to Jesus Christ and eternal life He won at so great a cost.

Evening of the Resurrection

St. John, writing a generation later than St. Luke, likewise describes the sudden appearance of Jesus to the Apostles in the Upper Room in the evening of "the first day of the week." He recalled the shut doors behind which he and the other disciples had locked themselves out of fear. In his old age John recalled their cowardice in Gethsemane and beyond. Yet he recalled that Jesus, Who had brought peace in Gethsemane by healing Malchus' ear after Peter had cut it off (see Luke 22:50-51; John

18:10), also proclaimed "Peace be with you" when He appeared in the locked Upper Room (see John 20:19). His "peace" was addressed to fearful men who had once abandoned Him and still lived in fear.

As in Luke 24:39–40, Jesus then "showed them his hands and his side," thereby demonstrating that He is truly the same Lord and King of the Jews who was crucified and gloriously raised from the dead. As they joyfully saw Him, He again proclaimed, "Peace be with you" (John 20:21a).

Only after having brought them peace and joy does Jesus commission the disciples to go into the world: "As the Father has sent me, even so I send you" (John 20:21b). On many occasions Jesus had taught that the Father had sent Him into the world:

> For God so loved the world that he gave his only
> Son, that whoever believes in him should not perish
> but have eternal life. For God sent the Son into the
> world, not to condemn the world, but that the world
> might be saved through him. (John 3:16–17)

> "These very works which I am doing, bear me witness
> that the Father has sent me. And the Father who sent
> me has himself borne witness to me." (John 5:36–37)

> "Yet even if I do judge, my judgment is true, for it is not I
> alone that judge, but I and he who sent me." (John 8:16)

> "And he who sent me is with me; he has not left me alone,
> for I always do what is pleasing to him." (John 8:29)

> " Truly, truly, I say to you, he who receives any one
> whom I send receives me; and he who receives
> me receives him who sent me." (John 13:20)

> "As you [Father] sent me into the world, so I
> have sent them into the world." (John 17:18)

Now, on the day of the Resurrection, Jesus sends the disciples just as the Father sent Him, since Jesus does what the Father does (see John 5:19; John 8:28; John 9:4). Therefore, Jesus sends them out on His mission to save the world by preaching the word that the Father had given Him.

This mission from God requires the Holy Spirit to empower and direct them, therefore Jesus continued the Paschal commission: "He breathed on them, and said to them, 'Receive the Holy Spirit'" (John 20:22). Jesus did not expect them to depend on mere human ability; He was well aware that they did not have much natural courage. Jesus' mission to the world required a strength not yet theirs, so He breathed upon them the Holy Spirit, the Counselor Who "will teach you all things, and bring to your remembrance all that I have said to you" (John 14:26), "the Spirit of truth, whom the world cannot receive" (John 14:17). This Holy Spirit of truth "will guide you into all the truth" (John 16:13) and will "bear witness" to Jesus (John 15:26), Who is the truth (John 14:6). These and more passages from the Last Supper Discourse are necessary to understand Jesus' gift of the Holy Spirit, so we will explore them more fully in the next chapter.

Jesus' commission continued, "If you forgive the sins of any, they are forgiven; if you retain the sins of any, they are retained" (John 20:23). The Church understands this verse as the occasion in which Christ established confession, the Sacrament of Reconciliation. The word *confession* emphasizes the penitent's act of expressing sorrow for sin, while *reconciliation* emphasizes God's act of forgiving the sinner and restoring him or her to full communion within the Church. As with the rest of God's gifts, it includes risks with the benefits.

One risk is that a sinner might use the confession of sin to assuage a guilty conscience without taking the necessary steps to cease committing the sin or to avoid reconciliation with the people he or she has offended. Furthermore, since the "seal of confession" is absolute, they might confess their sins so as to ensure that the priest or bishop confessor will never divulge the secret sin. Any misuse or abuse of this sacrament is ultimately the responsibility of the person who comes to a priest; priests assume that the penitent is truly sorry and wants to change. Priests assume that their role is to minister the mercy of God to people. However, not only was Our Lord aware that it was possible to make a bad confession, but He also made the Apostles aware of it by giving them the authority to "retain" sins if they had evidence of a lack of repentance.

In the sex abuse crisis, too many failures to judge the abusers correctly have occurred. While some people assume that the bishops and superiors were trying to hide their own poor governance by reassigning abusive priests, that may not have been the motive for most of the bishops who acted that way. Some of them may well have tried to hide cases in order to protect their own careers, the Church's reputation, or some of their priest friends.

However, many of them had sent the abusers for therapy at centers that did not understand the depth of the problem. In a number of cases, the priests were deemed "cured" and were recommended by psychological professionals for reassignment. Then some of these priests committed the same offenses against children and adolescents. The bishops did not "retain" the sins of offending priests so as to prevent them from being reassigned. This was often due to naivete regarding the seriousness of sex abuse, failure to understand the depth of the abusers' psychological disorder, and inexperience with a new and shocking phenomenon.

Over the years since the 1990s, the leaders in the Church have learned a lot, though mostly from errors of judgment in the early stages. Meanwhile, as bishops and superiors learned from their mistakes, many more vulnerable people suffered greatly and still bear the wounds. Perhaps, just as it was the Risen Lord, still bearing the wounds in His hands, feet, and side, Who could empower the Apostles to forgive and retain the sins of others, so might it be necessary for the victims of abuse to take part in the reconciliation of the abusers. This can be done only at the pace that the victims' levels of healing will permit, and they can never be forced to do something that harms them further.

Nor is the goal to make it possible for abusers to ever again work with the young. No matter how sorry an abuser might be, the protection of the vulnerable is paramount. Nonetheless, the exposure of victimizers to the pain, tears, anger, outrage, fears, and psychological damage in the victims, with those very victims taking the initiative to extend forgiveness, may break through the retention of guilt toward healing reconciliation. Along with the psychological and character strength needed by both sides of the crisis, the crucified and Risen Lord is the source of authentic forgiveness.

The Eighth Day: Thomas' Conversion on the Sunday After the Resurrection

The Apostle Thomas was not ready to accept the testimony of the other ten Apostles regarding Jesus' Resurrection. He may have experienced a combination of guilt over his own failure to stay with Jesus to the end — especially since he had decided to accompany Jesus to Bethany to raise Lazarus from the dead. While Jesus' purpose was so that the disciples "may believe," Thomas had told the disciples, "Let us also go, that we may die with him" (John 11:15–16).

Apparently, Thomas was unimpressed with Jesus' knowledge of the Lazarus's situation, and he saw doom in their future. Even after Lazarus was raised from the dead and after the Resurrection, Thomas does not yet have faith, either in Jesus' promise of the Resurrection nor in his fellow disciples' ability to truthfully witness to the Risen Lord. St. John explained Thomas' absence from Jesus' first appearance to the other ten disciples:

> Now Thomas, one of the twelve, called the Twin, was not with them when Jesus came. So the other disciples told him, "We have seen the Lord." But he said to them, "Unless I see in his hands the print of the nails, and place my finger in the mark of the nails, and place my hand in his side, I will not believe." (John 20:24–25)

Thomas rejected the testimony of the other ten Apostles and then established his own criteria to believe—touching the marks of the wounds in Jesus' hands, feet, and side. Of course, he would not have known about these wounds except from the testimony of the "beloved disciple" who, unlike Thomas, had stood at Jesus' Cross. He may have taken into consideration the report of the other disciples who had seen Jesus' glorified wounds (John 20:20). Still, he wanted to fulfill his own criteria of touching the wounds himself.

While a lack of faith is certainly not universal among sexually abusive and manipulative clergy, or among embezzlers and other sinners, it is often enough a factor. Lack of faith in the Church's ancient testimony to the Resurrection, the hope of the resurrection of all people, and faith in God's final judgment, whether to eternal life or eternal damnation, is a factor in the lives of some clergy. Yet a strong commitment to this faith is the basis for a love of Jesus Christ that is strong enough to motivate living out the virtues of celibate chastity and unstinting service.

Skeptics and cynics have always existed within the Church, but in the 1960s, skepticism about the Resurrection and the miracles of Jesus began to be taught in Catholic seminaries, convents, and schools. Scripture professors included the writings and ideas of modern scholars such as Rudolf Bultmann and others who rejected the truth of the Resurrection on the basis of the philosophy of Martin Heidegger. Heidegger's idea of man as a "being toward death," who finds authentic faith only when facing the inevitability and finality of death, influenced these theologians, who viewed the Resurrection as an escape from death's finality. Miracles of healing and the Resurrection thereby robbed people of the anxiety over death that led to authentic faith. For them, not only could the Resurrection be untrue, it *should be* untrue, along with miracles. Bultmann boasted of his "demythologization" process as necessary to the promotion of a more modern and mature Christianity. Of course, like Thomas, the Pharisees, and the chief priests, Bultmann had no evidence that the Resurrection was not true. He did not discover Jesus' body, a claim to His bones, or any other such fact. Historicity was not as important as an authentic faith that faced anxiety over death.

It is worth noting that the philosophy underlying this theology did not prevent its inventor from grave immorality. Heidegger joined the Nazi party on May 1, 1933, a few days after becoming the rector of the University of Freiburg, hoping to "bring a concentration on the Germans' Western historical essence." He lectured to the students: "Let not theories and 'ideas' be the rules of your being. The Fuehrer himself and he alone is German reality and its law, today and for the future." He treated shamefully his former mentor, Edmund Husserl, a Jew who had converted to Christianity, and in general believed that there was "a dangerous international alliance of the Jews." The inability of Heidegger's philosophy to prevent him from becoming a dues-paying Nazi party member until the end of the war indicates the weakness of his view of humanity in ethical guidance, yet alone in Christian faith.

Theological reinterpretation of the Gospel through a Heideggerian lens led to denial of the most basic tenets of

Jesus' death and Resurrection among seminary professors and students. Such a watered down Christian faith may be one factor among many that lies at the roots of moral breakdown. Particularly those clergy who publicly profess the Church's faith in the Resurrection in the liturgy but do not believe in it may open themselves to ethical inconsistencies as well. If there is no Resurrection, no divine judgment, reward, or punishment, then self-interested misbehavior in sexual, financial, and other areas of life may seem logical possibilities.

Again, this would be one factor; a number of the perpetrators of sexual misconduct would strongly hold to orthodox Catholic teaching without living it. However, that fact does not negate the role of a lack of faith in other cases. Further, even among the orthodox believers, their sexual misconduct is linked to a compartmentalization of their faith that does not integrate their beliefs with their morals. They seem to need a deeper faith in the truths of Jesus' death and Resurrection so as to form an intellectual support for authentic Catholic morality. That helps people better integrate the spiritual and moral aspects of life.

On the Sunday after the Resurrection, Jesus appeared again to the Apostles in the Upper Room, this time with Thomas present. He began with His standard greeting, "Peace be with you" (John 20:26). Had He appeared on the following Friday or Saturday, He would have honored the end of Passover or the Jewish Sabbath. By appearing on a Sunday, "eight days later," He identified Sunday as the "eighth day," as in the Letter of Barnabas:

Your new moons and your Sabbaths I cannot away with. Ye see what is His meaning ; it is not your present Sabbaths that are acceptable [unto Me], but the Sabbath which I have made, in the which, when I have set all things at rest, I will make the beginning of the eighth day which is the beginning of another world. Wherefore also we keep the eighth day for rejoicing,

in the which also Jesus rose from the dead, and having been
manifested ascended into the heavens. (Barnabas 15:8–9)

The idea of the eighth day concept was even incorporated
into early Christian architecture, as churches and baptistries
were built with eight sides to commemorate the Resurrection
as the eighth day. This way of numbering stems from the Jewish
accounting of Sunday as the first day of creation, when God
said, "Let there be light, and there was light" (Gen. 1:3). On
the eighth day, which is the Sunday following the first day of
creation, Christians celebrate the fact that Jesus has begun a new
creation by His Resurrection, as St. Paul teaches: "Therefore, if
any one is in Christ, he is a new creation; the old has passed away,
behold, the new has come" (2 Cor. 5:17). In this new creation
we celebrate the Resurrection on the eighth day—that is,
Sunday—as Jesus chose to do in His Resurrection appearances
and on Pentecost.

Another aspect of the full week in between appearances is the
parallel with the week described by St. John in the beginning of
the Gospel. From the first appearance of St. John the Baptist
through to Cana, a week passes by, with each day or marker of
days being noted by the evangelist. Now, after the resurrected
Jesus appears, another week is noted in this Gospel as a parallel
to the week of Jesus' appearances at the beginning of His public
ministry.

Thomas Comes to Faith

Then he said to Thomas, "Put your finger here, and see my
hands; and put out your hand, and place it in my side; do not
be faithless, but believing." Thomas answered him, "My Lord
and my God!" Jesus said to him, "Have you believed because
you have seen me? Blessed are those who have not seen and yet
believe." (John 20:27–29)

This passage opens with Jesus expressing His full awareness that Thomas demanded proof of the Resurrection, even though He was not present when Thomas had made his demand (John 20:24–25). Frequently Jesus knew what people were thinking even without them having said anything to Him directly (see, for example, John 6:64; Matt. 12:25; Mark 8:17; Luke 5:22; Luke 9:47). Now Thomas is about to learn personally that Jesus knows his heart and mind and can address those deepest concerns.

The Lord Jesus still knows all of the thoughts of our minds and hearts, even thoughts of which we are barely aware. Some people want to forget their past thoughts and suppress thoughts that do not fit into their self-image. Yet Jesus knows them with absolute certainty and clarity. We cannot hide our thoughts, our lack of faith, our sinful desires, or our past memories from God. He knows those areas of life in which conversion has not yet taken place, and He wants to address them as He addressed Thomas, the Pharisees, and the disciples. His goal is to present us with a choice at these hidden, deep personal levels that we keep locked away even from our self-knowledge: "Will you believe me and follow me?" Such a conversion to faith in Jesus raised from the dead is one of the two key themes of each appearance of Christ to His disciples. The other theme is that once people believe that He is alive, He commissions them to share this Good News with others.

Jesus summoned Thomas beyond his lack of faith: "Be not unbelieving!" Thomas was willing to make that decision, and he answered Jesus, "My Lord and my God!" Thomas knew that no one could know his inner thoughts except God and that only God could raise the dead. He therefore confessed even more faith than the other disciples had by proclaiming the Risen Jesus to be Lord and God.

Jesus accepted his act of faith with a rhetorical question that challenged his initial lack of trust: "Have you believed because you have seen me? Blessed are those who have not seen and yet believe" (John 20:29). Jesus proclaims a beatitude that places people who believe without seeing on a higher level of faith than Thomas.

St. John concludes this episode in a way that includes all of us who read this Gospel and believe: "Now Jesus did many other signs in the presence of the disciples, which are not written in this book; but these are written that you may believe that Jesus is the Christ, the Son of God, and that believing you may have life in his name" (John 20:30–31). Faith that Jesus has risen from the dead easily leads to faith that He "is the Christ, the Son of God." This faith leads believers to "life in his name": just as He suffered much and entered into His glory, so will believers join Him in suffering, but will find within it a glory in this life. Faith in Jesus gives them perspective on their suffering and hope for its resolution in this life and the next. For that reason, all who suffer in this life can turn again and again to the Gospels, find themselves and their own life within its pages, and find themselves moving through the Paschal Mystery to salvation.

The Resurrected Lord Jesus Appears in Galilee

St. John and St. Matthew both write about appearances of the Risen Lord in Galilee at two of His most significant locations—the lake and the mountain. We will examine John 21 first, where Jesus meets the Apostles at the Sea of Galilee, and then Matthew 28, where He meets them on a mountain.

Jesus Appears at the Sea of Galilee

Just as Jesus' presence was required for the conversion of Thomas, so now His presence is required for the Apostles to make the transition from being tempted to return to their former careers rather than accept Jesus' mission. Seven of the disciples were together—Simon Peter, Thomas called the Twin, Nathanael of

Cana, the sons of Zebedee (James and John), and two unnamed disciples—when Simon Peter told them, "I am going fishing," and they followed him (see John 21:1–3).

This is a highly risky point in the career of the disciples. They had seen the Risen Lord on two occasions, but these two encounters may not have made that kind of determinative impact on them so as to change the whole direction of their lives. Almost as if they were religious tourists seeing a marvelous resurrection and taking a few notes, these few disciples readily followed Peter back to the fishing boat they had once left behind. This contrasts with Jesus' earlier invitation to follow Him and become fishers of men: "Follow me, and I will make you fishers of men" (Matt. 4:19; see also Mark 1:17; Luke 5:10). Despite Jesus' call to become fishers of men, and despite having seen Jesus risen from the dead, they return to casting nets for fish unsuccessfully. Did Jesus' summons or His death and Resurrection make a permanent impact on their lives or not?

Jesus came to the disciples on the lakeshore at daybreak in order to resolve the issue, since only He could break through to them. As always, He took the initiative and engaged them in a dialogue about their success at fishing:

> "'Children, have you any fish?' They answered him, 'No.' He said to them, 'Cast the net on the right side of the boat, and you will find some.' So they cast it, and now they were not able to haul it in, for the quantity of fish." (John 21:5–6)

Simon Peter jumped from the boat into the sea and swam to shore while the others dragged the net full of fish to shore. There they found a charcoal fire with fish and bread cooking on it (John 21:7–9). Jesus asked them to bring some of their 153 large fish to cook alongside the other fish and eat a breakfast with the bread Jesus brought to them. An uncomfortable silence prevailed, since no one was brave enough to ask Him who He was. "They knew it was the Lord" (John 21:12).

After breakfast, Jesus turned to Simon Peter and asked three questions. The background to these questions is itself threefold: Peter's threefold denial of Jesus; Peter's call to be a fisher of men (Luke 5:10); and Peter's confession of faith, when Jesus designated him the rock on which He would build His Church (Matt. 16:16–19).

The most important background for the threefold questions is Peter's denials during Jesus' trials.

> Jesus said to Simon Peter, "Simon, son of John, do you love me more than these?" He said to him, "Yes, Lord; you know that I love you." He said to him, "Feed my lambs." A second time he said to him, "Simon, son of John, do you love me?" He said to him, "Yes, Lord; you know that I love you." He said to him, "Tend my sheep." He said to him the third time, "Simon, son of John, do you love me?" Peter was grieved because he said to him the third time, "Do you love me?" And he said to him, "Lord, you know everything; you know that I love you." Jesus said to him, "Feed my sheep." (John 21:15–17)

Jesus did not ask why Peter denied Him, nor did He ask for an act of faith or an affirmation of loyalty. Rather, three times Jesus evokes love from Peter as His way to undo the three denials. Peter had realized the gravity of his sin as soon as Jesus "turned and looked" at him, which drove him to leave the courtyard and weep bitterly. Such profound sorrow and grief still require reconciliation, and this comes from Christ's initiative.

In the context of the sex abuse scandal, as in all situations needing profound reconciliation, the power of the Risen Lord offers insight into the process of overcoming past hurts. The abusive clergy and religious, the neglectful hierarchy and superiors, and anyone who has made false accusations against innocent people all need reconciliation with their various victims. They often cannot get out of the problem by offering their own sorrow for their past deeds, since it can appear merely as a way to avoid the consequences for what they have done wrong.

In many ways, those who have suffered at the hands of others can take the initiative for reconciliation when they feel ready to do so. Similar to the Resurrection, and empowered by its graces, victims who have come to terms with the pain of their abuse and its various effects have a moral authority with which to approach those who hurt them. The Risen Lord offers a path beyond seeking an apology, and shows that mercy is in fact a restoration of love. In the Parable of the Prodigal Son (see Luke 15:11–32), a father keeps a watch for his runaway son to return, reconciles him, and mercifully restores him to his place in the family, thereby remaining a father to that son instead of letting him fall to the level of a servant with himself as his master. Here in John 21:15–17 Jesus lives out that parable with Simon Peter by evoking a profession of love to undo each of his denials of knowing Jesus. In so doing, Jesus restores both Peter to Himself and Himself to Peter.

The second background passage is Simon Peter's confession of faith that Jesus is the Christ, the Son of the living God. In response, Jesus changed his name to Peter, meaning "rock," because he was to be the rock on which Jesus built His Church, and the one to whom the keys of the Kingdom of God are given, the one with the power to bind and loose on earth in such a way that it is bound or loosed in heaven (see Matt. 16:16-19). By evoking Simon's love three times, Jesus reaffirms Peter's leadership within the Church.

The third background element to this episode is when Jesus tells Peter after his first extraordinary catch of fish, "Do not be afraid; henceforth you will be catching men" (Luke 5:10). In the first part of this episode, Peter had led other disciples to return to fishing (John 21:1-3). Though Jesus had called him to be a fisher of men, he has returned to fishing for fish, even after having witnessed the Risen Lord. Therefore, Jesus' loving questions of reconciliation now restore Simon Peter to leadership, but he needs a change of imagery in order to better understand the role. Instead of being a fisher of men, Jesus tells him to "feed my lambs," "shepherd my sheep," and "feed my sheep." Just as the image of holding the "keys" of the Kingdom indicate that Peter has the role of a prime minister for Jesus the King (see Isa. 22:22), so now Peter is to act as a shepherd for Jesus' lambs and sheep, sharing in Jesus' own identity as the Good Shepherd.

Jesus' teaching about being the Good Shepherd ended with a prediction about laying down His life for His sheep: "For this reason the Father loves me, because I lay down my life, that I may take it again. No one takes it from me, but I lay it down of my own accord. I have power to lay it down, and I have power to take it again; this charge I have received from my Father" (John 10:17–18). Then, having reconciled Simon and restored him to leadership, Jesus predicts that Peter would die by crucifixion (see John 21:18–19) and calls him to follow Him.

Here at the Sea of Galilee, Jesus predicted that Simon Peter would die on a cross. Reconciliation does not mean that the former sinner can return to past sins, infidelity, and foolishness. Reconciliation entails future suffering and toil rather than an easy forgetfulness of the past. Yet reconciliation also brings the peace that is strong enough to center a person in God no matter what opposition, risks, and dangers may arise.

Thirty-five years later, after a number of arrests in Jerusalem (see Acts 3 and 4), a near execution by Herod Agrippa I (see Acts 12), and travels to Antioch, Greece, and Rome, St. Peter was executed by crucifixion under Emperor Nero. The transformation from Simon son of John in the Gospels to St. Peter the martyr required further transformation. This was accomplished by the gift of the Holy Spirit poured out upon him, the other Apostles and disciples, and thousands of their converts, to which we will turn in the next chapter.

Jesus Appears on a Mountain in Galilee

Jesus had instructed the eleven Apostles to meet Him in Galilee at an appointed mountain (see Matt. 28:16). The local Christian tradition identified it as the same mountain where He had delivered the Beatitudes and the rest of His initial long sermon (Matt. 5-7). It is a short walk from Capernaum and stands across the ancient road from the place where Jesus had met the disciples fishing (see John 21). Despite His appearance among them, the disciples remain divided between worshiping Him and doubt (see Matt. 28:17). The issue of faith was as lively a decision in this final Galilee appearance as it was for Thomas on the day of the Resurrection and as it remains in modern times. As St. Paul wrote:

"But if there is no resurrection of the dead, then Christ has not been raised; if Christ has not been raised, then our preaching is in vain and your faith is in vain. If the dead are not raised, 'Let us eat and drink, for tomorrow we die.'" (1 Cor. 15:13)

Throughout His public ministry Jesus had claimed to have all authority (see Matt. 11:27). He repeated the claim after His Resurrection: "All authority in heaven and on earth has been given to me" (Matt. 28:18). Just as He had given an initial introduction to the life of the Trinity in Matt. 11:27, His claim to all authority led to another Trinitarian teaching, this time linked to His authoritative command to make disciples and baptize them:

"Go therefore and make disciples of all nations, baptizing them in the name of the Father and of the Son and of the Holy

Spirit, teaching them to observe all that I have commanded you; and lo, I am with you always, to the close of the age." (Matt. 28:19)

Jesus' own baptism in the Jordan had been a very Trinitarian experience, with the Father speaking of His love for the Son being baptized and the Holy Spirit hovering between them. Now He instructs the disciples to let each baptized person experience the power of the same Holy Trinity in each individual's Baptism.

CHAPTER 8

———— ∞∞∞ ————

CHRIST ASCENDS, AND THE HOLY SPIRIT TRANSFORMS THE DISCIPLES

The Ascension of Jesus Christ is described in Luke 24:50–51, in Acts 1:1–11, and in the so-called "Long Ending" of Mark (16:9–20). These narratives of the Ascension are not simply Jesus' departure story, but rather offer a depth of insight into the mission of the Apostles, their successors, and the whole Church throughout time. In addition to these narratives, Jesus taught about the meaning of the Ascension in the Last Supper Discourse, particularly in John 14—16. In the context of teaching about His "departure," He taught about the role and necessity of the Holy Spirit and the hope of eternal life that strengthens disciples to persevere in ministry and service. We will examine these texts to better grasp how the Holy Spirit and the virtue of hope will help Christians make their way through the present clergy sexual abuse crisis.

Jesus Teaches About His Ascension and the Holy Spirit During the Last Supper

St. John did not compose a narrative of the Ascension, but he includes Jesus' teaching about His return to the Father and its meaning for the disciples. This is not unlike his lack of a

Eucharistic institution narrative while including a detailed teaching about the Eucharistic in John 6.

He presents Jesus' teaching about the role of His absence, His ongoing spiritual presence, and the role of the Holy Spirit in the Church. On three prior occasions Jesus had announced His departure, but the crowd failed to understand Him each time: first, they thought He was going to the Diaspora Jewish communities spread throughout the Mediterranean world (see John 7:33–35), or they thought He would commit suicide (see John 8:21–22), and finally, they simply lacked the faith to accept His words (John 12:34–43). During the Last Supper, Jesus mentioned His "departure" four more times to the eleven Apostles, but they failed to understand Him any better than the crowds had earlier.

These teachings are important for the Church's efforts to reform the clergy during the sex abuse crisis. The Holy Spirit is absolutely essential in centering each and every Christian on the active presence of Jesus Christ in the Church. Every Christian needs the Holy Spirit to stir their conscience about the truth of Jesus' teaching, the need to have sin pruned from daily life, and to empower the weak to be steadfast in faith and virtue. The moral failure of the sexual perpetrators and the irresponsible exercise of Church leadership can be rectified, but the Holy Spirit is the guide that Jesus promised for the time after His departure. Therefore we will examine Jesus' Last Supper teachings to His first bishops with a view to considering those teachings as remedies for contemporary bishops and priests regarding the sexual abuse crisis.

The First Announcement of Jesus' Departure

Precisely at the moment when Judas departed the Last Supper, Jesus made the first announcement of His own departure and highlighted the necessity of love, faith, hope, and the Holy Spirit: "Little children, yet a little while I am with you. You will see me; and as I said to the Jews so now I say to you, 'Where

I am going you cannot come'" (John 13:33). He follows up that announcement with four important instructions. First, He commands them to love one another:

> "A new commandment I give to you, that you love one another; even as I have loved you, that you also love one another. By this all men will know that you are my disciples, if you have love for one another." (John 13:34–35)

Jesus used the Greek verb *agapao*, not the word for romance (*eros*), familial love (*storge*), or friendship (*philia*), all of which are human loves that entail emotions and a tendency to become self-serving. Agape love directs disciples to freely choose to love one another as Jesus loves them, accepting other persons with their faults and failures, and with a vision of what they could be. This love seeks other people's greatest good in light of God's eternal love for them, and Jesus wants this kind of love to characterize the Church.

Agape love is absent from abusive relationships, and it is basic to any reform of bishops, priests, and laity alike. Those who believe they deserve gratification, compensation, and rewards in this life will tend to excuse abuse. Those who believe that other people are objects and tools to meet their own needs will justify their sins with excuses and self-righteousness. They will not humbly admit their weaknesses and faults, and they will not confess them before Jesus Christ crucified, Who is the only source of authentic justification. As Jesus indicates, their refusal to obey the commandment to love is rooted in a lack of faith.

The second instruction on Jesus' departure offers hope for a place in heaven for the disciples who had faith in God and in Him:

> "Let not your hearts be troubled; believe in God, believe also in me. In my Father's house are many rooms; if it were not so, would I have told you that I go to prepare a place for you? And

when I go and prepare a place for you, I will come again and will take you to myself, that where I am you may be also. And you know the way where I am going." (John 14:1–3)

Jesus will ascend to heaven "to prepare a place" where many rooms will be ready for His disciples. This offers hope to sustain them during their many and difficult labors for the Kingdom of God, which they will do without commensurate reward during their earthly life. More importantly, during persecutions and martyrdom, they can look beyond the suffering and the shortening of their lives to an eternal home in heaven, a hope that has sustained the 75 million martyrs throughout Church history.

However, this hope depended on the disciples' relationship of faith in the Father and Jesus during the time of Jesus' departure. As Jesus told Thomas, "Blessed are those who have not seen and yet believe" (John 20:29).

Jesus personifies the way to the Father; to know Him is to know truth and life and the Father Himself. This emphasizes the need for every disciple to keep focused on the Person of Jesus Christ rather than on merely doing a job, promoting an ideology, or pursuing self-interests. A priest who loses that love for Jesus will either live as an idealist who cares more for ideas than for God or the people he is called to serve, or he will turn to pursue gratification and selfishness.

Jesus gives a third instruction about His departure: the disciples will not only do the same works as Jesus, but they will do even greater ones, if they ask in Jesus' name.

"Truly, truly, I say to you, he who believes in me will also do the works that I do; and greater works than these will he do, because I go to the Father. Whatever you ask in my name, I will do it, that the Father may be glorified in the Son; if you ask anything in my name, I will do it." (John 14:12–14)

In fact, stories about healing the sick and paralyzed and even raising the dead will fill the pages of Acts of the Apostles. Peter, Paul, and the others clearly state that they were able to do those "works" only by the power of the Holy Spirit, showing that they eventually grasped Jesus' teaching about the Holy Spirit in the fourth instruction about His departure to heaven:

"If you love me, you will keep my commandments. And I will pray the Father, and he will give you another Counselor, to be with you for ever, even the Spirit of truth, whom the world cannot receive, because it neither sees him nor knows him; you know him, for he dwells with you, and will be in you." (John 14:15–17)

Jesus prepares the disciples to receive the promise of the Holy Spirit of truth by commanding them to love Him. That love includes a major implication of keeping His commandments. In any authentic agape love, the lover seeks the good of the beloved and never wants to offend. Therefore, disciples will do everything possible to keep His commandments so as to avoid offending Jesus' love.

Then, for those who love and obey Him, Jesus promises to ask the heavenly Father for the gift of the Counselor Who is the Spirit of truth. The Greek word *parakletos* etymologically means "someone called to one's side," and it described an advisor, advocate, or counselor for the defense in a law court—that is, a defense lawyer. Jesus uses the phrase "another Counselor" or Paraclete, because Jesus Himself is their first Paraclete, as John teaches in his first epistle: "If any one does sin, we have an advocate [paraclete] with the Father, Jesus Christ the righteous" (1 John 2:1).

This other Paraclete is "the Spirit of truth," Who has two characteristics. First, He is an invisible Spirit capable of entering the disciples' hearts and minds. Second, He is characterized by truth, which Jesus will clarify in John 16. However, since Jesus already identified Himself as "the way, the truth and the life" (John 14:6), it is obvious that the Spirit of truth is closely connected to Jesus the truth.

Identifying the Holy Spirit with truth explains why "the world cannot receive [him], because it neither sees him nor knows him" (John 14:17). The world has been incapable of accepting the truth Who is Jesus, so it will certainly be incapable of accepting the Spirit of truth.

Jesus' departure to heaven is here and is connected with the coming of the Holy Spirit. While Jesus' departure will seem to be an abandonment, in fact it makes possible intimacy with the Holy Spirit. Jesus made it clear that the disciples can only accept His "economy of salvation" if they love Him and each other selflessly, if their labors are sustained by hope for an eternal dwelling in heaven, and if they have faith in Jesus and God the Father. Vatican II develops this by saying that celibate priests renounce "the companionship of marriage for the sake of the kingdom of heaven (cf. Matt. 19:12)" and "they embrace the Lord with an undivided love altogether befitting the new covenant," with a view "to the resurrection of the world to come (cf. Luke 20:36)."

This celibacy is "a most suitable aid for the continual exercise of that perfect charity" in which they become "all things to all men in their priestly ministry," and they should accept it "gratefully" "as a precious gift of God for which they should humbly pray." It is the Holy Spirit Who enables them to "freely and generously hasten to respond to this gift" and "consecrate themselves to the Lord by a complete gift of body and soul" (*Presbyterorum Ordinis* 10).

The Second Announcement of Jesus' Departure

Jesus' second announcement of His departure included the promise that He was not abandoning the disciples—the Holy Spirit of truth will remain with them as a Paraclete:

"I will not leave you desolate; I will come to you. Yet a little while, and the world will see me no more, but you will see me; because I live, you will live also. In that day you will know that I am in my Father, and you in me, and I in you. He who has my commandments and keeps them, he it is who loves me; and he who loves me will be loved by my Father, and I will love him and manifest myself to him." (John 14:18–21)

The *Revised Standard Version* translates the Greek word *orphanous* as "desolate" in order to emphasize the disciples' interior reaction rather than a father-child relationship to Jesus. Jesus' emphasis regarding His departure to heaven was His ongoing union with His heavenly Father. In consequence, the disciples will remain united to Him like branches to a vine (see John 15:1–8). By union with Christ, they will also be united with the heavenly Father, with a new status as His children. No matter where they go or what their circumstances might be, they will not be desolate, helpless orphans because of their intimate connection "in my Father, and you in me and I in you." This teaching is closely connected to Matthew 28:20, where, after instructing the disciples to teach all the nations "to observe all that I have commanded you," He promised the disciples, "I am with you always, to the close of the age."

In the context of promising the indwelling of the Father and Son within the disciples, He promises to send the Holy Spirit as their Paraclete. Thereby all three Persons of the Blessed Trinity will indwell the Christian: "These things I have spoken to you, while I am still with you. But the Counselor, the Holy Spirit, whom the Father will send in my name, he will teach you all things, and bring to your remembrance all that I have said to you" (John 14:25–26).

Jesus emphasizes that the "Counselor" is the Holy Spirit Whom the Father will send in Jesus' name. His role is to teach the disciples "all things" and empower them to remember all that

Jesus has said. This was Jesus' message when He instructed the disciples on their first mission to the villages of Galilee:

"When they deliver you up, do not be anxious how you are to speak or what you are to say; for what you are to say will be given to you in that hour; for it is not you who speak, but the Spirit of your Father speaking through you." (Matthew 10:19–20)

The gift of speech from the Holy Spirit appeared often among the disciples. On Pentecost, the disciples "were all filled with the Holy Spirit and began to speak in other tongues, as the Spirit gave them utterance" (Acts 2:4), and then the Holy Spirit inspired St. Peter to address a large crowd. When Peter was put on trial for the first time before the Sanhedrin, the Holy Spirit gave him the ability to speak (see Acts 4:8). It was the same with St. Stephen: "But they could not withstand the wisdom and the Spirit with which he spoke" (Acts 6:10; see also 7:55–56). Based on such experiences, St. Peter taught:

It was revealed to them that they were serving not themselves but you, in the things which have now been announced to you by those who preached the good news to you through the Holy Spirit sent from heaven, things into which angels long to look. (1 Pet. 1:12)

First of all you must understand this, that no prophecy of scripture is a matter of one's own interpretation, because no prophecy ever came by the impulse of man, but men moved by the Holy Spirit spoke from God. (2 Pet. 2:20–21)

The ability to remember Jesus' words at the times one needs them is indeed a gift of the Holy Spirit, demonstrating that Jesus did not leave us orphaned.

The Third Announcement of Jesus' Departure

Jesus introduced the third announcement of His departure with a promise of His gift of peace that drives out fear, enables the disciples to rejoice over His return to his Father, and evokes faith:

> "Peace I leave with you; my peace I give to you; not as the world gives do I give to you. Let not your hearts be troubled, neither let them be afraid. You heard me say to you, 'I go away, and I will come to you.' If you loved me, you would have rejoiced, because I go to the Father; for the Father is greater than I. And now I have told you before it takes place, so that when it does take place, you may believe." (John 14:27–29)

Abiding peace is the disciples' inheritance as Jesus departs. This is not the type of peace that the world gives, and each Christian will need to discern the difference between the peace of Christ and that of the world. The world's peace may seem initially exhilarating or exciting, but it fades away. The peace of Christ remains in us, even when external circumstances, such as persecution or rejection or loss come about.

In the case of some individuals, the sexual abuse crisis arose from feelings of loneliness and abandonment. They may have expected an experience of intimacy to bring them peace, but it did not. A sure sign that these acts come from the world and from the evil spirit is the pain felt by the victims and the disorder that turned those acts into an international crisis. Both the offenders and the victims need the authentic peace of Christ that comes from union with Him and the Father. Those who continue to experience the temptations, whether to homosexual or heterosexual encounters, whether with minors or adults, need to center on Jesus as the source of true, lasting peace. Any worldly offers of intimacy and peace will not merely evaporate, but will sour into a catastrophe for both the perpetrator and the victim, since that is the way of the world.

The Fourth Announcement of Jesus' Departure

Jesus' fourth announcement began with a promise that the Holy Spirit is the one "whom the Father will send in my name." Here Jesus said that the Paraclete proceeds from the Father (see John 15:26). Jesus points out that the Holy Spirit proceeds from both the Father and the Son; through the gift of the Holy Spirit each disciple is drawn into the life of the Blessed Trinity's infinite love.

Next Jesus warned the eleven Apostles against falling away from Him on account of persecution from those who do not know the Father like they do:

> "I have said all this to you to keep you from falling away. They will put you out of the synagogues; indeed, the hour is coming when whoever kills you will think he is offering service to God. And they will do this because they have not known the Father, nor me. But I have said these things to you, that when their hour comes you may remember that I told you of them. I did not say these things to you from the beginning, because I was with you. But now I am going to him who sent me; yet none of you asks me, 'Where are you going?' But because I have said these things to you, sorrow has filled your hearts. (John 16:1–6)

Jesus' destination is "the one who sent me," the Father of Whom He had spoken throughout the Gospel. This is not so much a journey to a place as it is to a Person He loves. In His great prayer in John 17, he taught that the Father is the destination for all disciples who love Him. At this point Jesus returns to His promise of the Holy Spirit in John 16:7–15, which can be broken down into in three sections.

The first section (John 16:7) introduces the importance of

the coming of the Holy Spirit to the disciples: "Nevertheless I tell you the truth: it is to your advantage that I go away, for if I do not go away, the Counselor will not come to you; but if I go, I will send him to you." Jesus' absence is an advantage precisely because He can and will send the Paraclete/Counselor to them. Jesus does what the Father does: both send the Holy Spirit, and neither sends Him in contradiction to the other or without the other (see John 14:16, 26; 15:26).

These verses indicate that God's self-giving love involves all three Persons of the Trinity in complete, total, and infinite union with one another. Unlike the pagan deities, who were constantly reduced to the image and likeness of human jealousies, envies, anger, lust, and other vices, the Holy Trinity is completely holy, self-giving, and loving. Humans, created in God's image and likeness, are thereby called to be self-giving and harmonious, like the Persons of the Holy Trinity. They do not use each other, but rather give of themselves to each other. That is the character of true love instead of abuse.

The second section (John 16:8–11) treats three tasks the Holy Spirit will accomplish when He comes to the disciples: "And when he comes, he will convince the world concerning sin and righteousness and judgment: concerning sin, because they do not believe in me; concerning righteousness, because I go to the Father, and you will see me no more; concerning judgment, because the ruler of this world is judged."

The inability of the world to receive the Spirit of truth is not solely because of ignorance but also because of animosity, similar to the hatred that the world has for Jesus, Who is Himself the light of the world and the truth:

> For every one who does evil hates the light,
> and does not come to the light, lest his
> deeds should be exposed. (John 3:20)

> "The world cannot hate you [unbelieving

brothers], but it hates me because I testify of
it that its works are evil." (John 7:7)

"If the world hates you, know that it has hated
me before it hated you. If you were of the world,
the world would love its own; but because you are
not of the world, but I chose you out of the world,
therefore the world hates you." (John 15:18–19)

"He who hates me hates my Father also. If I had not
done among them the works which no one else did,
they would not have sin; but now they have seen and
hated both me and my Father. (John 15:23–24)

The Greek word *elenchein* means to "convince" or "convict"
someone, proving that the person is wrong on a subject. The Holy
Spirit will demonstrate the world's falsehood in the face of His
divine truth, the way a Paraclete—that is, a defense lawyer—proves
the falsehood of the accusers. He will specifically demonstrate that
the world is wrong about "sin and righteousness and judgment."

First, the Holy Spirit will prove the world wrong about "sin,
because they do not believe in [Jesus]." The world rejected faith
in Jesus and came to hate Him (see John 3:20; 7:7; 15:18, 23–24),
showing that neutrality toward Jesus is impossible. Rejecting faith
in Jesus necessarily becomes a rejection of love for Him and then
hatred, and this is the world's most basic sin.

Second, Jesus said the Holy Spirit will convict the world
"concerning righteousness, because I go to the Father, and
you will see me no more" (John 16:10). This phrase requires
an understanding of the word *righteousness*, which in the
Old Testament refers to moral correctness, or having correct
standards. Israelite courts did not decree a person "guilty" or
"not guilty," as in English common law; rather, they declared
a guilty person to be "wicked" and an innocent person to be
"righteous" (see Exod. 23:1,7). The Holy Spirit will prove that

Jesus is "righteous" (John 16:11); that is, innocent of the charges of blasphemy that had been laid against Him throughout His public ministry. This would also apply to Jesus' upcoming trials before the High Priests Annas and Caiaphas, as well as before Pilate, which were trials by the "world."

The Jewish leaders accused Jesus of blasphemy before Pilate and the world: "We have a law, and by that law he ought to die, because he has made himself the Son of God" (John 19:7). Being condemned to crucifixion, an accursed way of dying (Deut. 21:22), was supposed to prove that He was not the Son of God. However, Jesus rose from the dead and ascended to the Father, which proved Him "righteous" or innocent of blasphemy. The Holy Spirit thereby convicted the world and prove them wrong about Jesus' righteous innocence.

Third, the Holy Spirit will convict the world "concerning judgment, because the ruler of this world is judged" (John 16:11). Because the Holy Spirit is the Paraclete/Counselor who defends the disciples as their defense attorney, He is able to convict the world and its ruler, Satan, of wrong judgment. On Palm Sunday Jesus gave the key evidence that convicted the world and its ruler:

> "Now is the judgment of this world, now shall the ruler of this world be cast out; and I, when I am lifted up from the earth, will draw all men to myself. He said this to show by what death he was to die." (John 12:31)

That key evidence is Jesus' Crucifixion, when He is "lifted up" because it causes the "ruler of this world," Satan, to lose power. During Jesus' trial on Good Friday the crowd demanded that Pilate crucify Jesus. When Pilate asked, "Shall I crucify your king?" the high priests responded, "We have no king but Caesar." However, the Holy Spirit will convict the world that Satan is the "ruler of this world," as the devil told Jesus in the wilderness:

> And the devil took him up, and showed him all the kingdoms of
> the world in a moment of time, and said to him, "To you I will
> give all this authority and their glory; for it has been delivered to
> me, and I give it to whom I will." (Luke 4:5; see also Matt. 4:8-9)

The Holy Spirit will prove wrong all those who condemned Jesus to death, especially after He rises again and defeats the "ruler of this world." The Paraclete will prove the truth of Jesus' words about the devil and the world (see John 8:44; 1 John 4:4; 1 John 5:4–5). The Holy Spirit of truth will give the disciples the ability to overcome the evil one and the world, and that will be the conviction that the Holy Spirit brings to their minds.

In the third section (John 16:12–15), Jesus promises that the Spirit of truth will teach the disciples those things they cannot bear yet: "When the Spirit of truth comes, he will guide you into all the truth; for he will not speak on his own authority, but whatever he hears he will speak, and he will declare to you the things that are to come." The disciples were very limited in their ability to understand and accept Jesus' teachings, either because they had "little faith" or were "hard of heart." In the same way, everyone who has trouble understanding and accepting Jesus' teachings needs to examine his or her conscience to determine whether the failure to accept Him comes from a lack of faith or a hardness of heart.

Next, Jesus informed the disciples that the Holy Spirit, Who is the "Spirit of truth," has the authority to guide them into all truth because He has received everything that belongs to Jesus, and Jesus has received everything He has from the Father. In explaining the source of the Paraclete's truth, Jesus also taught that the one God includes three Persons, Whose internal relationships are characterized by total self-giving. Each Person completely gives of Himself to the others, and then they share their love and truth with human beings. The Divine Persons' self-giving is inherently infinite: each Person gives infinitely of Himself to the other persons, and each infinite Person also accepts the infinity given to Him. No Person holds back anything and no Person rejects anything from the other. This is the quality of the unity within the Blessed Trinity.

When Jesus included the Holy Spirit in the self-giving and receiving of God, He thereby asserted that God is not a duality of Father and Son but a Trinity of three Persons absolutely one in their divinity, their infinite self-giving, and their acceptance of the other Persons.

As the Holy Spirit led St. John into "all truth," he was later inspired to write in his first epistle a key ramification of Jesus' teaching about the self-giving of the three Divine Persons, namely, that "God is love" (1 John 4:8; 16). If the Divine Persons are not giving themselves to each other and accepting that gift of each other, how can St. John write that "God is love?"

Divine love is not some transitory feeling but is an eternal self-gift and acceptance of the other. These three Persons exist eternally, neither beginning nor ending. Only infinite and eternal love is appropriate to divine nature. The wonder is that Jesus has introduced humans to that love and challenges us to love God with our whole heart, mind, and soul. The consequence of accepting God's love is sharing it with our neighbors. Such would be the message of the Apostles as they proclaimed Jesus' Gospel to the whole world after His Ascension.

In the fourth section (John 16:16–22), Jesus explains: "A little while, and you will see me no more; again a little while, and you will see me" (John 16:16). At this point, Jesus' absence refers to His imminent death. The Apostles would see Him again when He appeared in the Upper Room, gave them His peace, and breathed the Holy Spirit on them, showed His wounds to Thomas a week later, and appeared to the disciples who had gone fishing. Still, the Apostles were perplexed about His departure, and discussed the problem among themselves: "What is this that he says to us, 'A little while, and you will not see me, and again a little while, and you will see me'; and, 'because I go to the Father'? .... We do not know what he means" (John 16:17, 18).

The disciples, along with the rest of the world, will think that Jesus is gone, but they do not understand that His absence is temporary. His return will cause the disciples great joy, as is true of a woman in childbirth whose sorrow is turned into joy:

> "Truly, truly, I say to you, you will weep and lament, but the world will rejoice; you will be sorrowful, but your sorrow will turn into joy. When a woman is in travail she has sorrow, because her hour has come; but when she is delivered of the child, she no longer remembers the anguish, for joy that a child is born into the world. So you have sorrow now, but I will see you again and your hearts will rejoice, and no one will take your joy from you." (John 16:20–22)

In the fifth section of this final discussion of the departure (see John 16:23–27), Jesus makes the important point that He is leaving the world and going to the Father so that they can ask the Father for all things in Jesus' name:

> "In that day you will ask nothing of me. Truly, truly, I say to you, if you ask anything of the Father, he will give it to you in my name. Hitherto you have asked nothing in my name; ask, and you will receive, that your joy may be full. I have said this to you in figures; the hour is coming when I shall no longer speak to you in figures but tell you plainly of the Father. In that day you will ask in my name; and I do not say to you that I shall pray the Father for you; for the Father himself loves you, because you have loved me and have believed that I came from the Father. I came from the Father and have come into the world; again, I am leaving the world and going to the Father." (John 16:23–28)

His departure will benefit the disciples because He will intercede for them, as their first Paraclete or Advocate, whose name will make their prayers to the Father effective. Prior to His departure He assures them that the Father loves them on account of their love for Jesus. They can trust in that love and in Jesus' presence with the Father, from whom they seek all good things.

Finally, the whole unit concludes with the disciples claiming to believe Him and His words. Jesus knows better than they that they do not yet fully believe, so He adds a warning that a time of persecution is coming very soon, even that very night (see John 16:32). He reassures them, though, that in Him the disciples will have peace, telling them to "be of good cheer, I have overcome the world" (John 16:33).

This last teaching applies to clergy throughout the ages, who, like the Apostles, have faith, but it is often not yet strong enough to center their lives. They do understand and believe at some levels of their minds and hearts, but Jesus is not fully integrated into all of their ideas and decisions. For that reason, some of them "go off the rails" in the sexual realm and sin against chastity. Instead of praying as they ought, they might relax alone with pornography, or enter into sexual relationships with other adults, or engage minors in abusive relationships. Only Christ can center their lives and integrate every aspect of their existence. He integrates the creative powers of sexuality, and through forgiveness and mercy, He integrates human failures and sins into redemption.

The process of letting Christ be the center of life who integrates all of its components is a lifelong development, moving through every stage of life's changes and growth. However, Jesus is the truth who is powerful enough to integrate people at every stage of life's development. Though He has departed into heaven, He truly leaves us the Holy Spirit to effect these stages of growth and give us "good cheer" through all tribulation.

The Ascension

As seen in the above discussion, Jesus spent more time preparing the disciples to understand the meaning of His Ascension and the coming of the Holy Spirit than the Gospels spend in describing the Ascension. Mark and Luke mention Jesus ascending to heaven (see Mark 16:9–20, a section not found in the oldest manuscripts, and one most scholars speculate is a later summary). Another very short summary of the Ascension is found in Luke 24:50–53:

> "Then he led them out as far as Bethany, and lifting up his hands he blessed them. While he blessed them, he parted from them, and was carried up into heaven. And they returned to Jerusalem with great joy, and were continually in the temple blessing God."

A distinctive element in Luke's description of the Ascension is Jesus' act of raising His hands to bless the Apostles before He departed to heaven. This stance indicates His priestly role, since "Aaron lifted up his hands toward the people and blessed them" (Lev. 9:22), as did Simon the high priest in the 190s BC: "Simon came down, and lifted up his hands over the whole congregation of the sons of Israel, to pronounce the blessing of the Lord with his lips, and to glory in his name" (Sir. 50:20).

Pentecost and the Coming of the Holy Spirit

Pentecost is a Greek name for the Israelite Feast of Weeks (*Shabuoth*), which God commanded to be celebrated as a pilgrimage feast (see Ex. 23:16; 34:22; Lev. 23:15-21; Deut. 16:9-12), along with Passover and the Autumn Feast of Booths (*Succoth*). In these Old Testament passages, it is translated literally as "Feast of Weeks" (*e`orth.n e`bdoma,dwn*), but in Tobit 2:1 and 2 Maccabees 12:32, written in the third and second century BC respectively, the Greek word *Pentecost* appears, meaning "fiftieth day." The Old Testament connects the feast with the late spring wheat harvest, while later Judaism emphasized the feast as the commemoration of Moses receiving the two stone tablets containing the Ten Commandments on Mt. Sinai. Since this feast was so important, many Jews from other countries came to Jerusalem to celebrate it.

> When the day of Pentecost had come, they were all together in one place. And suddenly a sound came from heaven like the rush of a mighty wind, and it filled all the house where they were sitting. And there appeared to them tongues as of fire, distributed and resting on each one of them. And they were all filled with the Holy Spirit and began to speak in other tongues, as the Spirit gave them utterance. (Acts 2:1–4)

This description of the coming of the Holy Spirit has parallels and important differences with the Mount Sinai manifestation of the Lord when He gave Israel the Ten Commandments (see Exod. 19:16). Both manifestations of God in a "theophany" (or appearance of God) include sounds and visible phenomena; fire appears at both, with powerful sounds. However, at Mount Sinai the fire comes with smoke, trumpet blasts, and thunder, which the people of Israel observed from a distance as they trembled in fear. Further, Moses ascended the mountain alone as the Lord descended with fire, smoke, and a shaking of the mountain. This event was the key to Moses' most important role as the mediator of the covenant that established a new relationship between the Lord and Israel (see Exod. 19:5–6).

At the Christian Pentecost, the Holy Spirit manifested Himself in flames of pure fire without smoke or thick cloud, and the flames parted like tongues of fire upon each person in order to fill each one with the Holy Spirit. This interior filling of the early Christians with the Holy Spirit contrasts with Sinai's gift of the Law on tablets of stone, as St. Paul wrote:

> You yourselves are our letter of recommendation, written on your hearts, to be known and read by all men; and you show that you are a letter from Christ delivered by us, written not with ink but with the Spirit of the living God, not on tablets of stone but on tablets of human hearts. (2 Cor. 3:2–3)

As a result, the first Christians received the ability "to speak in other tongues, as the Spirit gave them utterance" (2 Cor. 3:4), enabling them to speak with the crowd of pilgrims outside the Upper Room who gathered as they heard the sound of the loud wind. This gift was only the beginning of the signs of power, prophecy, and teaching that are related throughout the Acts of the Apostles and the history of the Church.

The Apostles Take It Outside

Pentecost, or the Feast of Weeks (*Shavuoth*), is one of the three great Jewish pilgrimage festivals, which explains the presence of devout Jews "from every nation under heaven" in Jerusalem at that time (Acts 2:5). That "multitude came together, and they were bewildered, because each one heard them speaking in his own language," even though they knew that the Apostles were Galileans who did not know the many disparate languages of Mesopotamia, Asia Minor, North Africa, and Europe in which to speak of "the mighty works of God" (Acts 2:6–11).

The Apostles did not use the opportunity to brag about their abilities or special position, but rather exercised this new gift to proclaim the Gospel. They told of Jesus' ministry, death, and Resurrection, in light of Old Testament prophecies from Joel and David. Having learned from Jesus, they now instructed the congregation of Israel gathered in Jerusalem about the fulfillment of the Old Testament in Jesus Christ. The result was the conversion and baptism of three thousand people and the continuation of the Church community life by devotion to "the apostles' teaching and fellowship, to the breaking of bread and the prayers" (Acts 2:41–42).

The Acts of the Apostles tells the story of the development of the Church from Jerusalem, to Judea, Samaria, and to the ends of the world. The Holy Spirit transformed the Apostles, who no longer bickered about their self-importance or acquisition of rewards. Rather than hide from their enemies, they boldly proclaimed the Gospel of Jesus Christ before the Sanhedrin, governors, and kings. Luke concludes Acts in AD 62, with St. Paul's imprisonment in Rome as he awaited trial before the Emperor Nero. Though he includes the martyrdom of St. Stephen (see Acts 7) and St. James the Apostle (see Acts 12:2–3), he did not yet know of the martyrdom of Peter, Paul, and the others, including his own, that would occur within a few years. He shows the transformation that the Holy Spirit effected in the once very frightened Apostles and disciples, and through them the Spirit transformed the world.

Growth in the Gifts of the Holy Spirit

The fact that St. Peter and the others did not boast about having the gifts of the Holy Spirit stands in great contrast to their behavior before receiving gifts of the Holy Spirit. What had changed in the Apostles after their reception of the Holy Spirit?

More than twenty years later, St. Paul wrote that the fruits and gifts of the Holy Spirit had transformed the believers, not only in external acts of healing, miracles, and other wonders, but interiorly with an increase in virtues — i.e., the fruit of the Holy Spirit. Peter, Paul, and the rest knew that this was the operation of God's grace, since they were all well aware of their own failures to be virtuous, courageous, and self-giving. They included stories of their personal failures throughout the New Testament so as to make clear that the Holy Spirit had transformed them. Today's bishops and priests need the Holy Spirit's transformation as the only way out of the present crisis.

The Interior Gifts of the Holy Spirit

First, let us examine the gifts that transform people interiorly. The earliest list of the gifts of the Holy Spirit comes from the prophet Isaiah. He describes the Messiah as "shoot from the stump of Jesse," that is, a member of David's family tree, Who will possess various intellectual gifts and virtues from the Spirit of the Lord:

> And the Spirit of the Lord shall rest upon him, the spirit of wisdom and understanding, the spirit of counsel and might, the spirit of knowledge and the fear of the Lord. And his delight shall be in the fear of the Lord. (Isa. 11:2–3)

Wisdom and understanding are gifts that build upon knowledge in order to gain insight into God, His ways, and human life. Counsel is the ability to explain wisdom to other people, while "might" or courage empowers one to act upon that wisdom and understanding. "Fear of the Lord" is the recognition of God's majesty and greatness by small and otherwise insignificant human beings. Modern people far too often treat the "fear of the Lord" as a negative virtue, but Scripture considers it the "beginning of wisdom" (see for example Prov. 1:7; 9:10; 15:33). The end point of fear of the Lord is profound love of God or piety, but humans need to start where it is most effective and salutary for their greater good.

Next, we turn to a list of the fruits of the Holy Spirit found in Galatians 5, in an exhortation to live according to the Holy Spirit and to reject gratification of the flesh:

> But I say, walk by the Spirit, and do not gratify the desires

of the flesh. For the desires of the flesh are against the Spirit, and the desires of the Spirit are against the flesh; for these are opposed to each other, to prevent you from doing what you would. But if you are led by the Spirit you are not under the law. Now the works of the flesh are plain: fornication, impurity, licentiousness, idolatry, sorcery, enmity, strife, jealousy, anger, selfishness, dissension, party spirit, envy, drunkenness, carousing, and the like. I warn you, as I warned you before, that those who do such things shall not inherit the kingdom of God. But the fruit of the Spirit is love, joy, peace, patience, kindness, goodness, faithfulness, gentleness, self-control; against such there is no law. And those who belong to Christ Jesus have crucified the flesh with its passions and desires. If we live by the Spirit, let us also walk by the Spirit. Let us have no self-conceit, no provoking of one another, no envy of one another. (Gal. 5:16–26)

This passage can easily serve as an examination of conscience for every Christian: "Have my actions served to gratify the disordered desires of my flesh or are they manifestations of the fruit of the Holy Spirit?" Some of the works of the flesh come from a disordered use of one's sexuality: "fornication, impurity, licentiousness," and some attack the control of the intellect and will, such as "drunkenness, carousing." Others sin directly against God's majesty, such as "idolatry, sorcery," while others destroy human community, such as "enmity, strife, jealousy, anger, selfishness, dissension, party spirit." One can examine the priest abuse scandal from the perspective of this list of the works of the flesh and perceive the activity of these sins and the deadly effects they have on individuals and on the whole of society.

On the other hand, the fruit of the Spirit avoids "conceit," provocation of others, and envy because the Holy Spirit empowers the disciple to become holy and virtuous. Therefore, the first fruit of the Spirit is love for God above all and for other humans as oneself. While the culture uses the word "love" frequently, it is often a cover for the self-centered use of other people. The love that grows as a fruit of the Holy Spirit reflects God's nature as love and thereby seeks the good of the other for the sake of that person, with respect for his or her inherent dignity. For that reason joy, peace, patience, and chastity flow from it. The Holy Spirit grants this love to His disciples so as to transform them from persecutors like Saul into saints like the Apostle Paul.

Contemporary bishops and priests need the same kinds of conversion as the early Apostles and disciples experienced, transforming them from self-centered people to those who share the love of God, loving one another as Jesus loves them. In addition, the fruit of the Holy Spirit will continue to grow and develop within them throughout the whole extent of life, making them into the saints who are much needed today.

External Gifts to Build Up the Church

Modern Christians continue to need the Holy Spirit and His gifts to empower the Christian life and mission as an antidote to the enervating effects of cynical individualism, self-indulgence, and isolation, which are far too common in modern society.

When listing these gifts of the Holy Spirit, St. Paul also describes their purpose, which is unity within the Church (see 1 Cor. 12:4–7, 11–13). The gifts vary among themselves, but they derive from the Trinity. The goal of these gifts is to unite all of the baptized into the one "body of Christ," which is the Church. The variety of gifts overcomes the differences among individuals that appear insurmountable to human society, such as the differences between Jews and Greeks, slaves and free people, male and female, Scythian or barbarian, but are no obstacle to God: "for you are all one in Christ Jesus" (1 Cor 12:13; Gal. 3:28; Col. 3:11).

Interestingly, as in a human body, the greater and more complex the unity among the members, the greater the diversity of organs.

Simpler organisms, such as oysters, succeed as a species with simple elegance. However, more complex creatures also become more interesting; that is the reason that people choose dogs and cats over oysters as pets and companions. Humans enjoy even greater complexity, which makes them fascinating as friends, spouses, and family. The Church is also a complex body, which is why it has the potential to transform the world through the ages.

The unity among the different members of the Church makes its diversity possible. Just as when a body part is disconnected from the body through an accident or a surgery, the separated part soon decays and is reduced to its constituent chemical parts. Those individual chemicals—iron, calcium, sodium, and so on—then resemble all other elements of the same type. When a member of the body remains united to the whole, it maintains its complex diversity, with the other parts complementing it. Likewise in the Church, the separation of individual members from the whole Church through heresy, schism, or some other serious sin diminishes the individual, who then looks like the rest of the sinners. When a person is united to the Church by the Holy Spirit, his or her distinctive gifts arise, and uniqueness characterizes their sanctity. That is what makes the saints so very interesting.

St. Paul addresses the same principle of unity in the other lists of spiritual gifts found in Romans 12:4–5 and Ephesians 4:1–7. Note that the unity of the body of Christ can be sustained only with virtues of humble patience motivated by love for one another. After listing the diverse gifts of the Holy Spirit (see Eph. 4:8–11), he points out that their purpose is to equip Christians for service to build the Church in unity, knowledge, and maturity in Christ. Humble service that builds up the body of Christ is the purpose of the Holy Spirit's gifts. The gifts are meant to help Christians attain "unity of faith and knowledge of Christ," not arrogant, individual self-expression. Ultimately, their goal is maturity defined as "the stature of the fulness of Christ," Who unifies the Church in love.

Only in the context of these goals and values ought Christians study the lists of the gifts of the Holy Spirit, with the idea of asking the Holy Spirit to grant them as a way to love other people and to aid all in maturing to the stature of Jesus Christ. The first list is in 1 Corinthians 12:8–10:

> To one is given through the Spirit the utterance of wisdom, and to another the utterance of knowledge according to the same Spirit, to another faith by the same Spirit, to another gifts of healing by the one Spirit, to another the working of miracles, to another prophecy, to another the ability to distinguish between spirits, to another various kinds of tongues, to another the interpretation of tongues.

St. Paul then follows up with a prioritizing of the gifts in the context of their role in the whole body of Christ:

> Now you are the body of Christ and individually members of it. And God has appointed in the church first apostles, second prophets, third teachers, then workers of miracles, then healers, helpers, administrators, speakers in various kinds of tongues. (1 Cor. 12:27–28)

The second list is in Romans 12, which presents seven different charisms with exhortations on exercising them for the common good:

> Having gifts that differ according to the grace given to us, let us use them: if prophecy, in proportion to our faith; if service, in our serving; he who teaches, in his teaching; he who exhorts, in his exhortation; he who contributes, in liberality; he who gives aid, with zeal; he who does acts of mercy, with cheerfulness. (Rom. 12:6–7)

The third list is the shortest: "And his gifts were that some should be apostles, some prophets, some evangelists, some pastors and teachers" (Eph. 4:11).

No list is exhaustive, as seen by the fact that only prophecy is found in all three. Rather, each list includes gifts not mentioned in the others. Some gifts are more oriented to the organization of the Church, such as apostles and administrators. Some are more extraordinary for their miraculous quality, such as healing, miracles, and speaking in tongues. Some appeal to the intellect, such as evangelists, teachers, those who exhort, or those who have a word of knowledge or word of wisdom. Some appeal to acts of charity, such as helpers and those who contribute or give aid. That fact indicates that the Holy Spirit might reveal new charisms for the upbuilding of the Church. That is why religious orders of priests, brothers, monks, sisters, and lay organizations have taken on various charisms to teach, evangelize, aid the sick, poor, and needy, and so on. New expressions of these charisms arise with the developments of cultures, technology, and various needs and opportunities. The Church continues to seek the guidance of the Holy Spirit and His gracious generosity so that we might be His instruments in building the Church and maturing in Christ Jesus.

As in every age, no one ought to think more highly of oneself than a sober assessment in the light of faith would permit (see Rom. 12:3). St. Paul had warned both the Jews (see Rom. 2—4) and the Gentiles (Rom. 11:7–24) against thinking too highly of themselves. Every believer, clergy or lay faithful, needs to think humbly about himself or herself. The antidote to the temptation to pride is love, without which the spiritual gifts avail nothing:

But earnestly desire the higher gifts. And I will show you a still more excellent way. If I speak in the tongues of men and of angels, but have not love, I am a noisy gong or a clanging cymbal. And if I have prophetic powers, and understand all mysteries and all knowledge, and if I have all faith, so as to remove mountains, but have not love, I am nothing. If I give away all I have, and if I deliver my body to be burned, but have not love, I gain nothing. (1 Cor. 12:31—13:1–3)

Such love is never self-serving, as has been the case in all forms of sexual abuse, nor is it mere affection, romance, or shared interest. It is a gift of God's grace that empowers a person to give of the self for the good of the other person, who is accepted for his or her own sake. That makes love the "more excellent way" (see 1 Cor. 13:4–13). This definition of love serves as an antidote for clerical abuse, and it lies at the core of correcting the crisis of clergy who have loved themselves and have sought self-gratification at the expense of others, whether minors, the disabled, or adults.

CHAPTER 9

⸺ ∞∞∞ ⸺

THE VIRGIN MARY DRAWS
THE DISCIPLES NEAR

The New Testament records three events in which the Blessed Virgin Mary made an impact on the Apostles: the wedding feast of Cana (John 2:1–11); as Jesus hung upon the Cross (John 19:25–27); and Acts 2:12–14). Sacred Tradition remembers a fourth interaction, namely, the assembly of the Apostles at the time of her Dormition and Assumption. Inclusion of these episodes in Sacred Scripture and Tradition not only indicates her importance in the Christian revelation, but points to her importance in the lives of priests. Devotion to Mother Mary has characterized saintly priests throughout the centuries, and it remains essential in present era.

Tragically, devotion to Mary declined from the late 1960s until the mid 1980s, even though the New Testament and Vatican II recommend Marian devotion to everyone, particularly priests. Usually, priests neglected Mary rather than openly rejecting her in order to promote ecumenical relations with some of the mainline Protestant churches and to address feminist issues in some sectors of the Church, including seminaries and convents.

During this time children were not catechized about Mary,

the Rosary, or Marian prayers and hymns. Many adults in the 1980s and later admitted that they did not even know that there were Mysteries of the Rosary, let alone what they were or what purpose they served. This indicates how widespread was the neglect of Marian devotion. Blessed Mary became a small part of personal prayer, and she was not preached much; typically, on Marian feasts the homilies portrayed her as an example of faith, but not much more.

Importantly, the pattern of sexual misbehavior and predation, which has been predominantly homosexual, showed a marked increase in this same period. While it may be incorrect to argue *post hoc ergo propter hoc* in this regard, still consideration of and devotion to Mary will be an important source of grace in this time of scandal among bishops and priests. She will help increase love for Jesus and obedience to His teaching among those who have done harm, for the victims of that harm, for those falsely accused, and for everyone who is tempted to sin.

It is also worth noting that despite this neglect of Marian devotion in the post-Vatican II era, the Holy Spirit, Who led the Blessed Virgin Mary on her own pilgrimage of faith, has inspired a return to Marian devotion throughout the Church, including among priests. For that reason one does well to reconsider the teaching of the Second Vatican Council and Scripture so as to further ground and deepen love of the Blessed Virgin Mary and to seek her help in the present crisis in the Church. Pope St. John Paul II became famous for his journeys throughout the world and was frequently photographed kissing the ground of each nation he visited. He always included a consecration of every country he visited to the Blessed Virgin Mary and a formal consecration of the whole world to her. In this he, who had attended Vatican II as a very young bishop, lived out that council's Marian teaching and expounded upon it in his encyclical *Redemptoris Mater*.

Vatican II presents a rich instruction on the role of the

Blessed Virgin Mary in the Constitution of the Church (*Lumen Gentium*), dedicating the whole of chapter VIII to "The Blessed Virgin Mary, Mother of God in the Mystery of Christ and the Church." It opens by claiming that "the faithful must in the first place reverence the memory 'of the glorious ever Virgin Mary'" (*LG* 52, citing the Roman Canon of the Mass) and calls her the Mother of the Church (*LG* 53). Its twofold purpose is to set forth "the role of the Blessed Virgin in the mystery of the Incarnate Word and the Mystical Body, and the duties of the redeemed towards the Mother of God" to show true devotion in accord with the Magisterium of the Church" (*LG* 54, 66–67).

The document on the priesthood (*Presbyterorum Ordinis*) specifically advises priests about veneration of the Blessed Mother:

> They will always find a wonderful example of such docility in the Blessed Virgin Mary, who was led by the Holy Spirit to dedicate herself totally to the mystery of man's redemption. Let priests love and venerate with filial devotion and veneration this mother of the Eternal High Priest, Queen of Apostles and Protector of their own ministry. (*PO* 18)

Such devotion flourishes best when it is nourished by Sacred Scripture and Tradition, the Fathers of the Church, the liturgy, the Magisterium, and when it "proceeds from true faith" and "always refers to Christ, the source of all truth, sanctity, and devotion" (*LG* 67). Again, at this time of sexual and financial scandal among bishops and priests, we do well to accept the Vatican Council's teaching and apply it to the spiritual life of the clergy as well as teach it to the laity.

The purpose here is to examine three interactions between the Blessed Mother and the Apostles in the New Testament and one from the Tradition as sources of spiritual insight and help for the various persons suffering in the priest abuse scandal. The pain of the victims and their families is always primary. However, each Catholic can apply these events to their own circumstances, whether it be the faithful who have been scandalized by the crisis, the priests who were falsely accused, or the bishops, priests, and seminarians who carry a certain type of corporate guilt even though they had not participated in the scandal.

The spiritual consideration of these four interactions is meant to stimulate reflection on the Blessed Mother's role in gaining wisdom and healing through this crisis. Both are needed today, and Mary Seat of Wisdom, whose many appearances over the past two hundred years have sanctified many shrines for healing, is Our Lord's gift whose presence offers both.

Cana and Faith

The first Gospel episode is at the Wedding Feast of Cana, when the wine ran out and Jesus' mother mentions the problem to her son. Jesus responded, "What is it to me and to you, Woman? My hour has not yet come" (John 2:4). By this response He indicates that His "hour" of suffering and death had not yet come, but the working of a miracle would set the hour in motion. Mary does not claim to know about His hour, so she has no explanation. She simply and confidently told the servants, "Do whatever he tells you" (John 2:5). Jesus instructed them to fill the six stone jars with water and take some of it to the chief steward. They heed Mary's words and follow Jesus' instructions, resulting in a large amount of water being turned into the best wine (John 2:4–10). Upon witnessing this first sign of Jesus' glory, "his disciples believed in him" (John 2:11).

St. John Paul II teaches that "Mary's maternal task" appears when she becomes "the spokeswoman of her son's will" to manifest His salvific power:

At Cana, thanks to the intercession of Mary and the obedience of the servants, Jesus begins "his hour." At Cana Mary appears as believing in Jesus. Her faith evokes his first "sign" and helps to kindle the faith of the disciples. (*Redemptoris Mater*, 21)

After the Vatican Council, many clergy, religious, professors at seminaries, and lay faithful recapitulated the Apostles' act of faith and then ongoing lack of faith. The challenges to believing were associated with a feeling that the Christian Faith had to adapt to modernity. The post-War society was dealing with the shock of Nazi atrocities and questioned everything, including the existence of God. Existentialist philosophy questioned whether life had meaning or purpose. Some scientists reduced reality to mathematical models and the measurement of data accompanied by claims that none of the universe has direction or purpose; the cosmos is not particularly beautiful or purposeful, but rather came into existence through accidents of history. Determinists concluded that human beings have no free will, while existentialists believed that all people have is free will to choose whatever they want.

In that context, Christianity itself seemed without purpose. As explained in chapter 7, Rudolph Bultmann, who denied Jesus' miracles and Resurrection, greatly influenced graduate schools and seminaries alike. Fr. Charles Curran and others rejected the Church's teaching on the integrity of the sexual act with its procreative purpose and changed the focus of sexuality to love apart from procreation. They publicly rejected Pope St. Paul's encyclical *Humanae Vitae*, which led to the rejection of much of the Church's other teaching on sexual morality precisely as the culture underwent a sexual revolution inspired by Alfred Kinsey's reduction of human sexuality to animal urges. Kinsey preached to the public and to legislators that sexual acts were simply part of nature and society ought not regulate sex through moral codes and laws. At his urging, many American and foreign legislatures decriminalized sex acts, opening the way for an increase of evil behavior, including pedophilia—an act which the Kinsey Report actually stated is good for children.

In contrast to the modern spread of doubt about God, Jesus Christ, and basic morality, present-day disciples need to return to Cana and discover the Blessed Mother's faith in her son in service of other humans in need. She shared her faith in Jesus with the servants by telling them to do whatever He told them; her faith inspired faith within the first disciples because they could witness that Jesus was more than a teacher.

Modern disciples, including bishops, priests, and deacons, need a greater devotion to the Blessed Mother so she can inspire within them more faith at the service of those in need. The inclusion of the Wedding Feast at Cana among the Rosary's Mysteries of Light is a great providence that will help the Church grow in faith that the dirty waters of modern infidelity and immorality might be transformed by Jesus Christ into the best wine of a Christian culture that brings joy to the entire world. A culture built on the kind of faith that does whatever Jesus tells us will give divine purpose to science and technology, art, recreation, and all other aspects of modernity.

Jesus Shares His Mother with the Beloved Disciple

A second interaction of Jesus' mother occurred with an individual disciple as she stood by her son at the Crucifixion.

> When Jesus saw his mother, and the disciple whom he loved standing near, he said to his mother, "Woman, behold, your son!" Then he said to the disciple, "Behold, your mother!" And from that hour the disciple took her to his own home.
> (John 19:26–27)

Other relatives are named in the Gospel, but none of these

kin are chosen to care for her after Jesus' departure. Rather, His choice is the "disciple whom Jesus loved." From the Cross, which is the new tree of life, Jesus addressed Mary as "Woman," the name given to the mother of all humanity before she fell into the serpent's temptation to disobey God. Archbishop Fulton J. Sheen appropriately noted that had Jesus identified the disciple by his name, it may have limited her motherhood to that one man. However, He addresses this saying to "the disciple whom he loved," thereby extending her motherhood to every beloved disciple.

Sheen and many others through the centuries have focused on Mary's blessed motherhood with priests, though without excluding the rest of the Church. Priests do well to accept Christ's entrustment of them to His mother, as well as accepting her entrustment to them "take her to [their] own home." This means incorporating Marian devotion in a variety of ways. The most standard practices include daily praying of the Rosary and joyful celebrations of Marian feast days in the Liturgy of the Hours and at Mass. Both the Rosary and the liturgy draw a person into the variety of mysteries of Christ's life, but they do so from Our Lady's perspective. All Christians need a balanced incorporation of all aspects of Christ's life, from His Incarnation and childhood, His public ministry, His suffering and death, and His glorious Resurrection. The Rosary helps call to mind the application of these mysteries to the grief, pain, and resolution of the present sexual crisis in the Church.

Another wonderful way to "take Mary into our homes" is through a personal consecration to Jesus Christ through her. St. Louis de Montfort preached this vigorously in early eighteenth-century France, and his success became poignantly apparent in the 1790s when the French Republic viciously persecuted those French people who remained faithful to the Church in the regions where he had preached. Within a short time the French government martyred two hundred thousand of its own citizens who protected their priests and nuns and rejected the false Catholicism invented by the revolutionary government. Their consecration strengthened them in normal life and in persecution; priests who make the consecration will likewise be strengthened to resist temptations of all kinds, including the cynicism or despair about failed bishops and priests. Such a consecration motivates priests to excel in zeal, not unlike those knights of old who were motivated to excel by the ladies, for whose love they strove to be worthy.

Consecration to Jesus through Mary is best undertaken with significant prayerful preparation, and three books provide a method of prayer and meditations that dispose the soul to make this commitment: *33 Days to Morning Glory: A Do-It-Yourself-Retreat in Preparation for Marian Consecration* by Fr. Michael Gaitley; *Totus Tuus: A Consecration to Jesus Through Mary with Blessed John Paul II*, by Fr. Brian McMaster; and *Preparation for Total Consecration According to St. Louis de Montfort*, by Fr. Hugh Gillespie, SMM. Each of these offers a month or so of organized meditations and reflections, drawing on Scripture, the writings of St. Louis de Montfort, Pope St. John Paul, and other resources to guide a person to live more closely to Christ with the Blessed Mother's help. At the end, the person makes the consecration to Jesus through Mary.

Those who make this consecration discover that they have more energy and enthusiasm to keep their commitments. Our Lady guides and motivates them to be more centered on Christ instead of on careerism or other distractions. Bishops and priests are typically kept busy doing good things for the Church and for people in need while their time for prayer suffers. In my book *Father, Forgive Me, for I Am Frustrated*, I named a chapter after an old saying about the spiritual life: "If the devil can't make you bad, he makes you busy." These many good things consume time for quiet contemplation and prayer, which draw one into an intimate relationship with God. If a priest becomes defined by his good actions, God and the Church become his employers rather than an awesome Lord and Father and a beloved Spouse.

A priest needs love and intimacy in his life as much as any other person does. However, the Lord has called him to celibacy "for the sake of the kingdom of God" (Matt. 19:12), so his experience of intimacy differs from that of marriage and family. Having close friends is extremely important, as when Jesus formed a band of Twelve Apostles and sent them on mission in pairs rather than alone. Priests need fellowship with each other and with other close friends, while at the same time maintaining proper boundaries that do not infringe on their commitment to a celibate and chaste life.

However, as with every Christian, including married couples, the need for intimacy includes a deep, loving relationship with Jesus Christ and His mother. Prayer engages a person with the Lord and His saints, allowing profound thoughts and deep secrets to be brought into the relationship. In prayer, people can speak of problems, sins, worries, and fears that might overwhelm fellow humans but are accepted by the Lord God.

Individuals choose patron saints with whom they identify, those who had similar occupations, struggles, and temptations, and they feel they can be spiritual friends with these saints. This is most true of the Blessed Virgin Mary, not because of our ability to identify with her occupation in life, but because she knew Jesus so intimately and can help us know Him better than any other human being.

One further advantage of making a consecration to Jesus Christ through the Blessed Virgin Mary is that her exalted dignity helps Christians treat all women with greater respect. Mothers teach their children respect for women by providing them with a model of feminine dignity. In particular, they teach their boys not to treat women as maids or other types of servants for a man's use, but to aspire to deserve a woman's authentic love. Women are not useful tools whose labor gratifies a man's indolence or greed, or who satisfy his lust. The Blessed Mother continues that education in the importance and dignity of all women and is therefore especially important to celibate priests.

One aspect of her role in helping priests mature is in having recourse to her during temptations to lust. No man wants his mother, wife, or daughter to catch him looking at pornography or engaged in fornication or adultery. No man wants a much beloved woman to witness him approaching other women out of mere lust, and if he falls into such sins, they will correct his bad behavior in accord with their authentic love for him.

Similarly, a priest needs the Blessed Mother within his spiritual life as an antidote to the temptations to lust and as a model of that purity of heart that enables one to "see God" (Matt. 5:8). Of course, the Blessed Virgin Mary will do much more than that, as witnessed by her many other titles, such as "Seat of Wisdom" and "Destroyer of Heresies." Like all women, Blessed Mary is rich and complex in her influences on a man. She will help a priest mature in his ministry, avoid falling into lustful behavior, and refrain from being a source of scandal so as to be a tower of Catholic strength in the world.

The Blessed Mother in the Early Christian Community

The first chapter of the Acts of the Apostles mentions Mary's presence immediately after the list of eleven faithful Apostles and before the choice of Matthias as the replacement for the dead Judas Iscariot. Vatican II points out that God did not "manifest solemnly the mystery of the salvation of the human race until he poured forth the Spirit promised by Christ." In preparation for that outpouring of the Holy Spirit, the Apostles were "with one mind in prayer with the women and Mary the mother of Jesus, and with his brethren" (Acts 1:14). Blessed Mary, who had already been overshadowed by the Holy Spirit at the moment of the incarnation of the Messiah, was now "prayerfully imploring the gift of the Spirit" between the Ascension and Pentecost (*LG*, 59). St. John Paul II mentions the "unique correspondence between the moment of the Incarnation of the Word and the moment of the birth of the Church." The one "who links these two moments is Mary: Mary at Nazareth and Mary in the Upper Room at Jerusalem." "Her discreet yet essential presence indicates the path of 'birth from the Holy Spirit.'" She became "by the will of the Son and the power of the Holy Spirit present in the mystery of the Church" as "a maternal presence," in line with Jesus' words from the Cross: "Woman, behold your son!"; "Behold, your mother" (*Redemptoris Mater*, 24).

As the Blessed Virgin shared this fellowship in the early Church, it is fair to assume that she shared the fruit of her own contemplation and prayer with the disciples. She was the only living witness to the events of the birth of John the Baptist and of Jesus. Especially important are the lines "Mary kept all these things, pondering them in her heart" (Luke 2:19) and "his mother kept all these things in her heart" (Luke 2:51). Certainly, after the circumcision of John the Baptist, many people talked about the amazing events of John's father's muteness and then his sudden ability to speak (see Luke 1:65–66).

However, none of those people were present in the Upper Room with the Apostles; the only living witness to the birth of John was Mary, and she shared these episodes with the disciples. In addition to sharing her memories, which were the fruit of thirty-four years of contemplation, she remained with the community during their nine days of praying for the coming of the Holy Spirit on Pentecost.

Though she had received the Holy Spirit in a powerful way at the Incarnation when He overshadowed her so that Jesus could become flesh in her virginal womb, now she would receive Him again with the rest of the Church community. In receiving the Spirit in the form of a tongue of fire, she receives the Holy Spirit in a different way, and as such shows herself as a member of the Church. St. Luke never portrays her as having preached like Peter and the other Apostles, but she certainly remained part of the community as "they devoted themselves to the apostles' teaching and fellowship, to the breaking of bread and the prayers" (Acts 2:42).

Pope St. John Paul II brings up in this context his own contemplation of Our Lady as she heard Peter, John, or one of the other Apostles celebrate the liturgy and speak Jesus' words, "This is my Body" and "This is the cup of my Blood." Imagine her attentiveness as she recalled the fact that His Body and Blood had first taken shape within her womb and that He was now present to the community in the Eucharist. Enter into her devotion to her Son as she received His Body and Blood in Holy Communion!

The Assumption of Mary

A final experience of the Blessed Virgin's fellowship with the Apostles is described in the later accounts of her passing into eternity. Though this event is not found in the New Testament, the story is told in a number of ancient books from the Eastern churches, the oldest being the Ethiopic text known as the *Liber Requiei Mariae* (The Book of Mary's Repose), *De Transitu Virginis Liber* (The Book of the Passing of the Most Holy Virgin, the Mother of God), attributed to St. Melito of Sardis, and *The Six Books Dormition Narrative*. The earliest traditions date at least to the third century but are written later.

The Catholic Church depends on the vision of the glorious Mother of Christ in Revelation 12 as its doctrinal source, along with the teachings of various Church Fathers such as St. Epiphanius, St. Gregory of Tours, St. John Damascene, and St.

Modestus of Jerusalem. Pope Pius XII defined the dogma of the Assumption in his Apostolic Constitution *Munificentissimus Deus*. However, the various ancient narrative traditions have provided the Church with an imaginative sense that has inspired icons and other artwork depicting the Assumption of Mary.

The oldest narratives date the Blessed Mother's dormition to the AD 30s and place her in Jerusalem, near the site of the Upper Room. Eventually a Byzantine church, and presently the Benedictine monastery of the Dormition of Mary (built 1898–1911), commemorated the traditional site of Our Lady's home. The traditional site of her tomb had been a Jewish Christian church in a cave on the Mount of Olives, then a Byzantine church, a Benedictine convent during the Crusades, and presently an Armenian Orthodox church, with Greek and Ethiopian chapels inside. Our Lady's Assumption is a tradition much venerated by a variety of Christian communities from the first century until the present.

The ancient narratives always include a gathering of "all the Apostles of the Lord Jesus Christ" to join the Blessed Mother before her death and to be present at her Assumption. The Church does not define whether the Blessed Mother died before being assumed into heaven, but the early traditions present her imitating her Son, Jesus Christ, Who died and was buried before His Resurrection. It is likely that she also passed through death before being raised up and assumed into heaven.

De Transitu Virginis Liber describes the Blessed Mary and the Apostles praying and praising God together until the Lord Jesus came "with a multitude of angels and a great light" to invite His mother to "enter into the treasury of eternal." In adoration of Jesus she proclaimed, "You know, O King of Glory, that I have loved You with My whole heart. Receive Me, Your Maidservant." At that point she gave up her spirit, and the Apostles took her body to a new tomb at the base of the Mount of Olives, near the

Garden of Gethsemane. Later, the Lord Jesus Christ arrived and united the Blessed Virgin's soul with her body so that she who had not sinned would not "suffer the dissolution of the body in the tomb." She rose up from the grave, and the angels led her to Paradise.

None of these or the other details of the various descriptions of Our Lady's Assumption are considered to be sources of the dogma; that is reserved to Revelation 12, to the patristic sermons on the Assumption, and to the liturgical celebrations over the centuries. However, the impact of these narratives on Catholic art and devotion offers insights into the Blessed Mother's relationship with the Apostles and their successors through the ages.

Particularly important is the gathering of the Apostles around her deathbed. Eastern icons portray the Apostles in liturgical vestments as they surround her funeral bier during her Dormition. Along with the three New Testament passages discussed above, this scene points to the importance of the bishops' and priests' devotion to Mary in living out their ministry.

Why is Marian devotion so important for priests and bishops? No one answer can exhaust all of the elements of the mystery, but some aspects can be described. Priests devoted to Mary will discover her importance throughout their whole lives, and they will develop insights into Mary's importance as they grow closer to her.

One of the great and many gifts all women possess is their ability to center the people around them. An example of this is seen when a husband and father dies; the family typically goes to "Mom's house" for the holidays and other family gatherings; when a wife and mother dies, Dad joins the children at a daughter's or daughter-in-law's home. Men do not center the family's attention the way women do. In the Church, particularly for bishops and priests, the Blessed Virgin Mary offers the maternal center of our Christian family. In peaceful quiet, such as people so gently sing in Christmas carols like "Silent Night," she tenderly centers the Church in order to lead people to Jesus, whether in a simple manger or into heaven's glory after her Assumption.

While her womanly gifts help to center the Church, her unique personhood inspires us as an immaculately conceived, sinless, and perpetually Virgin Mother. Her holiness truly "magnifies the Lord" (Luke 1:46) and evokes from people of all generations the acclamation "Blessed" (Luke 1:48). She is the holiest of all creatures, and her ability to center the Church acts as a call to greater holiness. The image of the Blessed Mother summoning the Apostles before her death brings out this role not only to draw priests to the center of the Church, but also to evoke greater holiness and virtue from the priests.

Modern priests live in a sexually glutted culture loaded with innuendo and explicit sexual content throughout the media. Turning away from those influences in order to contemplate Mary's purity and holiness is an important antidote to the temptations presented by society and its implicit permission to comply with the acceptable sins. Of course, once a person does give in to these temptations, society attacks the sinner in order to maintain control over them; this is a "rope a dope" tactic to neuter the influence of bishops, priests, and the whole Church. The Blessed Mother is a holy antidote who centers us in Jesus, Who is "our wisdom, our righteousness and sanctification and redemption" (1 Cor. 1:30).

Another gift of the Blessed Virgin Mary is the Church's celebration of her feasts, each of which points to Jesus Christ in some important way, such as His Incarnation during the Annunciation or His death on Our Lady of Sorrows. Other feasts necessarily include the Virgin Mary—the Nativity, Epiphany, Good Friday's reading of the Passion of St. John, and others. This points to the inclusion of Mary in liturgical and prayerful consideration of the mysteries of Jesus Christ and our salvation. The priests who celebrate these feasts and mysteries in the Liturgy of the Hours and around the altar need to develop a close relationship with the Blessed Mother in their personal prayer life so as to be an aid to her role of centering the Church. For her part, she will help priests to develop their fatherly role of caring for the people of God. That itself will help them avoid the temptations to take advantage of the people, including through sexual temptations.

Another extremely important means of daily devotion to the Blessed Virgin Mary is the Rosary. By giving attention to each Mystery, one focuses on Jesus instead of abstract ideas about Him or service programs or even one's own self-centeredness. In praying the Rosary, one begins to see Jesus through His mother's eyes, a perspective of unconditional love that strengthens one to love Him for His own sake. Furthermore, meditating on the Mysteries of the Rosary draws one's attention to all of the events of one's salvation. Sometimes Catholics have focused on one aspect of salvation, such as the Incarnation, or Jesus' suffering and death, or the Resurrection, or some other favorite mystery. By daily praying of all the mysteries, we gain a fuller, more rounded understanding of Jesus Christ and His mother. This gives us more opportunities for spiritual and even theological balance in regard to salvation.

Other authors will provide far deeper insights than these. However, this is possible only if we observe the faith of the Blessed Mother and then grow in our own faith, as the disciples experienced at Cana. We stay close to Jesus in His suffering, as the Blessed Mother did at the Cross, and we remain as open to the Holy Spirit as she and the disciples in the Upper Room did at Pentecost. Then we can pray the words of the Salve Regina:

Turn then, most gracious Advocate, your eyes of mercy toward us and after this, our exile, show unto us the blessed fruit of your womb, Jesus. O clement, O loving, O sweet Virgin Mary.

This prayer is like a national anthem for priests. May praying it in the Rosary, Night Prayer of the Liturgy of the Hours, and in private devotion evoke from them a selfless greatness of love that makes them as apostolically motivated as were the first disciples to give themselves ever more to Jesus Christ as their Lord, to the Church as his Mystical Body on earth, and to the service of all people.